IN THE TIME OF SILENT CAL

IN THE TIME
OF SILENT CAL

by JULES ABELS

G. P. Putnam's Sons

NEW YORK

CONTENTS

IN THE TIME OF SILENT CAL

Chapter I

CALVIN COOLIDGE

His build and stature were meager, as if more would be to give way to the sin of waste. The features of his thin face were aquiline; he had a cleft chin and a broad forehead surmounted by sandy hair which was almost red; his lips were pursed into a thin line. He rarely smiled. His expression, according to a widely reported quip, was of having been "weaned on a pickle" and, according to another description, of "looking down his nose to locate that smell which seemed forever to affront him."

He was President of the United States from 1923 to 1929, a period of ebullient optimism and robust living, a period of hyperactivity which has often been called the Jazz Age or the Roaring Twenties. It was an age of many contradictions, and that it was also known as the Coolidge Era seems, *on the surface,* the greatest anomaly of all. In a period that was pulsating with color and drama he appeared drab and colorless, in a time of soaring hopes he stood before the world joyless and bloodless, in an age increasingly given to play he knew only work, in an age of extravagance he practiced and preached extreme frugality, and in an age that was noisy and raucous with the blare of radios and auto horns and talk, he was publicly silent—so much so that he earned the sobriquet of Silent Cal.

He arrived in Washington in 1921 as Vice President, having been elected on the Republican ticket as the running mate of Warren G. Harding. It was not long before the capital realized that Mr. Coolidge was a strange bird. A good part of the Vice President's duties at the time was attendance at dinners, and Mr. Coolidge was not derelict. However, in accordance with his privilege he was the last to arrive and the first to leave. The Vice President sits at the right of the hostess and is traditionally the fount of wisdom and wit. Mr. Coolidge, however, had nothing whatever to say and was not the slightest bit self-conscious about it. Edward Lowry wrote that year in the *New Republic:*

> To the whole of social and political Washington he presents an impenetrable blank. He dines out with the best of them. Never a night passes that the big, closed car placed at his disposal by the fond taxpayers does not convey him to a dinner party. No soup, however thick or thin, deters him, no fish however disguised by a pallid, viscous goo the chef seems to like, daunts him, and thence south through the entree to the ice leaving only a waste behind him. And all in perfect silence. . . .
>
> I have been eager to pluck out the heart of Mr. Coolidge's mystery, to discover what sort of man he is, to establish a basis for an appraisal. All in vain, for he has disclosed nothing. He has been observed as intently as possible under the circumstances, in the crush preceding the largest and noisiest of dinner-parties, standing quite still and saying not a blessed word although all about him was babble, laughter and conversation. He doesn't seem ill at ease or embarrassed or tongue-tied. He was just still. Silent upon a peak at Darien is no word for it. He gave no appearance of being about to say something presently. He was an absolute calm. Old Ironsides at anchor lay in the harbor of Mahon, the waves to sleep had gone. Not a leaf stirring. . . .

He assumed the office of the Presidency on the death of Harding in August, 1923. His personality did not change a whit. Yet this strange, frigid, withdrawn man, regarded by many as a museum piece, lacking all the outgoing traits of personality of the American politician, turned out to be one of the most popular Presidents in our history—during his time.

He was a "darling of the gods," wrote H. L. Mencken. "No other American has ever been so fortunate, or even half so fortunate." Indeed, luck was his constant handmaiden—until, after his Presidency, the nation's business structure, which he himself had called our "temple," came crashing down to tarnish his name for succeeding generations.

On the day that Coolidge was nominated in June, 1920, as Harding's running mate, a Boston newsman at the Chicago convention bet the company assembled that if Harding were elected, he would be assassinated before he completed his term. "I am simply telling you what I know. I know Calvin Coolidge inside and out. He is the luckiest goddam blank blank in the whole world." Others had the same hunch. In the *Outlook* magazine for June 12, 1920, Frederick M. Davenport wrote from the convention that a Bostonian friend of Coolidge told him that if the Republican ticket were elected, "I wouldn't take the Presidency for a million dollars." Asked why, he replied, "Because I would die in a little while. Everything comes to Calvin Coolidge in a most uncanny and mysterious manner."

He was born on July 4, 1872, in Plymouth, Vermont. As a critic put it, he showed a "foresight sound and characteristic, having chosen as the day of his advent one which the neighbors were bound to celebrate."

The log-cabin tradition has become so much of the folklore of the Presidency that it was often said of Coolidge that he rose from poor farmboy to the White House. As a matter of fact, his father, Colonel John C. Coolidge (the title was given to him as a member of the governor's staff), was a familiar figure of the American countryside, the rural tycoon. Such a man owns the general store; he is the extensive landowner always on the lookout for profitable deals; he is the local notary and gives legal advice. All these were functions performed by Coolidge's father. He had held the office of town selectman, constable, deputy sheriff, school commissioner, and roads commissioner. When Coolidge was three years old, his father was elected to the state legislature, where he served two terms in the lower House and a term in the State Senate.

Coolidge's mother had been Victoria Josephine Moor. Photographs show an extremely lovely-looking girl with fine features. She was an invalid as long as Calvin could remember her and died at the age of thirty-nine, when Calvin was twelve. "The greatest grief that can come to a boy came to me," he wrote in his *Autobiography*.

The silence, repression, and frugality of Coolidge have often been explained as the prototype of the Vermont farmer. But

11

there have been many other Vermonters who did not have these characteristics. There was Jim Fisk, lusty buccaneer, gambler, and womanizer of the Robber Baron era; there was the voluble Little Giant, Stephen A. Douglas; there were the Mormon leaders Joseph Smith and Brigham Young; there were the two Deweys, Admiral George Dewey, hero of the Spanish-American War, and educator Dr. John Dewey; there was Senator Warren Austin, verbose and emotional, speaking for the United States in the United Nations.

One wonders if the silence of his home did not have much to do with repressing Coolidge. An ever-present sadness was there because of the invalidism of his mother and her wasting away month by month, probably because of tuberculosis. He had only a sister, Abigail, three years younger than he, who was even more quiet. His father was a silent, uncommunicative man. A neighbor once said of him, "Compared to the father, the son is a positive chatterer." The son regarded the huge, hulking figure of his father with the reverence accorded to an Old Testament patriarch. "My father had qualities that were greater than any I possess. I cannot recall that I ever knew of his doing a wrong thing."

The house must have been dead as the night, no noise, no laughter, no babble of childish voices. Then there was the harsh discipline. He would be taken out of bed at night to be chastened for petty derelictions, such as leaving his playthings on the road, and Grandmother Coolidge would punish him for not heeding her by shutting him up in a windowless, spidery attic.

He attended a semiprivate academy at Ludlow, Vermont, from the time he was twelve, and at nineteen entered Amherst College in Massachusetts. A slight youth, called Red because of the color of his hair, he attracted little notice, though he displayed a capacity for wit and was selected to deliver the humorous oration in the graduation festivities. In later years few of his classmates could remember him. Those who could had comments such as this: "A drabber, more colorless boy I never knew than Calvin Coolidge when he was in Amherst. He was a perfect enigma to us all." Another recollection was that of a "very retiring, silent individual with few friends." He did not take part in extracurricular activities, though he was glad to be tapped by a newly formed fraternity in his junior year, Phi Gamma Delta. When asked in a later year whether he had participated in athletics, he answered whimsically, "Yes, by holding stakes." He did particularly well in his studies in his last two years and was graduated *cum laude.*

Like several other Presidents, he dropped his first name. He had been chistened John Calvin after his father, in college he had been J. Calvin, and he was merely Calvin Coolidge as he embarked on his chosen career of the law. A vagary of chance, the first in a series, swerved him from a course that would have doomed him to lifelong obscurity. While at Amherst he had written to former Governor William P. Dillingham of Vermont asking him whether he could study law in his office in Montpelier. Not having received a reply, he applied to the firm of Hammond and Field in Northampton, Massachusetts, and was accepted. A few days later he received a letter from Dillingham apologizing for the delay and accepting Coolidge's application.

In the law office of Hammond and Field he started a career of hard, unremitting toil unencumbered by recreation, sports, or girls. He did not date during and after his college career, and after graduation he was so wrapped up in study that he did not even visit his father in Plymouth for two years even though his home was not distant. In July, 1897, when he was twenty-five, he was admitted to the Massachusetts bar on oral examination.

He had not planned to make a political career, he later said. His goal had been to be a prosperous small-town lawyer with the chance of attaining a judgeship. However, for an unknown, struggling young lawyer politics is a useful launching pad, and as an ardent, unmarried Republican, he had a lot of free time in the evenings. As soon as he arrived in Northampton, he became enmeshed in politics at the ward level. In 1900, after three years as a lawyer, he was appointed city solicitor, a job paying $600 a year, which did not interfere with his expanding law practice. It was the first of a long string of positions on the public payroll. At dinner when he was Vice President, a dowager by his side said, "Mr. Coolidge, what is your hobby?" to which he replied laconically, "Holding public office."

When he was twenty-nine, he wrote his father, "If I ever get a woman some one will have to support her, but I see no need of

13

a wife as long as I have my health." Three years later he was elected chairman of the Republican City Committee, and his law practice could support a family. The following year he courted and married the first and, we can be reasonably sure, the only woman in his life, Grace Goodhue, a graduate of the University of Vermont who was in Northampton as a teacher at the Clarke School for the Deaf. She was the antithesis in personality of her groom, extremely vivacious and full of spontaneous, unaffected laughter. They went to Montreal for a two-week honeymoon, which Coolidge terminated after a week, saying that he was eager to return to exhibit his "prize." He probably was eager to spend an extra week on his campaign for the local school board, in which he was turned down by the voters, the only defeat he ever knew for public office.

The next year he was elected to the lower house of the legislature, the General Court, and was reelected the following year. Then he became mayor of Northampton. It was evident that he had prowess at the polls though he was not the conventional backslapper. "To the people I seemed in some way that I cannot explain to represent confidence." His dour exterior certainly was not vote-appealing. A letter, introducing him to the speaker when he arrived at the State Capitol, read, "Like the singed cat, he is better than he looks." He ran for the State Senate in 1911 and won. From that time on his rise to state and then to national prominence was rapid.

After two terms in the Senate one of the lucky events occurred that led many to believe that Coolidge was a favored child of fortune. He had already decided to retire from the Senate. Then he heard a rumor that the president of the State Senate, Levi P. Greenwood, would run for lieutenant governor. Since the president of the Senate was the second in power only to the governor, Coolidge decided to run for a third term in order to have a chance at the post. Greenwood changed his mind, but then it was too late for Coolidge to withdraw his candidacy.

At midnight on election night Coolidge got a telephone call from Boston. Levi P. Greenwood had lost his seat in the Senate! He had been the victim of women suffragettes who had concentrated on him as an object lesson because of his opposition to votes for women. Coolidge fought for the job. That very night he went by auto to Springfield, where he caught a train to

Boston arriving at dawn. He had breakfast with a powerful friend, United States Senator Winthrop M. Crane, canvassed members of the Senate living in Boston by personal visit, called members around the state by telephone. Within a few days he had the requisite number of pledges needed for election to the post and was a state power.

At this point Frank Waterman Stearns, the wealthy president of a large dry goods firm of Boston, stepped in as the guiding angel of Coolidge's career. In some occult way Mr. Stearns became convinced that Calvin Coolidge was a man of destiny. In some part the hero complex was traceable to Harvard-Amherst rivalry. Devotion to his alma mater Amherst was a religion to Stearns, and he intensely resented the fact that Harvard graduates had preempted the places of honor in Massachusetts political life. Stearns began preaching Coolidge all over the state. Thus, "I have become convinced that the salvation of the Commonwealth and the country demands that Calvin Coolidge should be kept in active public life and as near to the top as possible."

No one was more baffled about this than Coolidge himself, as he often wrote to Stearns. Taking no chances, Coolidge had an intermediary sound out Governor David I. Walsh about a place for him on the Public Utility Commission when he retired from the Senate, but the Democratic governor was cold to the idea. Destiny could not be foiled. Incumbent Lieutenant Governor Grafton Cushing, a Republican, made the highly ill-advised decision to contest the Republican nomination for governor with Samuel McCall, who, though defeated by Walsh in the last election, was considered by the Republican organization to merit another chance. Cushing lost his bid but made his contribution to history by opening the door to Coolidge to take his job and rise another step to the top.

Stearns managed Coolidge's campaign in the primary. He obtained workers by using Amherst alumni and got them to put up money while spending freely out of his own pocket. He pleaded with Coolidge to defrost, writing to him, "When you meet people, and especially when they are invited to meet you, if you would give them a pleasant smile, even without speaking, it would make the trick complete, and you can do it, because you sometimes do." Coolidge won the primary and ran ahead

15

of Samuel McCall, who was elected governor in the general election in November.

To Stearns, this was only the start. He wrote to Coolidge, "Every step must be taken with great care, because the opportunity is wonderful." To Coolidge's friend and classmate at Amherst Dwight W. Morrow, who was now a partner in J. P. Morgan & Company, Stearns wrote about "higher things" since "Calvin Coolidge is the political heir of Abraham Lincoln." To all and sundry, Stearns would pronounce, "I know I'm not sane on the subject but. . . ." As for Coolidge, he looked on the Stearns mania with good humor and the philosophy: "If chance will have me king, why, chance may crown me." Often he warned Stearns that he might wind up tragically disappointed. Nonetheless, in 1918, after serving two terms as lieutenant governor, Coolidge was elected governor.

The relationship between the two men was a peculiar one. They were always "Mr. Coolidge" and "Mr. Stearns" to each other. When Stearns had something on his mind, he found it more effective to write Coolidge a letter than to talk to him. When Coolidge became President, Stearns had a permanent suite in the White House and became familiar to the press as the "Floorwalker of the White House." Coolidge liked to have him around like Old Dog Tray and would call him to his office, ignore him, and, after a while, say, "Thank you, Mr. Stearns," on which words Stearns would depart. Once Coolidge received a copy of *The Intimate Papers of Colonel House,* containing the correspondence between Wilson and his adviser Edward M. House, and said solemnly to Stearns, "Mr. Stearns, an unofficial adviser to the President of the United States is not a good thing and is not provided for in our form of government," an instance of Coolidge's deadpan spoofing since both knew that Stearns could not qualify as a Colonel House. Coolidge used him for trivial responsibilities, such as arranging travel plans or sounding out men on whether they were available for government jobs.

The Boston police strike of 1919 was the event which projected Coolidge into the national limelight. After the Armistice in 1918 there was a riptide of inflation in which the chief vic-

16

tims were those with fixed incomes, such as civil servants. The salaries of the members of the Boston police force were very low. The maximum was only $1,600 a year, and out of that the men had to buy their own uniforms. Under the two-platoon system the working day was twelve hours. A movement began to unionize the force, and the American Federation of Labor was asked for a charter, which was granted as it had been to the police force of several other cities.

The police commissioner, who was legally responsible to the governor, was a proper Bostonian, Edwin U. Curtis. He announced that it was impossible for a police officer to belong to a labor union and at the same time to perform his sworn duty, and he threatened to suspend the ringleaders from duty. The mayor of Boston in a three-cornered division of authority was a good-natured bumbler, Andrew J. Peters, who took the well-traveled course of appointing a committee to find a solution. The Citizens' Committee of Thirty-four after feverish activity came up with a compromise—arbitration of the dispute with punishment of the offenders to be delayed indefinitely. Curtis refused to accept the finding, and Peters and the committee called on Governor Coolidge at the statehouse in Boston asking him to force Curtis to accept the plan. Coolidge flatly refused.

On the deadline date of Monday, September 8, Commissioner Curtis suspended 19 ringleaders. The police force by a vote of 1,134 to 2 voted to strike the next day. In another conference that afternoon with Mayor Peters, Coolidge again refused to intervene and also refused to call out the state guard.

The next day at 4:45 P.M. police streamed out of the station houses, clad in the uniforms, which they owned, but without clubs and badges, symbolic of their authority. The walkout included 1,117 out of 1,544 in the force. That night there were many disorders, including the pillaging of stores. The next day Mayor Peters found that he had been guilty of an oversight and that he had the legal authority to call up units of the state guard located in Boston without the sanction of the governor. This guard was augmented with volunteers, including Harvard students. In a pitched battle that night six rioters were killed, but law and order had prevailed.

The threat posed by the police strike had been beaten back

17

with no help from Governor Coolidge. Nonetheless, the following day he acted. He called out the entire state guard and issued an executive order taking over the police department, superseding Peters' authority, and reinstating Curtis, whom Peters had just removed as commissioner.

Discussing the strike in *American Heritage* (October, 1963), Francis Russell subtitled his article "By doing nothing Gov. Calvin Coolidge emerged as a national hero." The same view was expressed by the *Nation* magazine at the time. "Coolidge sat discreetly on the fence until he saw on which side public sentiment was gathering. When this had manifested itself, he climbed down from the fence on the side of the crowd and issued a proclamation needlessly mobilizing the entire State Guard."

Upon closer examination, Coolidge's actions reveal his harsh, granitelike character. In his *Autobiography* he said, "If he [Curtis] were to be superseded, I thought that the men he had discharged might be taken back and the cause lost." A principle was at stake, as Coolidge saw it. If Coolidge had not taken over and Peters had remained in charge, there would undoubtedly have been a love feast, customary after such strikes, and all would have been forgiven. In Coolidge's view the punishment must fit the crime, and desertion from duty was a crime.

Because of Coolidge, all the 1,117 men who left the force on September 9 to go on strike lost their jobs permanently; *not a man was taken back*. In his *Autobiography*, Coolidge said, "I helped these men in securing other employment." In answer to a storm of protest over his Draconic action he issued a proclamation rebuking those who called for forgiveness. "Those who would counsel it join hands with those whose acts have threatened to destroy the government. There is no middle ground. Every attempt to prevent the formation of a new police force is a blow at the government. That way treason lies."

In his *Autobiography* he also wrote that "the wages of sin are death"; that he meant this literally and not figuratively is shown by his adding that those of his Amherst classmates who were "sports" were already dead. Observe the face of this man in a photograph—his thin, compressed lips and bony, angular features. This is the face of a man who in another context of history would in complete devoutness and self-righteousness have been another Calvin sending Servetus to the stake, another Torquemada in the Spanish Inquisition, or a Robespierre dooming his comrades to the scaffold.

When the president of the AFL, Samuel Gompers, wired him urging him to reinstate the men pending arbitration, Coolidge refused, and in answer to a second plea he said, "There is no right to strike against the public safety by anybody, anywhere, anytime." Many men have worn out their lungs, their legs, and also their stomachs in a futile bid for the Presidency. Calvin Coolidge won it with one epigrammatic sentence.

One cannot appreciate the impact of the Boston police strike on American public opinion without taking into account the hysterical atmosphere of the times. Labor disputes were epidemic in 1919 with millions on strike at one time or another. It was alleged that the foreign-inspired IWW was fomenting unrest and that the Bolsheviki were planning revolution.

With no regard for the facts, Coolidge was acclaimed in the national press as "the man who defied Bolshevism and won." While the strike was on, the Boston *Herald* said, "We are in the eye of the nation. If the Soviet theory succeeds here it will spread to other battlegrounds and become nationwide." The Philadephia *Evening Public Ledger* said while the strike was in progress, "Bolshevism in the United States is no longer a specter. Boston in chaos reveals its sinister substance. In their reckless defiance of the fundamentals of morality, in their bullying affront to the structure of civilization, wherein do the police of the New England metropolis differ from the mad minority which overthrew Kerensky and ruined Russia?" After the strike was over, it said, "The nation has chosen. If it ever was vague in its conception of the Bolshevik horror, the vision is clear-cut now." When Coolidge was overwhelmingly reelected in November, he was congratulated by President Wilson, even though they were of opposite parties.

There was a mild boom for Coolidge for President which seemed to fade away as Coolidge veered from the role of active contender. He accurately decided that there would be a deadlock in the Republican convention of 1920 between Governor Frank O. Lowden of Illinois and General Leonard Wood, and his only hope was as a dark horse rather than an active campaigner, and even that hope was shattered when the senior Senator, Henry Cabot Lodge, deserted his favorite son cause. On the first ballot in Chicago he had only 28 out of the 35 votes from Massachusetts, and his vote drifted downward in subsequent ballots.

After Harding's nomination for President, Coolidge received the nomination for Vice President through an unprecedented occurrence, a runaway convention. A good deal of friendly sentiment for Coolidge had been generated by the missionary work of the *fidus Achates* Stearns, who at his own expense had widely distributed a book of Coolidge's speeches entitled *Have Faith in Massachusetts* and had given each of the delegates a pocket volume entitled *Law and Order*. However, with Lodge dominating the convention, Coolidge now thought his chances for the second spot were nil—Lodge had not even brought up his name for President in the "smoke-filled" room. During the tenth and final ballot for the Presidential nomination, the Senators who controlled the convention met in an alcove under the rostrum and decided on a fellow Senator, Irvine Lenroot of Wisconsin, for Vice President and then gave orders that word be transmitted over the "grapevine" that he was the man.

Senator Lodge, the permanent chairman, thinking it was all over but the empty formality of the vote, turned the gavel over to Senator Frank B. Willis of Ohio and left the floor. Then things went haywire. The delegates were hot and tired and they were resentful of the fact that the platform and Harding as Presidential candidate had been dictated to them. During a seconding speech for Lenroot, on the words "Lenroot of Wisconsin," a delegate shrieked, "Not on your life." To party regulars Wisconsin, as the home state of maverick Robert M. La Follette, was anathema—and Lenroot shared in the odium even though he had broken away from Senator La Follette.

A stocky man in the Oregon delegation shouted to be recognized. Senator Willis perfunctorily did so, thinking that he wanted to add his voice for Lenroot. Judge Wallace McCamant did not go to the rostrum but, standing on his chair, spoke a few words, "On behalf of the Oregon delegation I name, for the exalted office of Vice President, Governor Calvin Coolidge of

Massachusetts." A roar came from the crowd, greater in the opinion of newspapermen than any acclaim that the name of Harding had received. Old guardsman H. H. Rummel, head of the Arkansas delegation, who had just seconded the nomination of Lenroot, executed the swiftest about-face in political history as he sensed the applecart being overturned, and he seconded Coolidge's nomination. In a bandwagon rush other states joined in, and Coolidge was named on the first ballot before the stunned Senate leaders could regain control of the situation.

In the November election the ticket of Harding and Coolidge overwhelmingly defeated the Democratic ticket of Cox and Roosevelt. On election night the first radio station in the world, KDKA in Pittsburgh, started operating in time to broadcast election returns, thus inaugurating the radio age which was to be as much as anything else the symbol of the Age of Coolidge.

Coolidge was a most unobtrusive Vice President in a job then designed for Throttlebottom. With growing boredom he presided over the Senate, which his predecessor, Thomas Marshall, had termed the Cave of Winds. Aside from that he was ex officio president of the Smithsonian Institution. By special dispensation from Harding he sat in on Cabinet meetings but remained silent. According to Senator James Watson of Indiana, who was a member of the ruling Republican hierarchy, there was talk of dumping him in favor of a more colorful personality in the 1924 Presidential campaign. Then fate took a hand.

On June 20, President Harding set out on a transcontinental journey before going on to Alaska. It was a weird trip to be indelibly engraved on the memory of all those with him. Samuel Hopkins Adams wrote in "The Timely Death of President Harding":

> From Tacoma on, the President was in a state of chronic jitters.
> He could not be quiet five minutes on end. His one thought was
> to escape from thinking. To this end he organized a bridge game
> with Secretaries Wallace, Work and Hoover, Speaker Gillett and
> Admiral Rodman. The President played to exhaustion twelve,
> fourteen, and fifteen hours a day, with brief time out for lunch
> and dinner . . . his nervous demoralization was painfully apparent.
> It reached a point where he felt the need for real relief. He sought

21

out Secretary Hoover. "Mr. Secretary," said he, "there's a bad scandal brewing in the administration." . . .

While making a speech in a stadium in Seattle, he suffered a sharp spasm of pain in his chest. He was rushed aboard the train. On reaching San Francisco, the weak and haggard man was half-carried into the Palace Hotel, where he was put to bed. On the night of August 2, he was listening to his wife reading an article by Samuel Blythe about him in the *Saturday Evening Post,* "A Calm Review of a Calm Man." When she paused, he said, "Go on, go on," and then gave a convulsive shudder. The nurse pulled back the covers and started rubbing his chest, Mrs. Harding ran screaming into the corridor for a doctor—but all was in vain. The President was dead.

Across the continent, Coolidge and his wife were at his father's house in Plymouth. They had retired at nine o'clock, saying that it was as good a way as any to beat the heat. At 10:45 P.M. the Western Union office at Bridgewater, ten miles away, received the news of Harding's death, and a Model T Ford set out over the moonlit road to the Coolidge home. Colonel Coolidge in a nightgown answered the door and in a trembling voice called out to his son upstairs. Cars were clattering over the narrow, rocky road from Ludlow, where newsmen had been quartered in case of the dire event which had come to pass. Coolidge wrote out a brief statement and the newsmen departed for Ludlow believing that the oath would not be taken until the morrow. Congressman Porter H. Dale said to Coolidge, "The United States has no President. Mr. Coolidge, the country should never be without a President." Coolidge said, "Father, Mr. Dale thinks I should take the oath immediately and here. You are still a notary, aren't you?" His answer was, "Yes, I am."

At 2:47 A.M. the dramatic swearing in by kerosene light took place. The father, standing a head taller than his son, a shirt covering his nightshirt but without collar and tie, administered the oath to his son. By the side of the new President was his wife. Four others were in the room, including a twenty-two-year-old "stringer" for the Associated Press, an editor of a small Vermont paper, who wrote the press account for the world.

There was nothing so dramatic in the Coolidge Presidency as the entering upon and the leaving of it. Sketches of the oath taking appeared widely on the front pages of newspapers, and reproductions of a painting of the event by Arthur Keller were displayed and hung in homes. To Republican leaders it was a godsend, the Lincoln touch, the kerosene lamp being the effective substitute for the log cabin. It was characteristic of Coolidge's luck that if Harding had died a day later, Coolidge would have been spending the night in the baronial mansion of his wealthy friend Guy Currier at Peterboro, New Hampshire.

There was so much in the twenties that was tinsel romance, so much that was illusory, so much that corresponded to W. S. Gilbert's ditty "Things are seldom what they seem." The dreamlike tableau which ushered in the Coolidge regime was one of these. Actually, the oath administered by his father was null and void. After being informed by Attorney General Harry M. Daugherty that his father had no authority to swear in a federal official, Coolidge on August 16 took a new oath administered in his office by Justice A. A. Hoeling of the Supreme Court of the District of Columbia. This did not come to light until years afterward, when Daugherty's memoirs were published.

Soon after Coolidge became President, the Teapot Dome scandal erupted, the facts having been brought to light by a Senate committee headed by the bulldog Senator Thomas J. Walsh. This concerned the transfer of valuable government oil reserves to private oil companies, the principal one being at a queer-shaped hill in Wyoming called Teapot Dome. Albert B. Fall, Harding's Interior Secretary, had been bribed to make the transfer.

Coolidge professed his holy indignation. "If there has been any crime, it must be prosecuted—no one will be shielded for any party, political or other reasons . . . if there has been any guilt, it will be punished, if there has been any fraud it will be revealed." At the same time, with consummate skill, he tried to minimize the involvement of Republicans. "A few public officers were guilty participants, but the wonder is not that there was so much and so many, but rather that there have been so little and so few." Members of the Senate demanded that Attorney General Daugherty be fired since he seemed to be implicated. Coolidge rode out the storm of protest, and after weeks had gone by and public interest had become stale, he dismissed Daugherty on an unrelated issue, that the Attorney General refused a Senate committee access to Justice Department files. Walter Lippmann wrote, "There have been Presidents in our time who knew how to whip up popular enthusiasm. There has never been Mr. Coolidge's equal in the art of deflating interest."

Coolidge had no difficulty at all in obtaining the Republican nomination in the Presidential election of 1924, smothering all opposition in the primaries. The Democrats had thought that they could win in 1924 with a one-sentence platform, "Thou shalt not steal," but they were stymied by Coolidge's masterful handling of the situation, his own shining Puritanism, and his apparent cooperation with the investigations. They staged a donnybrook in Madison Square Garden in New York, where after two weeks and 103 ballots they came up with a candidate who offered no real alternative to Coolidge, since John W. Davis was a big corporation lawyer who had recently boasted, "I have J. P. Morgan, Standard Oil Company and other foremost American concerns on my list of clients. I am proud of them. Big business has made this country what it is."

The only feeling injected into a dull campaign was the candidacy backed primarily by the railroad brotherhoods of the old-time Progressive Senator Robert M. La Follette, "Fighting Bob." His platform, which he wrote himself, differed little from Theodore Roosevelt's in 1912 although he now proposed government ownership of the railroads and the Congressional right to reenact any law that the Supreme Court had declared unconstitutional. Since the Supreme Court was then as sacred as the flag and motherhood, this gave Republican orators the golden opportunity to denounce La Follette as a "Bolshevist" who wanted to overthrow American institutions. It was "Coolidge or chaos" since a vote for Davis might enable La Follette to deprive Coolidge of an electoral vote majority and throw the Presidential contest into the House, thereby delaying the setting up of a new administration indefinitely.

Beyond his acceptance speech, Silent Cal had nothing to say during the campaign. He did not think that it befitted a President to beg people to vote for him, and besides, he told his press conference, "I don't recall any candidate for President who ever injured himself by not talking." This silence exasperated Davis, who said of his campaign, "It reminds me of nothing as much as the words of Tennyson, 'The dead oared by the dumb went upward with the flood.' "

The major issue agitating the nation was the Ku Klux Klan, 5,000,000 strong, flourishing in the North, as well as the South. The Democratic convention in a dramatic cliff-hanging vote had refused to condemn it, but Davis lashed out against it in ringing denunciation. In answer to repeated requests for Coolidge to make known his position, his secretary and political majordomo, C. Bascom Slemp, sent out replies, "Concerning the Ku Klux Klan, the President has repeatedly stated that he is not a member of the Order and is not in sympathy with its aims and purposes." Newspapers commented editorially that, as a matter of fact, Coolidge himself had never stated that he was not in sympathy with the Klan. So Slemp released a new form letter which merely said that Coolidge's "position as to the Klan is well known to his intimates." Coolidge did receive good support from the Klan in the Midwest and border states. Billboards bore the slogan "Keep Kool with Koolidge," and from afar only KKK stood out to the viewer.

The 1923–1924 Congress had treated Coolidge most disrespectfully, and he had got only one minor measure through. The Omaha *World-Herald* put it, "Throughout the session the Republican Congress has devoted itself to bludgeoning the President's nose, boxing his ears and otherwise maltreating him." Nonetheless, the Coolidge myth was already emerging, the picture of a strong, resolute man at the helm of the ship of state, guiding it unharmed through all types of villainous attack. Cartoons appearing at this time, as they appeared all through his administration, depicted him as a teacher instructing an unruly gang of Congressional gamins or using a rod on them.

In the election, Coolidge won in a landslide, polling 15,725,000 votes to 8,387,000 for Davis, while La Follette polled the remarkable total of 4,823,000, running second to Coolidge in nine states. It was a humiliating defeat for the Democrats, who polled only 105,000 votes in California compared to 424,000 for La Follette. The Kansas City (Missouri) *Star* commented,

25

"If Calvin Coolidge is a myth, it is the cleverest myth ever set up in the political arena."

The inaugural the following March was, according to Coolidge's wishes, a barebones one. The parade was skimpy, only fifty minutes long, and Coolidge watched it apathetically. For the first time in many years there was no inaugural ball. There was no inaugural banquet, no inaugural concert, nothing beyond Coolidge's speech and the parade. Even at Lincoln's inauguration in 1861, when the life of the Republic hung in the balance, there were more festivities.

The new Vice President stole the show. Charles G. Dawes was an explosive character who had given his name to the Dawes Plan whereby the United States lent Germany the money to pay its reparations to the Allies, who, in turn, used the money to pay the United States their war debts.

In 1923 he had made a memorable appearance before a Congressional committee investigating war expenditures. Charges had been made before the committee of fabulous prices paid for war supplies, of mountains of food and equipment lost or wasted. Dawes, who had been a brigadier general in charge of supply, put on a performance which could not have been better stage-managed by David Belasco. He started off meekly, drawing slowly on his corncob pipe. He led on the committee members to nag him with trivial questions, carping criticisms and insinuations. Then he suddenly leaped to his feet. "Hell'n Maria. We were winning the war," he shouted, "not keeping books. Suppose we did lose a few carloads, what of it? We won the war, didn't we? Can't you understand that men were dying under shellfire? When we got a call from a field hospital, do you think we stopped to put it in the right column of the right ledger? Hell'n Maria, no. We shot it along." He almost blew the members out of their seats and blew himself into a national hero.

The Vice President in an inauguration is supposed to be subdued and even surreptitious—but not Dawes. In his inaugural speech in the Senate he lashed out at that chamber for its archaic rules, such as license for the filibuster. The tirade was delivered to the accompaniment of his pounding on the lectern with one hand as he leveled an accusing finger at the Senators with the other. The members gazed at him with stupefaction and afterward buzzed among themselves about the ignominy they had endured. Said Senator Henry F. Ashurst, "It was the most acrobatic, gymnastic speech I have ever heard in the Senate." Senator James Reed said, "His melody of voice, grace of gesture and majesty of presence were excelled only by his modesty."

Six days later Dawes had his one big opportunity to render a service to the Coolidge administration, and he ignobly struck out. As successor to Attorney General Harlan Fiske Stone, whom Coolidge had just elevated to the Supreme Court, Coolidge sent up the name of Charles B. Warren of Michigan. Opposition sprang up among Democrats and Progressives on the ground that when he was president of the Michigan Sugar Company, he had been allegedly involved in violations of the antitrust laws. The vote on confirmation was expected to be very close. On the afternoon of March 10 the debate was nearing its end, but Senator Albert B. Cummins had begun a speech in behalf of Warren which was expected to last four hours. He finished sooner than expected. Dawes was absent. He had gone to the Willard Hotel to take a nap, and a messenger was dispatched to find him. The vote was a tie, 40 to 40, which Dawes could have broken in Warren's favor if he had been there instead of charging down Pennsylvania Avenue in a taxicab. A delay was obtained in the Senate by taking another vote, and it was again 40 to 40. Just as Dawes entered the Senate chamber, the lone Democrat for Warren, Senator Lee S. Overman, shifted his vote, and the nomination was lost.

There were a good many quips about Dawes. Newsmen used the term "dawsing" for napping on the job. He had formed a controversial organization of ultraconservative businessmen, the Minute Men, and it was said that the "Minute Man was two minutes late." Dawes was never taken seriously after that as a political force in the Republican Party.

It was a galling rebuff for Coolidge, for it was the first time since Reconstruction that a President's choice for a Cabinet post had been defeated. Coolidge sent up the name of Warren again, and this time it was turned down by a big margin. Coolidge had trouble throughout his administration in getting his appointments approved by the Senate. As an act of gratitude for

27

nominating him in the 1920 convention he appointed Wallace McCamant of Oregon to the federal Circuit Court of Appeals, but the Senate turned it down because of the hostility of Senator Hiram Johnson of California.

Although the impression was widespread in the era that Coolidge was firmly in control, it was closer to the truth that the President and Congress were virtually stalemated. These were years of Republican ascendancy, not Republican domination. In the Congresses of 1922, 1924, and 1926, the Republican majority was so thin that it rested on the help of nominal Republicans, the Progressives of the West. In the years of Coolidge, 1923–1929, the record of Congressional inaction is remarkable —the only legislation that can be said to have had any enduring significance was the passage of the Federal Radio Act of 1927, which led to a subsequent statute setting up the Federal Communications Commission; the granting of funds for building Boulder Dam; and the appropriation of $325,000,000 for Mississippi River flood control.

A contributing factor was legislative resentment of Coolidge for being showered with praise while there were only brickbats for Congress. Typically, the St. Louis *Globe-Democrat* said, "The people are sick and tired of Congressional inefficiency and turmoil, they are sick of the lack of cohesion and purpose, sick of the domination by blocs and cliques, sick of its mistakes and failures." Coolidge was St. George in the public mind holding the Congressional dragon at bay. When he announced in August, 1927, that he did not "choose to run" again, it was treated as a national catastrophe, and when he left the White House, he was accompanied by hymns of praise from a grateful people.

Memory can distort over four fitful decades, and Americans tend to exaggerate their judgments. If Calvin Coolidge was overexalted in his lifetime, he has been too denigrated since his death. The patron saint of prosperity has come to be regarded as an antediluvian troglodyte in thought whose nonaction was responsible for the Crash. As a result, an inaccurate picture of Coolidge as a person has emerged.

For example, in *The Aspirin Age* published in 1949, Irving

Stone wrote, "He aspired to become the least President the country has ever had; he attained his desire. By forcing the government to lie supine, he paved the way for a world depression which led blocks of nations to demand forms of government which would control everything . . . he was as responsible as any individual of his age for the socialist revolution now sweeping over Europe and Asia." He went on. "In the White House he napped every afternoon through one of the most dangerous periods in modern history. . . . The Washington Monument pierces five hundred and fifty-five feet into the sky to symbolize the greatness of George Washington's contribution to his country. Calvin Coolidge's monument should be a hole dug straight into the ground to commemorate all the things he failed to do for his country."

In this, as well as in many other assessments, there is an inherent contradiction. If Coolidge was weak and ineffectual, how could his influence have been so strong, "forcing the government to lie supine"?

Throughout the twenties misconceptions about Coolidge were already rife. He was quite aware that the news media manufactured a quaint image of himself for the edification of the public. At the Gridiron Dinner in 1923 he told the newsmen, "The usual and ordinary man is not the source of very much news. But the boys have been very kind and considerate to me, and where there has been a discrepancy, they have filled it in and glossed it over, and they have manufactured some. They have undertaken to endow me with some characteristics and traits that I didn't altogether know I had. But I have done the best I could to live up to those traits." Coolidge was perfectly willing to pitch hay on his farm while wearing a business suit and patent-leather shoes, or to put on cowboy clothes, or to wear an Indian headdress, if the public enjoyed seeing him that way.

At the outset, Silent Cal was in large part pure myth. At the time there was a good deal of fun about him as a paradigm of silence—thus, "he can be silent in five languages," "when he opened his mouth a moth flew out," etc. In actuality, when Coolidge was at ease and not on public display, he was the most garrulous occupant that the White House has ever had. Herbert Hoover and Bernard Baruch both attest that in private conver-

29

sation they found it hard to get a word in edgewise. His secretary who succeeded Slemp, Everett Sanders, in after years wrote that it was a source of never-ending wonder to those around him in the White House that he could be known as "silent."

The transcripts of his press conferences, which took place in his office, were dug up and first published in 1964 in a volume entitled *The Talkative President*. They show that his answers to questions from newsmen went on endlessly. Here is an example. He was asked if he planned to visit New Orleans, and this was his reply:

> I don't recall now whether I have had an invitation to go to Louisiana next year. It seems as though someone came in and spoke to me about going to New Orleans. I would like to go down into the South, especially Louisiana, to go to New Orleans, because I have never happened to be there. I have been in most of the states of the Union, as far south as South Carolina. I haven't visited Florida. I judge from the current news reports that Florida is not in need just at the present time of additional guests [this was during the land boom] but I should like to go there very much. It is a wonderful country. I haven't been in Louisiana or Mississippi. I have been to Texas. I think those are all the states of the Union, with the possible exception of North Dakota, Montana and Idaho. When I went West once, I went over the Santa Fe and back another way, and another time over the Union Pacific and came back over the Canadian Pacific, so I didn't get into Idaho and Montana. I don't think I have been in North Dakota. The other states I have been in. But I haven't any plan about going South. It takes a considerable time to get there and back. I think it is very doubtful if I can pay a visit to that state during the coming winter.

Yet throughout his administration, in his public appearances, except when reading prepared speeches, Coolidge was frozen in silence. Foreign diplomats introduced to Coolidge had to be warned beforehand that the President's silence was not to be construed as displeasure. What accounts for these public silences? It is an interesting psychological question.

There might have been a traumatic experience sometime as a boy when he was forced to talk with strangers and thereafter developed a mental block whenever he felt that he was being similarly forced to talk. In a rare case of self-analysis on his part, he once said to Frank Stearns, "When I was a little fellow, I would go into a panic if I heard strange voices in the kitchen. I felt that I couldn't meet the people and shake hands with them. Most of the visitors would sit with Father and Mother in the kitchen, and the hardest thing in the world was to have to go through the kitchen door and give them a greeting. By fighting hard, I used to manage to get through that door. I'm all right with old friends, but every time I meet a stranger, I've got to go through the old kitchen door—and it's not easy."

Perhaps making a virtue of what he recognized as an ingrained quality, Coolidge often pointed out the advantage of silence and expressed his belief that reserve in speech enabled him to conduct his work more expeditiously. Governor Channing Cox of Massachusetts visiting him at the White House marveled that, "With all the people you see, you don't seem to be pressed for time, while I'm always fighting to get through so I can do some real work," to which Coolidge replied, "Channing, the trouble is that you talk back to them."

Belying his outer appearance, Coolidge was not emotionally cold. On the contrary, his sentimentality was excessive. Three days after he became President, he wrote to James Lucey, a cobbler of Northampton who had lined up Irish votes for him in his early campaigns, "Not often do I see you or write you, but I want you to know that if it were not for you I would not be here. And I want to tell you how much I love you." He was stickily sentimental about members of his family. He had no hesitancy about kissing his sons and his father in public. He always kept a photograph of his mother on his desk, and her photo in a silver case was found on his person at his death.

His love for his pets, particularly his collies Rob Roy, Prudence Prim, and Calamity Jane, was well known. When he napped in his bedroom in the afternoon, Rob Roy would sit on the window seat watching him, and when he arose, the dog would barkly wildly to announce to the world that his master was up. At mealtimes, Coolidge would shout, "Supper," and the three dogs would dash into the elevator and then would sit by the table accepting tidbits. Senator Watson related that once at breakfast, Rob Roy leaped up and grabbed a sausage from his plate. One of Will Rogers' favorite jokes in the theater was that when he was a guest at the White House, he had to get on all fours to get enough to eat; this provoked much merriment because it also contained the implication that Coolidge was parsimonious in feeding his guests.

On July 7, 1924, his son Calvin, Jr., age sixteen, died of blood poisoning a few days after he had developed a blister on his foot while playing tennis on the White House lawn. This happened in the days before penicillin, which could have effected a swift cure. A doctor at the bedside, Dr. John Albert Kolmer, writing in a medical journal many years later in 1955, said that anyone in the room where the boy lay would have been cured of any illusion about Coolidge's coldness. "At ten P.M. I announced that the boy was rapidly dying. The President sprang from his chair and took his dying son in his arms and shouted hysterically into his ears that he would soon join him in the Great Beyond and requested that young Calvin so inform his grandmother. A medallion of the grandmother was also placed in the hands of the dying boy."

After his Presidency, Coolidge took the unusual step of destroying his private papers. His *Autobiography* shows a studied attempt not to reveal himself. However, on the subject of his son Coolidge did open his heart. "We do not know what might have happened to him under other circumstances, but if I had not been President he would not have raised the blister on his toe which resulted in blood poisoning." Then this cry of anguish. "When he went the power and glory of the Presidency went with him. I do not know why such a price was exacted for occupying the White House."

The meaning seems clear. The Lord or whatever Providence he believed in had raised him above all other men, but in compensation, or perhaps to humble his pride, a fearful price had been exacted from him in the life of his son.

He did not display any affection whatever to Mrs. Coolidge in public. As a matter of fact, Coolidge both in public and in private seems to have treated his wife more coldly than any President's wife was treated, before or since. The answer seems to lie in his idiosyncratic personality or in some New England rural habit of regarding the woman as a housekeeper who must not intrude into men's affairs.

This charming, gracious, and lively lady (incidentally the first First Lady to smoke in the White House) obviously did not fit into his life as a partner but as an accessory. He never discussed his problems with her. Two years after his death, in 1935, she wrote, "Sometimes I wonder if Mr. Coolidge would have talked with me more freely if I had been of a more serious turn of mind. I do not think that he was favorably impressed with my education." Since she was a college graduate, this can mean only that he had contempt for her mind. He did not discuss with her at all his deliberations about whether to run for President in 1928, and after he had made the "I do not choose" announcement, he did not bother to advise her of it; she had to find out from another source.

It is doubtful that he talked to her at all. The evening was the only time he had free, but in a press conference, when asked if he had heard something on the radio, he replied, "My wife uses it [the radio] a great deal. I am usually in the evening engaged in some kind of work that keeps me in the library. My wife likes to knit or something of that kind and while she is knitting she turns on the radio."

She did not know his daily plans but had to keep her hat and coat handy in case she had to go with him somewhere. Once at breakfast she asked him if she could have his daily schedule, and he answered, "Grace, we don't give that out conspicuously." She did not even have the list of guests on the cruises on the Presidential yacht *Mayflower*. She had learned to make the best of it and once was heard to say, "I have never outgrown my childish enjoyment of the unexpected."

He would be quite abrupt with her in ordering her life. When he saw in the paper that Secretary of War Dwight F. Davis had arranged for her to take riding lessons at Fort Myer, he said acidly at breakfast, "I think you will find that you will get along at this job fully as well if you do not try anything new." When she bought a pair of culottes, before going on vacation in the Black Hills in 1927, he told her to return them. "No member of the Coolidge family has ever appeared in anything like that. Take it back where you got it."

He often indulged in sneers at her expense. Soon after their marriage she bought a book of household medical advice from

33

a door-to-door salesman. Leafing through it one day, she found
that her husband had written on one of the leaves, "This work
suggests no cure for a sucker." Before guests at dinner in Northampton he would make cutting remarks about her cooking such
as: "Don't you think the road commissioner would be willing
to pay my wife something for her recipe for pie crust?" Once
out of the blue he asked her, "When was Martin Luther born?"
She said she did not have the remotest idea, and he said, "Didn't
they teach you anything where you went to school?" These
details of her life with Calvin came from her own accounts.

Women played no part in Coolidge's existence. White House
chief usher Irwin "Ike" Hoover in his memoirs detailed the attitude of the seven Presidents he had served. Taft was a "ladies'
man pure and simple," Wilson "a great admirer of the ladies
but very discriminating," Harding "a sporting ladies' man"—
but Coolidge he dismissed with, "Coolidge had nothing to do
with the ladies."

Despite his sentimentality, there was a streak of sadism in his
nature. Though usually gracious to those with whom he worked,
he was capable of testiness and severity. Ike Hoover wrote that
he flew into terrible rages which made even such a choleric
predecessor as Theodore Roosevelt seem like a calm man. When
a memorial to Harding was completed at Marion, Ohio, he was
asked to dedicate it and declined. The shoddiness of the Harding regime was now clear to the world, and it would be politically unwise to do so. When pressure was put on him, he abused
the delegation. Though usually affable to the press, he opened
a press conference in the Adirondacks in the summer of 1927
by telling the correspondents that they should make their dispatches a serial entitled "Faking with the President," since all
he had read lately was a lot of hogwash.

In the White House files there is a note of November 11,
1924, to Secretary of the Navy Curtis D. Wilbur written an hour
and three-quarters after he had called about a commission for
the new Assistant Secretary Theodore Robinson which had not
yet arrived. Coolidge was obviously in high temper. "This is a
simple matter that should take no more than ten minutes. I
would like to have a report on this in a day or so." There is a
notation that the commission arrived just after Coolidge had

dictated the letter, but he ordered the note to be sent anyway, forcing the Secretary to make out a lengthy report. He often treated members of his Cabinet like lackeys. Thus, on June 27, 1927, he wrote to Secretary of War Davis, "I note your desire to go to France. . . . I do not like members of the Cabinet in Europe. Their presence is always misunderstood."

While the face he turned to the world was one of monarchical dignity, in private he was relaxed and often prankish. He would ring bells to summon all the White House janissaries, then walk off poker-faced. Colonel Edmund Starling, who took him for daily walks in early morning and evening, used to see him in his long nightgown peeking out of the Lincoln Room to discover whether the colonel was on duty. After he dressed, Coolidge would sometimes take the elevator to the basement to try to sneak out a side entrance to fool him, and Starling had to enlist the cooperation of the entire staff to catch him. Sometimes after the afternoon walk, Coolidge would invite Starling in for a bite. He took him to the butler's pantry and made cheese sandwiches "as strong as a billy goat." One day he said to Starling, "I'll bet no other President ever made cheese sandwiches for you." "No, indeed," Starling replied, "It is a great honor, Mr. President." Coolidge added glumly, "And I have to furnish the cheese, too."

Beneath the dour exterior there was considerable humor, which his class at Amherst had recognized in designating him the graduation humorist. Brevity was the soul of his wit, and it was given added flavor by being delivered deadpan. His reputation in that regard grew and along with it a body of apocrypha. For example, there is the famous story that on his return from church he was asked by his wife the subject of the sermon and said, "Sin," and, when asked further about it, replied, "He's against it." When Coolidge heard this, his wry comment was, "It would be better if it were true."

While he was presiding over the Massachusetts State Senate, a member complained angrily to him that another had told him to go to hell. Coolidge told him to calm down. "I've looked up the law on the subject and you don't have to go." At one of his press conferences he announced that he would attend a fair near his summer home the next day. When asked if he would say something, he replied, "No, I am going as an exhibit." When he was going to Florida to dedicate a "singing tower" constructed with funds from the philanthropist Edward Bok, he said, "Mr. Bok is dedicating it as a bird sanctuary and putting up these bells to interest the birds in music." His wit could be acidulous, "muriatic" to use a term of Mencken's. While he was driving in Rock Creek Park, he came across that independent character Senator William E. Borah taking his daily horseback ride. "I wonder if it bothers the Senator to be going in the same direction as his horse."

J. Russell Young, White House correspondent for the Washington *Evening Star,* delighted in telling about an incident that occurred during Coolidge's vacation at Swampscott, Massachusetts, in 1925. Accompanied by the press, Coolidge visited the farm of Clarence W. Barron, publisher of the *Wall Street Journal.* Barron showed him a prize bull. Coolidge asked him how much it was worth, and Barron replied, $30,000. Coolidge said nothing, but Young in his newspaper report put words in Coolidge's mouth: "Some bull." A few days later, Coolidge, accompanied by the press, drove to a place that required going up steep hills. When they arrived, Coolidge expressed to Young his surprise that his small coupe had been able to climb the grades. Young replied, "Mr. President, this little car can go anywhere your big limousine can go," to which Coolidge answered only, "Some bull."

Those who deem him reticent and a sluggard have to ignore the fact that Coolidge delivered more speeches (excluding political campaigns) and held more press conferences than any other President in our history. He could be hyperactive, as he was in getting the Republican nomination for himself in 1924. Harold Faulkner said in his book *From Versailles to the New Deal,* "Coolidge may have had a 'genius for inactivity' but this was not evident where his own political ambitions were concerned." Although he was responsible for little or no new legislation, behind the scenes he was hyperactive in ripping up the obstructions to business put up by administrative agencies.

He put in many hours at work. Although he did sleep long and nap afternoons, he worked evenings in the library and over weekends if he was not on the *Mayflower*. Compared to the 1,500 assistants which the President has today, he employed a pitifully small staff. There were only 40 in the whole Executive Office, and only 4 of these were above the rank of clerk. He combined in himself many of the functions now performed by highly specialized labor. He was his own press secretary; he was his own speechwriter with some research help; he was his own legal counsel; he was his own legislative liaison with Congress. Many times a member of Congress, told that the White House was calling, would pick up the phone to hear a nasal voice, "This is Mr. Coolidge speaking. . . ." He personally dispensed patronage and was acknowledged to have great skill in trading jobs for votes. Once Senator Selden P. Spencer of Missouri rose to ask unanimous consent to have inserted in the *Congressional Record* an article, "The Scientific Political Training of Calvin Coolidge." Democratic Senator Ashurst, who was sitting close by, rose and said, "I wonder if the Senator would speak more distinctly. Did I hear him to say that the article was entitled, 'The Scientific Political Trading of Calvin Coolidge'?"

Coolidge and Hoover were the last Presidents to write their own speeches. With the New Deal the practice began of a President's editing a speech written by others or merely endorsing its contents by reading it aloud. No one could mistake the Coolidge style which was a silhouette of his personality—spare, compact, without frills, devoid of adjectives. His sentences were epigrammatic and crisp—a statistician figured that he used 18 words per sentence, compared to 26.6 for Lincoln, 31.8 for Wilson, 41 for Theodore Roosevelt, and 51.5 for Washington. Repeatedly Coolidge used the antithesis construction—"not this, but that"; "this, although that"; "although this, yet that," etc.

Many regarded Coolidge as an effective writer, however windy his spontaneous speeches may have been. Among them was Chief Justice William Howard Taft, who privately expressed admiration for "his capacity for brief, cogent expression." Another was H. L. Mencken, who had nothing else good to say about Coolidge. Of Wilson, "The Archangel Woodrow," he wrote, "It is difficult to believe that even idiots ever succumbed to such transparent contradictions, to such gaudy processions of counterwords, to so vast and obvious a nonsensicality," and of Harding he wrote, "The learned doctor has acquired a gift for discourse that is to the public taste. It is a kind of baby-talk, puerile and wind-blown gibberish." But of Coolidge, he conceded, "He has a natural talent for the incomparable English language."

He once inscribed a book to a friend who had also lost his son, "To my friend, in recollection of his son, and my son, who by the grace of God have the privilege of being boys throughout eternity." In September, 1928, he was traveling through Vermont to inspect the repairs to the flood damage of the year before, and at Bennington he spoke, apparently spontaneously (although they sound more like his writing than like his speech), words that were widely reproduced in verse:

Vermont is a state I love.
I could not look
Upon the peaks
Of Ascutney, Killington,
Mansfield and Equinox
Without being moved
In a way that no other scene
Could move me.

It was here
That I first saw
The light of day.
Here I received my bride.
Here my dead lie,
Pillowed on the loving breast
Of our everlasting hills.

While the masses regarded Coolidge as a paragon of wisdom, hostile assessments appeared in the more literate journals. In the *American Mercury*, Frank Kent wrote, "To me the word that best describes him is 'thin.' He is physically and mentally thin—thin in body, thin in spirit, thin in mind. Not bad, Good Lord, no, just thin, a thoroughly commonplace, colorless personality, with a neat, one-cylinder intellect and thoroughly precinct mind." Mencken wrote also in the *American Mercury*, "He will be ranked among the vacuums. There is no principle in his armamentarium which is worthy of any sacrifice, even of sleep. There is no record that he ever thought anything worth hearing about any of the problems confronting him. His characteristic way of dealing with them is simply to avoid them, as a sensible man avoids an insurance solicitor or his wife's relatives."

Gamaliel Bradford wrote in the *Atlantic Monthly* an article entitled "The Genius of the Average." In the *North American Review*, John Spargo wrote, "His greatest strength is his commonplaceness, his lack of intellectual or other distinction separating him too far from the average man." According to Bruce Bliven in *Harper's*, he seemed "in many ways the common man himself. He photographs in the movies as well as possible from that point of view; he looks acutely miserable, self-conscious and ashamed."

However much Coolidge might have looked it, he cannot be accepted as "average." At a time when a far smaller percentage of the population went to college, he was graduated *cum laude* from a college of Ivy League quality. He would never have shocked his countrymen with a classical quotation, but he received a classical education. A high point of his college career was reading *Demosthenes on the Crown* in Greek; after graduation he diverted himself evenings by making his own translations of Cicero and read Dante's *Inferno* in the Italian. He participated in a nationwide contest among college seniors for an essay on the causes of the American Revolution and was awarded the first prize.

His excursions into culture were aborted by politics which caters to a low intellectual denominator, but his interest did not totally disappear. An English visitor Beverley Nichols related in his book *The Star Spangled Manner* his amazement that Coolidge, who was supposed to be an arch-Philistine, could discuss with him a modern art exhibition he had visited in Pittsburgh. "And as I looked at those pictures, I felt that I could see through them into the minds of the nations which had created them. If that nation's psychology was diseased, so was its art. The traces of neurosis were unmistakable."

The editors of his press conferences, Howard H. Quint and Robert H. Ferrell, stated in their introduction, "The President ranged over a wide variety of subjects with a degree of expertise that historians of a later generation have not always appreciated." Indeed, no one can read those transcripts in which Coolidge spoke off the cuff without being surprised that a President could be so well informed. Those who conversed with him have attested to that. The Democratic governor of South Dakota, William J. Bulow, who spent an evening with him during his 1927 vacation in the Black Hills, wrote, "I was surprised about the knowledge that Mr. Coolidge had on all kinds of subjects. . . . As the night wore on and he talked about so many different subjects, I thought about what the poet Goldsmith had said about the village schoolmaster, 'And still the wonder grew that one small head could carry all he knew.' "

The impression that Coolidge was a boor was created by stories such as the one that he dismissed the suggestion that the United States should forgive or reduce the Allies' war debts with, "Wal, they hired the money, didn't they?" The image is that of the narrow New England farmer determined not to be outslicked by big-city men or "furriners." The overwhelming probability is that this is part of the Coolidge apocrypha. Biographer Claude Fuess pronounced it a fairy tale. When the transcripts of his press conferences were unearthed, a search was made for the statement, and it was not to be found. Aside from the press, this was a subject he would have discussed only with members of his administration.

In actuality, Coolidge often discussed the problem in sophisticated terms during his unquoted press conferences. There was no precedent, he said, among civilized nations (which excluded Soviet Russia) for a repudiation of their external debts. Such things happened only among banana republics of Latin America. Moreover, it was to the interest of the European nations to pay the debts since an emergency might arise when they would want help again. "Unless money that is borrowed is repaid, credit cannot be secured in time of necessity." There was no One World concept at the time, and Coolidge's obligation was to the people of the United States. The foreign debts of approximately $10.3 billion amounted to half our national debt. "It has been pointed out time and again that this money has to be paid by our taxpayers, unless it is paid by the taxpayers of the countries which borrowed the money." While the European nations howled that they could not pay, they were spending hundreds of millions each year on armaments. "Nations which maintain huge armaments can afford to give consideration to their American obligations." When European nations put their money into armaments, the American taxpayer was hit twice because we were being forced into a competitive armament race. "I think that the practical policy to pursue at this time is not to enter into a competitive method of arming ourselves. . . . I should very much prefer that they would take their money and pay us, than on account of any action we took over here, feel that they should take their money and build battleships."

Coolidge was quite content if his views were represented as "Wal, they hired the money" if that was what the masses wanted. "He is a long-headed politician," wrote Chief Justice Taft to his wife. If it was politically smart to be "average," then this political animal would pose as average.

Colonel Starling was astonished when he became Coolidge's bodyguard to find that the man enjoyed no form of recreation —he did not play golf, ride horseback, fish, hunt, swim, bowl, or even play billiards, and he had no hobbies, even stamp collecting. In an era when more people spent more time at play than ever before, Coolidge must have decided that it was politically smart to achieve rapport with his countrymen.

Before his 1926 vacation in the Adirondacks, he told his press conference that fishing was for the old and infirm, but that summer he blossomed out as a fisherman—by holding the rod for the photographers, while Secret Service men baited the hook and unhooked the fish. The next summer, in the Black Hills of South Dakota, Coolidge became the nation's foremost trout fisherman. At Spearfish the state had a hatchery in which the trout were so tame that they ate out of a man's hand. At night, trout were put in tanks, driven to the creek where Coolidge fished, and penned up by wire netting on both sides. "The two miles of creek became the best trout fishing in the world. Those trout would fight and battle one another to see which could grab the President's hook first," related Governor Bulow.

Coolidge, as a fisherman, intrigued the nation. In the delicious satire by Sinclair Lewis, "The Man Who Knew Coolidge," Lowell Schmaltz of Zenith claims that he was a classmate of Coolidge in his first year at Amherst and on a visit to the White

House with his family tries to see Coolidge. He gets no further than an outer office, where a young man says that because of Schmaltz's close relationship with the President, he will tell him anything confidential he wants to know.

"Mr. Jones, what is the truth about the President's fishing? Is he a good fisherman?" and Mr. Jones confides to Schmaltz, "He's one of the best. His catch always compares favorably with that of any member of the party. But you must remember that he's constantly weighed down by the cares of the world."

Coolidge's philosophy may have been misguided and benighted, but contrary to the conventional caricature, he did have a philosophy and had full and incisive views on all issues. The *New Republic*, which ran a close race with Mencken's *American Mercury* and the *Socialist Call* to see which could appreciate Coolidge least, said, "Mr. Coolidge lives in a world which is thoroughly explored. It is laid out in uniform, rectangular blocks, which have all been meticulously surveyed, and in which every important place and object is definitely located."

Among Coolidge's firmest beliefs was his view that government should not play a significant part in our daily life. Government is nonproductive, and investment in government not only is sterile but drains the productive force of the nation of the capital needed for full economic activity. War prosperity induced by government spending was a counterfeit one. "Of course there was a large business during the War, but it was business that was paid for by using the capital of the country. The business of the past years has been paid for in the ordinary business way out of earnings." Today this may sound as ancient as Nineveh and Tyre, but then it was proclaimed and accepted as the gospel.

Business alone produces wealth and national well-being. In his acceptance speech in 1924 he adopted the philosophy of his Secretary of the Treasury Andrew W. Mellon that surtaxes on the incomes of the rich should be cut so that wealth could be invested in business, instead of going into tax-free state and local bonds. "I am not disturbed about the effect on a few thousand people with large incomes because they have to pay high surtaxes. What concerns me is the indirect effect on the rest of the people. Let us always remember the poor."

"Let us always remember the poor." The introduction of the plight of the poor in the discussion of what was palpably a tax relief measure for the rich is somewhat startling. Yet it is a sincere expression of the Hamiltonian philosophy as worked out in Coolidge's mind. The poor have a community of interest with the rich since, when the rock of industry is struck with the magic wand of capital, all drink of its waters.

Business, he proclaimed, "rests squarely on the law of service, reliance on truth, faith and justice. The growing tendency of American business to correct its own abuses has left the Government free to advance from problems of reform and repression [note the equivalence given the two words] to those of economy and construction." Lincoln Steffens commented that Coolidge had responded to the charge that government was a kept woman of business "by marrying Wall Street to Washington."

Government makes its contribution by being the least nuisance to business. He enthroned laissez-faire. "We have got so many regulatory laws already that I feel we would be better off if we did not have any more. . . . The greatest duty and opportunity of government is not to embark on any new ventures. . . . It does not at all follow that because abuses exist that it is the concern of the federal government to attempt their reform. . . . What we need is not more federal government but better local governments."

Every dollar saved from government was a dollar to turn the wheels of industry—therefore, the program that Coolidge called constructive economy. He set an example in the White House by ordering all unnecessary lights turned off; paper drinking cups were replaced by old-fashioned glasses; towels in lavatories were reduced from 175 to 88; there would no longer be free pencils for White House correspondents, who would have to buy their own. Democratic critics pointed out that nonetheless the *Mayflower*, which Coolidge used for weekend cruises, cost the taxpayers half a million dollars a year, and the cost was concealed by classifying the boat in the Navy budget as a light cruiser.

Budget Director Herbert M. Lord decreed strict enforcement

of economy in all government departments. Both sides of the paper were to be used for mimeographing; abbreviated addresses were to be placed on telegraphic, cable, and radio dispatches. A directive by Lord stated that the use of mechanical pencils instead of shaft pencils would produce "an annual per capita saving of three cents per employee."

Continuously, Coolidge preached and lectured to the nation in a stream of glittering aphorisms about the need for character. If America followed the creed of hard work and the tenets of virtue, it would be crowned with success. In his last annual message to Congress, he stated, "The main source of these unexampled blessings lies in the integrity and character of the American people." All this went down well, as Bruce Bliven wrote, since " 'Intellect' is at a discount compared to 'character' and 'good intentions.' There is a general feeling that intellect alone will lead us to Bolshevism."

Benighted Europe could not share in these blessings because it had lost the road to virtue and in fact had never been on it. We had saved ungrateful Europe from "starvation and ruin." In a typical sneer he said in an Armistice Day speech, "Europe is reported to hate us. This means that our interests have come within the European circle, whose distrust and suspicions, if nothing more, have been altogether too common. To turn such attention to us indicates at least that we are not ignored." Such colossal smugness helps explain why Coolidge was among the least popular Americans abroad.

All was stated apodictically; all was as right as right could be. The *New Republic* said that it had penetrated to the "heart of the Coolidge mystery" and found a windy "pedant." Once Senator George W. Norris exclaimed in the Senate, "He thinks he is a little Jesus Christ!" which he was persuaded to change in the *Congressional Record* to "He thinks that he is the embodiment of perfection."

But didactic, platitudinous pap was more generally acclaimed as supernal wisdom. The month after Coolidge's "I do not choose" statement in August, 1927, an article by Alice Pattison Merritt, "Why Women 'Choose' Coolidge," appeared in the *North American Review*. She said, "He has the faculty of grasping the fundamental truth in a situation and the greater gift of presenting it so that the people understand it and accept it. No one has stated the vital need of America so simply and vividly as he did in an address." What were the golden words of Coolidge she refers to? "We do not need more material development, we need more spiritual development. We do not need more intellectual power, we need more moral power. We do not need more knowledge, we need more character. We do not need more law, we need more religion."

Never had a President, except during the Era of Good Feelings under James Monroe a century before, enjoyed such solid support from the popular press. Normally Democratic papers, even William Randolph Hearst for the first time in his journalistic career, supported the incumbent President, and Hearst's Arthur Brisbane, the most popular columnist of that day, regularly exalted Coolidge as another Lincoln in character and another Napoleon in executive strategy.

This massive press buildup was assisted by the format of the Coolidge press conference. Twice a week the correspondents streamed into Coolidge's office and gathered in a semicircle around him. He put down his ever-present cigar, rose, and thumbed through the typewritten questions submitted to him, answering those he chose to. Under the rules set by Coolidge, no press transcript was available, no shorthand notes could be taken, no mention could be made of the questions that Coolidge did not choose to answer. And as far as the reading public was concerned, all information emanated not from Coolidge but from a mysterious and wraithlike creature who was known only as the White House Spokesman.

Often Coolidge talked vaguely; often what he had to say was deadly dull. As a writer said in the *Independent* magazine, "One goes into the President's office bouncing with spirit, one comes out dragging one's footsteps, tired of life." However, since there were no transcript, no direct quotes, and only indirect attribution to the President, the correspondents had loose rein and could doctor what the rapidly talking Coolidge said to make a report the public wanted to read, reflecting the unexcelled wisdom and courage of Calvin Coolidge. In 1963 Drew Pearson recalled, "Any newsman who tried to report that Calvin Coolidge wasn't the greatest President since Washington was likely to have trouble with his publisher."

His popularity was no accident. Despite the appearance he gave, despite superficial characteristics of a lackluster personality that seemed to set him apart from his contemporaries in a flamboyant age—his remoteness, joylessness, and saturnine aspect—Coolidge embodied the regnant political attitudes of the age: tiredness with war idealism, nationalism and xenophobia, economic conservatism, consuming faith in free enterprise, reverence for businessmen and the business system, apathy to political action, rejection of society's obligation to the individual, and smug optimism about the present and future. He was preeminently what the nation wanted. "He may not shoot off a lot of fireworks," said Lowell Schmaltz, as quoted by Sinclair Lewis, "but do you know what he is? He's SAFE."

This was truly the Age of Coolidge. In many ways the words of Ralph Waldo Emerson regarding an institution could be applied to the nation, that it was "the lengthened shadow of a man."

Chapter II

THE REACTION

There are some photographs that speak more eloquently than words, and one of them is that of President Woodrow Wilson addressing American troops on Christmas Day, 1918, at Humes in France. The gaunt, bareheaded man in fur-collared and fur-sleeved coat stands erect over a group huddled in the cold on the rostrum. In front of him, looking dolefully up, is a stray dog which has wandered onto the field. The soldiers are lined up at least twenty yards away. The mud is inches deep, and a wet snow is falling.

What Wilson was saying to the men in the faraway ranks was, "I find a comradeship with you today which is delightful." He talked of the "moral courage" needed to stay at home, away from the "Great Crusade." Their sacrifice would not be in vain because it would achieve "peace upon the foundation of right."

There is an ashen, dejected quality to the scene. The men could not have cared less what the President was saying. They had dined on baked beans for Christmas dinner and had marched for hours in the mud to greet Wilson. They wanted to go home.

The main character in Hemingway's *Farewell to Arms*, Lieutenant Henry, might almost have been commenting on this scene, when he said, "I was always embarrassed by the words sacred, glorious and sacrifice, and the expression in vain. We had heard them, sometimes standing in the rain almost out of earshot, so that only the shouted words came through . . . the things that were glorious had no glory and the sacrifices were like the stockyards at Chicago if nothing was done with the meat except to bury it."

The historian Samuel Eliot Morison has commented that no war was more popular in our history than the First World War while we fought it, and no war was so unpopular after. Seven men could be counted in our history who became Presidents because of their participation in previous wars; others had been nominated and many considered. But after this war no military figure of it was elected, none nominated and none seriously considered for the Presidency.

The war experience had been stripped of glory and idealism and revealed as stark death, bestiality, and filth. The quixotic adventure to save democracy became regarded as a sacrifice at enormous cost to pull Britain's and France's chestnuts out of the fire.

The spirit of disillusionment was directed at Wilson personally. Mark Sullivan described him as that "unhappy victim of the exaltation that had turned sour, personification of the rapture that had now become gall, sacrificial whipping-boy for the present bitterness." In 1924, Harry Elmer Barnes, writing in the *American Mercury,* said that "Woodrow Wilson produced more cynics than any figure in modern history." Our involvement in the war should have been convincing proof that the problems of the world community were something that we could not escape from thereafter. Franklin D. Roosevelt running as James Cox's running mate on the Democratic ticket in 1920 said with logic that was almost self-evident, "Every sane man knows that in case of another world war, America would be drawn in anyway, whether we were in the League [of Nations] or not." But the country, not wanting to be convinced, threw logic to the winds and overwhelmingly rejected the pro-League ticket in the Presidential election of 1920. Anti-League feeling was so strong that the State Department in the first year of the Harding administration feared even to acknowledge communications from the League.

This swift turnabout in national psychology is one of the most remarkable phenomena on our history. It rejected not only Wilson's international program to secure everlasting peace, but also the spirit of his domestic program. The reaction against Wilsonism swung America away from the reform that had been the keynote of our national policy from Theodore Roosevelt's time at the beginning of the century. The wave of progressivism which had produced such laws as the direct primary, popular election of Senators, the income tax, and stricter control of trusts and railroads was over.

The postwar era was actually not a return to "normalcy" (a word coined by Harding, who is believed to have misread "normality" in a speech). Instead, it was turning the clock back to the days of a more primitive approach to public problems. As the liberal magazine *Nation* put it in 1920, the new watchword was "Forward march—to the rear."

Reform had become an invidious term because it was associated with the frightful specter, that cesspool of revolutionary thought, Bolshevism. Attorney General A. Mitchell Palmer, who conducted a Red hunt under Wilson and deported aliens wholesale, wrote in 1920 of his success, "Like a prairie fire, the blaze of revolution was sweeping over every American institution of law and order. It was eating its way into the homes of American workers, its sharp tongues of revolutionary heat were licking the altars of churches, leaping into the belfry of the school-bell, seeking to replace marriage vows with libertine laws."

Postwar reaction found its dedicated apostle in Coolidge. He was particularly watchful for any insidious Bolshevist attempt to penetrate our institutions. When he was Vice President in 1921, he wrote for the *Delineator* magazine a series of articles showing how the new generation of college women was being corrupted by Bolshevism. At Wellesley, there was a club for the study of Socialism, a library in which books for and against Socialism were in "considerable use," and a professor of philosophy had admitted voting for the Socialist Eugene V. Debs for President. Radcliffe College was a hotbed of Bolshevism. The *Radcliffe News* had editorially criticized the attempt to exclude five Socialists from the New York State Assembly.

Throughout his Presidency, Coolidge was ever vigilant to identify liberal movements as part of the serpentine plots of

Bolshevism. When his Secretary of State Frank B. Kellogg in Congressional hearings described the program of the Calles government in Mexico, particularly measures to nationalize oil properties, as part of an international Bolshevist conspiracy, Coolidge's critic, Senator George W. Norris, derided him in a parody of James Whitcomb Riley's "The Goblins."

> Onc't there was a Bolshevik who wouldn't say his prayers,
> So Kellogg sent him off to bed, away upstairs,
> An' Kellogg heered him holler, an' Coolidge heered him bawl,
> But when they turnt the kivvers down, he wasn't there at all.

> They seeked him down in Mexico, they cussed him in the
>   press,
> They seeked him 'round the Capitol, an' ever'wheres I guess,
> But all they ever found of him was whiskers, hair and clout,
> An' the Bolsheviks'll git you, ef you don't watch out.

America was best. A tremendous surge of nationalistic feeling swept over the country. Coolidge expressed belief in our superiority in many ways. The British publication *Punch* sketched him in academic garb instructing a class, having written on the blackboard, "We lead the world in 1) wealth 2) generosity 3) humility 4) love of peace." The *Ladies' Home Journal* said editorially, "There is only one first class civilization. It is right here in the United States." A French visitor, André Siegfried, wrote of the American's view of himself, "As a people we are the wisest, politically the most free, and socially the most developed. Other nations may fail and fall. We are safe. Our history is the narrative of the triumph of righteousness among the peoples."

America was celebrated in a continuous rhapsody. Women's clubs opened their meetings by singing "America the Beautiful" and Rotary clubs with "My Country, 'Tis of Thee." In churches of the Episcopal Diocese of New York, there was a ritual performed called "Worship of the Flag," with psalms and responses from the congregation. Congress appropriated funds for Gutzon Borglum to carve the faces of our great men on the slopes of Mount Rushmore in South Dakota. Hollywood turned out epics of America, *Abraham Lincoln, The Covered Wagon, Union Pacific.* In 1928 the Musical America Prize was awarded to

Ernest Bloch for his *America* intoning America's glorious past and future, which was played simultaneously by six top symphony orchestras in the country. Legislatures of thirteen states passed laws requiring teachers in their schools to take oaths to support the Constitution. Laws were passed to ensure that schoolchildren would not be misled by lies about the unsullied past of our country. A New Jersey law forbade the use of any textbooks which "belittles, falsifies, misrepresents, distorts, doubts, or denies the events leading up to the Declaration of Independence or to any war in which this country has been engaged. . . ."

Having saved Europe from "starvation and ruin," America turned its back on the rest of the world and erected walls of insularity. Even before Wilson had returned from the Versailles Peace Conference, a movement had been launched in Congress to raise tariff barriers against world goods. Wilson protested that there was no need for haste, Europe would need years for rehabilitation from the ravages of the war and "no serious danger of foreign competition now threatens American industries." As soon as Harding took office in 1921, an Emergency Tariff Act was passed and was followed the next year by the Fordney-McCumber Act, which wiped out the tariff reductions made by the Underwood Tariff Act of 1913.

One of the most important developments in our history was the shutting of our doors to immigrants. Our policy had previously been one of welcome as expressed in the poem of Emma Lazarus graven on a tablet at the Statue of Liberty. "Give me your tired, your poor,/Your huddled masses yearning to breathe free. . . ." Now the fear was spread that foreigners were contaminated with radicalism, unassimilable and generally inferior. Sociologist Henry Pratt Fairchild wrote that the foreigner was responsible for boss rule in our great cities and mongrelization of our race. Madison Grant in his *The Passing of the Great Race* said that the "weak, the broken and the mentally crippled" would conquer the "great race" unless "inferior" peoples of southern and central Europe were barred from these shores.

Wilson vetoed a bill to establish a quota policy, but a law was enacted as soon as Harding took command, limiting immigrants to 3 percent of foreign born of that nationality resident in the United States according to the census of 1910, provided the total number did not exceed 350,000 in a year. Many felt that the figure was too high and that too large a proportion came from the southern and eastern parts of Europe. The newly revived Ku Klux Klan and the Daughters of the American Revolution put pressure on Congress, as did the American Federation of Labor, which believed that foreign low-cost labor threatened wage standards of American workers.

A new law was enacted in 1924, the Johnson Act, which was far more stringent and would cut the number of new immigrants by half. It restricted the figure to 2 percent of the foreign born of that nationality according to the census of 1890, which had the effect of making the quotas favorable to countries of northern Europe. One paper quipped that the nation should now sing:

> My country, 'tis of me,
> Nordic shall ever be.

Coolidge, signing the bill, said, "America must be for Americans." He did protest against one feature of the new law, a total ban on the immigration of Japanese, which was a completely gratuitous insult to a race sensitive about "face." If the quota system had been applied, only 107 Japanese would have been able to enter the country a year. The new law was an element in worsening Japanese-American relations until Pearl Harbor.

The most spectacular manifestation of reaction, nationalism, and nativism was the rebirth of the Ku Klux Klan, less a rebirth of the Ku Klux Klan of Reconstruction days in the South than the revival of the bigoted Know-Nothing Party, anti-Catholic and anti-foreign, which was formed in the 1850's. The new Klan began in 1915, when Colonel William J. Simmons and thirty others burned a cross on top of Stone Mountain near Atlanta, Georgia, and swore allegiance to the Invisible Empire, Knights of the Ku Klux Klan. It languished until 1920, when promoters Edward Clarke and Mrs. Elizabeth Tyler took it over and divided the organization into states run by King Kleagles and larger domains under Grand Goblins. It grew tremendously in the North, as well as in the South, after a Houston dentist, Hiram Wesley Evans, ousted Simmons. The Klan is not anti anything, proclaimed Evans; it is only pro-American. "Americanism is a thing of the spirit, a purpose and a point of view that can come only through instinctive racial understanding." Catholics, Negroes, and Jews "are simply racially incapable of understanding, sharing or contributing to Americanism."

The psychological reasons for the amazing growth of the Klan are complex. No doubt nationalistic feeling, left unsatisfied by the short war, had something to do with it. Charles W. Furgeson in *Confusion of Tongues* wrote, "We had indulged in wild, lascivious dreams. We had imagined ourselves in the act of intercourse with the Whore of the World. Then suddenly the war was over, and the Whore vanished for a time and we were in a condition of *coitus interruptus*," and so with consummation necessary, an imaginary whore had to be found. Samuel Eliot Morison in the same vein said that the "campaign of hate during the war got the people all hopped up for fighting Germany to an unconditional surrender, hanging the Kaiser, and all that; so when the war ended abruptly before even half the armed forces had seen action, the public, suddenly let down, turned its emotions against something else."

The Klan appealed to the American joiner instincts. Mencken saw the Klan as "no more than a manifestation of the poor hind's pathetic effort to raise himself out of his wallow, to justify and dignify his existence." At the local level its great strength lay in the fact that it was all things to all men, supporting Prohibition where Prohibition was strong, against the League of Nations where anti-League sentiment was strong. In Oregon, which had a population of 850,000, it had a membership of almost 100,000 by 1922 and ousted Governor Ben W. Olcott from office because he had publicly condemned it. It pushed through the state legislature a law forcing children between eight and sixteen years of age to attend public schools, a law declared unconstitutional by the Supreme Court in 1925 in *Pierce v. Society of Sisters*.

In the Democratic National Convention of 1924 the convention refused by a few votes to condemn the Klan by name. In August, 1925, 40,000 members of the Klan marched unhooded down Pennsylvania Avenue in Washington. But the Klan was already in a state of decline, and the next year its membership was down at least a third. As membership continued to dwindle, in February, 1928, it announced that it was dropping the use of masks and that its new name would be Knights of the White Forest.

An affair which had erupted in Indiana in 1925 was to be a potent factor in sealing its doom.

There is not much known of the early life of David Curtis Stephenson. He was born in Houston, Texas, in 1891, the son of Arizona D. Stephenson. One of the points in dispute is whether he attended a Catholic parochial school for part of what education he had. After little more than a grammar school education, he went into the printing business. Somewhere along the line he acquired a wife and child, whom he abandoned. He served in the war and in 1919 appeared in Evansville, Indiana, where he became a coal salesman. He was a candidate for the Democratic Congressional nomination in 1920 as a wet but was defeated. He then turned Republican. He was active in organizing veterans, and from that activity he turned to the embryonic Klan in Indiana.

He had great sales ability and became a top organizer for the Klan. He not only was an important figure in Indiana but was also Propagator for twelve Northern states with offices in Columbus, Ohio. He was so important nationally that in November, 1922, the night before a great Klonvocation in Atlanta, he and another Klan official woke up the Klan leader, William J. Simmons, and high-pressured him by threats and intimidation to resign the leadership in favor of Hiram W. Evans, who became Grand Wizard while Simmons had to accept the lowly post of Emperor. Stephenson became a chief aide to Evans. Records show that for the quarterly period starting March 17, 1923, he sent Evans the sum of $641,475 from the $10 Klecktokens paid by new Klan members. From each $10, Stephenson received $1.25 profit for himself and also got $3 from the sale of the Klan regalia of the nightshirt and ring.

Stephenson operated out of a suite of offices on the third floor of the Kresge Building in Klanopolis, otherwise known as Indianapolis. On a frosted door there was a sign CENTRAL STATES COAL COMPANY, and inside there was a room with an arched entrance over which there was imprinted "All bearers of evil tidings shall be slain." Although only thirty-two in 1923, Stephenson was known to most of his associates as The Old Man and often signed his letters that way. His mind moved rapidly, particularly when stimulated by drink. Despite his meager education, he spoke flawless English, and his tirades were punctuated by terrible oaths. His energy was boundless, and he once addressed a meeting of Klansmen for five hours with only one short break.

On July 4, 1923, there was a great Konklave of the Klan from three states at Kokomo, Indiana, attended by at least 100,000 Klansmen and their families in Melfalfa Park. In the afternoon a vast crowd waited in an open meadow. Soon a speck was discerned in the sky; it was a gilded airplane which landed, and out of it emerged a figure in a silken purple robe embellished with mystic symbols. Escorted to a dais, he flung back his visor and addressed the crowd: "My worthy subjects, citizens of the Invisible Empire, Klansmen all. It grieves me to be late. The President of the United States kept me unduly long counselling upon vital matters of state. Only my plea that this is the time and place of my coronation obtained for me surcease from his prayers for guidance," which was, of course, all poppycock.

Stephenson then read a document signed by Imperial Wizard Evans appointing him as the new Grand Dragon of Indiana. That night there was a parade, with thirty bands, but as in all Klan Klavalkades, there was no music, only the beating of drums. At regular intervals there were two Klan flags flanking an American flag. There was also a huge American flag, thirty feet long, with a dozen men holding it on each side. "Although hundreds of persons in the larger cities who had had no direct contact with the Klan felt that it could be laughed out of existence," wrote Morton Harrison, "few expressed that view after seeing a robed Klan parade. Bystanders watching a night parade of robed Klansmen marching four abreast were immediately quieted by the ghostly spectacle. The columns extended in the glare of one street lamp after another as far as there was any visibility. White-robed figures with heads and faces covered with pointed hoods, bodies completely draped in loose flowing cassocks—the dead whiteness of the uniforms and the dead silence of the marchers. . . . In the great mass of marchers there was not an eye or a face or hand in sight, nothing to read but a broken ripple of old shoes shuffling in and out of the shadow cast by the robes."

Under Stephenson's guidance the membership of the Klan in Indiana grew to 195,000, an enormous figure in view of the fact that the total male population of the state of all ages was 1,500,000. In the southern part of the state, close to Tennessee, where the population was almost 98 percent native-born, the migration of foreigners and Negroes into industry was viewed with deep suspicion. Stephenson built his campaign on hatred in the abstract—for the Jewish international bankers who bloodsucked huge profits out of the war, aliens who would overflow from the East and engulf Indiana and destroy American institutions, blacks who would move in waves from the South and take away jobs from Americans. The most potent image of fear was the Pope, who was preparing to move his headquarters from the Vatican to Washington. Photographs of the new Episcopalian Cathedral then being built on Mount St. Alban in Washington were circulated as proof of the Pope's new home, where he could command the capital city with field guns.

Every gimmick was employed to round up members for the Klan. Farmers and small townspeople were enlisted in a great moral crusade against vice. Stephenson unearthed a forgotten statute which authorized citizens to charter themselves into a Horse-thieves Detectives Association which could conduct searches without warrant, and thus Klansmen were empowered to raid suspected disorderly houses and drinking taverns. Businessmen were lured by the prospect that Jewish and Catholic shops would be boycotted, and anyway it was better to join than be harassed. Klan stores bore the TWK emblem (Trade with the Klan).

In the spring of 1924 Stephenson started his drive to take over the state government of Indiana. He backed for the Republican nomination for governor a party hack who was secretary of state, Ed Jackson, who had been given no chance. Stephenson's flavorful rhetoric is evident in these cards which were plastered over the state:

Remember

Every criminal, every gambler, thug, libertine, girl-ruiner, home-wrecker, wife-beater, dope peddler, moonshiner, crooked politician, pagan papist priest, shyster lawyer, Knight of Columbus, white-slaver, brothel madam, Rome-controlled newspaper, black spider is fighting the Klan. Think it over—which side are you on?

With the Klan's backing, Jackson won in the primary, and he went on to capture the governorship. The Republican State Convention that year was called a Klan Koncillium; in it the Klan named every candidate except the attorney general.

Stephenson started feuding with Grand Wizard Evans, the bone of contention being the funds that were shipped from Indiana to Atlanta. Evans attacked Stephenson, and Stephenson retaliated in a manifesto entitled "The Old Man's Answer to the Hate Vendors." It said in part, "The hour of fate has struck. The venality and jealousy of the men who carried the Rebel flag in '61 is now invading Indiana. It is a cowardly attempt on the part of a few yellow-livered Southerners who hate everything that is pure in Indiana. The present Imperial Wizard is an ignorant, uncouth individual who eats his peas with a knife. He has neither courage nor culture. He cannot talk intelligently. His speeches are written by hired intelligence."

Evans held a Konklave in Evansville which expelled Stephenson for immorality. Stephenson, nothing daunted, organized an independent Klan in Indiana and other Northern states. Observers had predicted that the national leadership was so weak that internal pressures would split the Klan and that was now happening.

When the legislature convened in January, 1925, the thirty-four-year-old Stephenson was regarded as the most powerful political figure in the state, and he played the part. Visitors to his office would hear him say into the phone, "Now you tell [United States Senator] Watson that I don't want [Postmaster General] Harry New to do that." A letter from the mayor of Indianapolis, J. L. Duvall, was later produced, written in February, 1925, in which Duvall wrote that in exchange for Stephenson's political support, he would appoint two named individuals as chief of police and captain and would appoint no members to the Board of Public Works without Stephenson's consent. At parties he gave, Stephenson would appear in Oriental dress and shriek, "I am the counterpart of Napoleon, the mastermind of the world. Drink her down."

Stephenson was hated, loved, and feared. He had his own paper, *The Fiery Cross*. Few had the hardihood to refuse to advertise in it. He organized auxiliary organizations to which he could sell regalia: Queens of the Golden Mask for women, Junior Klans for boys, and Triple K clubs for girls. He had a large home in the Irvington section of Indianapolis, a summer home on Buckeye Lake, Ohio, and a $75,000 yacht. He was believed to have greater ambitions. United States Senator Samuel M. Ralston was failing in health, and Stephenson was said to have expected Governor Jackson to appoint him Senator when Ralston resigned. He viewed himself as the logical Republican Presidential candidate in 1928, when he could sweep the South for the GOP.

All these hopes were suddenly exploded. In mid-January, at a banquet, Stephenson had met a twenty-eight-year-old unmarried girl, buxom Madge Oberholtzer, who was employed by the state superintendent of public instruction as manager of the Young People's Reading Circle. She was not attractive in the eyes of most men, but Stephenson disagreed. He tried to date her on several occasions, and she had had dinner with him twice at an Indianapolis hotel. On Sunday night, March 15, he called her at her home in Irvington, not far from his, and she returned the call at 10 P.M. He said he had something important to discuss with her and he would send someone over to get her. She did come over and found that Stephenson and his three companions had been drinking heavily. They forced drinks on her. He told her, "I want you to go to Chicago with me. I love you more than any woman I have ever known." The men armed themselves with pistols. Terrified and befuddled with drink, she accompanied Stephenson and a man named Gentry to the railroad station. "I think I am pretty smart to have gotten her," Stephenson told Gentry, who accompanied the couple aboard the train.

On the train they occupied a compartment. Gentry took the

upper berth. Stephenson pulled off her clothes and shoved her into the lower berth. He attacked her and chewed her all over, bit her neck and face, chewed her tongue, and chewed her breasts so hard that they bled. The next morning the three got off at Hammond, Indiana (possibly Stephenson was thinking of the federal Mann Act), and they checked into the Indiana Hotel.

After Stephenson had slept, they walked about the town, and she asked Stephenson for $15 to buy a hat. She bought the hat and then went to a drugstore, saying she wanted to buy some rouge. There she bought eighteen bichloride of mercury tablets. Back at the hotel room she swallowed six tablets, and in the afternoon, when she started spitting blood, told Stephenson's chauffeur, "Shorty," who had arrived, that she was dying. Stephenson was now thoroughly frightened. He wanted to take her to Crown Point, where they could marry, but she demurred. He then decided to return her to Indianapolis, and they drove there while she was vomiting blood. "You'll stay right here with me until you marry me," he said. "You must forget this. What is done has been done. I am the law and the power in Indiana."

That night, the sixteenth, she stayed in a room above his garage, and the next day she was returned to her home by Stephenson's men. Doctors were called immediately. She lingered on until April 14. Before dying she made a full statement which was legally admissible at Stephenson's trial. There was medical testimony that the taking of the tablets alone did not cause death; she could have been saved if she had been given medical attention. An added cause of death, if not the main cause, was infection from the bites on her body. Stephenson was convicted of second-degree murder and sentenced to life imprisonment.

Stephenson was stunned by the verdict. He thought that Governor Jackson would pardon him, but Jackson dropped him, as did all his old comrades. His lawyers claimed that Jackson even made it difficult for them to see him. From time to time Stephenson threatened that he would open up his "little black box" unless he were sprung, but to no avail. He finally revealed his secrets, and a Congressman, the mayor of Indianapolis, and the sheriff of Marion County went to jail while Governor Jackson escaped only by grace of the statute of limitations. Stephenson remained in jail, in effect a political prisoner, for thirty years. With good behavior he would have been paroled long before if Indiana governors had not regarded releasing him too much of a political liability.

The Stephenson case went far to kill the Klan. The pretensions of the Klan to guard our nation's purity became a subject for joke and ridicule, and the Klan could not survive ridicule.

Despite the Ku Klux Klan, the number of lynchings of Negroes declined throughout the decade. There were eighty-six in 1919, only nine in 1929. Civic programs for the betterment of the Negro's living standard were launched in the South, in large part selfishly motivated since the heavy migration of Negroes to the North was stripping the South of its cheapest labor supply.

Cases of violence to Negroes that did occur were flagrant enough:

In Columbia, Missouri, while a mob of several hundred, including many University of Missouri students and several co-eds, looked on, a Negro accused of attempting to assault a fourteen-year-old girl was hanged.

At Carteret, New Jersey, after a local pugilist was stabbed to death by some Negroes, a mob of white men, some masked, burned to the ground the First Baptist Church, which had all Negro parishioners, and the parson, his wife, and daughter had to flee to nearby Elizabeth. Then the mob drove 100 Negro families out of town.

Near Marshall, Texas, a Negro farm laborer was whipped to death by several whites because he had cursed his white employer.

Negro discrimination, which was fierce in the South, was practiced in the North, too, where a kind of apartheid was accepted. Negroes were economically a class of helots, who could not buy or rent real estate in certain districts of cities and who were excluded from theaters, hotels, and restaurants. In September, 1929, the Texas-born rector of a Brooklyn Episcopalian church asked from his pulpit that the Negroes sitting in his congregation leave. "The Episcopal Church provides churches for Negroes. Several of these churches are within easy reach of this locality." Heywood Broun in his newspaper column expressed his indignation. The reverend assumes "that the Lord's house which he tends is one of the better country clubs. There is no record that Jesus Christ ever said, 'Suffer the little Caucasian children to come unto me.' "

In F. Scott Fitzgerald's novel *The Great Gatsby*, Tom Buchanan, a scion of high society, expresses his fears about the ultimate disintegration of our civilization. "Nowadays people begin by sneering at family life and family institutions, and next they'll throw everything overboard and have intermarriage between black and white."

In November, 1925, a case raising that specter filled the papers and aroused intense public interest. The New York *Times* day after day reported the testimony on its front pages.

Leonard Kip Rhinelander, a descendant of a proud old family of French Huguenots and a bearer of one of New York's most distinguished names, brought a suit to annul his marriage to Alice Beatrice Jones on the ground that she had fraudulently concealed the fact that she was a mulatto, the daughter of a colored taxi driver of New Rochelle, New York.

Three years before, when Rhinelander was twenty-three years old, he was driving in a car with a friend who was an electrician. Rhinelander had been sent to an institution when he was seventeen years old. Mentally retarded and afflicted with a speech impediment that sometimes prevented him from speaking at all, he was extremely shy, particularly with girls. The car in which the two were riding broke down in New Rochelle, and while they were repairing it, a girl came along; the friend picked her up and went off with her. Some days later Leonard was sent to the girl's house to explain why his friend could not keep a date, and there he met her sister, who was Alice, then working as a housemaid.

It appears that Alice knew his background. Three days later she sent him a postcard. They met in New York to go to the theater but instead went to the Marie Antoinette Hotel, where they stayed together for five days, and later they stayed together for two weeks. They entered upon a fervid correspondence. From Panama and Havana where his parents had sent him, he wrote letters, full of smut, begging her to be faithful to him. She replied, "Listen, Leonard, I've had some sweethearts, but I've never been loved as you do. I never let a feller love and caress me as you do."

Her letters were crude and illiterate, full of passion and a curious admixture of love and money. "I dreamed of you last night. And hoped you loved me. You gave me piles and piles of brand new ten dollar bills, but you would not give me enough of them and every one of them were brand new." From the Adirondacks she wrote letters indicating that she was the most sought-after girl in the world. There was a "Harvard man" after her, and "I've had a chance for a thousand dates. . . . I was talking to Al Jolson today. He was in swimming but he is quite a flirt. Well, my darling, talk of men up hear. All a girl wants." Men loaded her with gifts. That "musical man," Irving Berlin, who had a cottage next door was paying her attention. (He testified at the trial he was not in the Adirondacks that summer.) It seems that her objective was only to have Rhinelander set her up in an expensive apartment, but that fall he married her.

On the stand, Leonard talked with violent effort in a tone of bewilderment, peering through heavy-rimmed glasses. The young man seemed to be acting under external compulsion, which was indeed so since his father, on whom he was dependent, had forced the suit. He claimed that she had explained her dark skin by saying that she was of a Spanish family. His counsel also claimed that she had concealed the fact that she was three years older than he and had previously been the mistress of another man. The wife's counsel said that he was suffering not from "mental weakness but blindness," since he had frequently visited the Jones family and had met her colored father often. Although Alice did not take the stand, in the jury room she bared herself to the waist to show that her color was black.

No doubt she had enticed him into marriage, but the plaintiff was unable to show fraud. Apparently the assumption was that it was so monstrous for a mulatto to marry a white in American society that she should have waved a red flag. The jury returned a verdict that there was no fraud. Rhinelander fought the case in the higher courts on the claim that since she had failed to take the stand, all he had said was true, but the Court of Appeals upheld the jury verdict.

In his book, published in 1929, *Our Business Civilization,* James Truslow Adams said, "In making the businessman the dominant and sole class in America, the country is making the experiment of resting her civilization on the ideas of businessmen. The other classes dominated by the business one are rapidly conforming in their philosophy of life to it." He was puzzled whether a great civilization could be maintained on "the philosophy of the counting house."

The way the businessman actually looked on society is reflected in various statements culled by James Warren Prothro in his *The Dollar Decade.* A spokesman, president John E. Edgerton of the National Association of Manufacturers, proclaimed that the true realization of the harmony of conflicting interests in America awaited the genius of American industry, which had achieved "the strangling of discontent by the baptism of general prosperity."

The first report in the twenties of the NAM's Committee for Industrial Development said, "History proves conclusively that the only hope for the mass is the development of able individuals." If the businessman was out to make a buck, there was no guilt in that. The leading business organ, *Nation's Business,* said, "The 100 percent American believes in the doctrine of selfishness, although he is often ashamed to admit it . . . a fact which leads him into bleary sentiment when he undertakes to define service. The American idea is that every man is out to promote his own interest." If some sweated at low pay while others prospered, if there was a wide gulf in earnings and living standards, that was due to innate inequality of talent.

In his book *Business in Politics,* Charles N. Fay wrote, "The main reason why the poor man is and remains poor is lack of brains, lack of wit to earn, thrift to save and knowledge as to how to use his savings." The sporting thing is for the masses to accept their lot. Wrote Fay, "We hear much of 'social discontent,'" but he revealed that this was only "a pompous phrase for what we used to call ordinary envy or jealousy." In *Nation's Business* a writer said, "Social discontent is allied to social parasitism. In nature it appears to be a characteristic of some parasites that they seek to devour their host regardless of the fact that the death of their host as the result of their short-sighted appetites will mean their own extinction."

The business philosophy could not have had a more avowed champion than Calvin Coolidge. It seemed to have been more than coincidence that his initials and those of the Chamber of Commerce were the same. Addressing the national Chamber, he said, "I have been greatly pleased to observe the many evidences that the attitude of the Chamber of Commerce very accurately reflects that of public opinion generally."

Behind an outer mask of lethargy, Coolidge most energetically proceeded to rip apart all the shackles that had been imposed on business in order to give it unmolested *Lebensraum.* Antitrust prosecutions of any import were halted. When Attorney General Stone received a report from the Federal Trade Commission that the Aluminum Company of America had a monopoly and Stone signaled that he would take action, Coolidge kicked him upstairs to a seat on the Supreme Court. His successor from Vermont, a dull oaf, John Garibaldi Sargent, testified before a Congressional committee that he had never heard of the case until "five or six or eight months" later, and then he had promptly absolved the company of guilt. Alcoa was controlled by Secretary of the Treasury Andrew W. Mellon.

The independent agencies were the main target for Coolidge. The Federal Power Commission was no problem since at that time it was composed of his own men, the Secretaries of War, Agriculture, and the Interior. The Federal Trade Commission was different. After the Presidential election of 1924, Coolidge changed the complexion of the commission by appointing to it his Western campaign manager, former Congressman William E. Humphrey, who denounced the Wilson concept of the commission as a policeman as "an instrument of oppression and disturbance and injury instead of help to business." He said the commission must no longer serve as a "publicity bureau to spread Socialist propaganda." Many changes were made in commission practice, which Humphrey zealously reported to Coolidge. Prosecutions were hamstrung by a new rule that information supplied by a firm under investigation could not be turned over to the Justice Department without the company's consent. The publicity weapon was rendered impotent by a new rule that there could be no publicity about a firm's violating a trade practice ruling until a final determination was made by the commission. Mr. Humphrey became a *cause célèbre* in the New Deal days when Roosevelt removed him summarily on the ground that he was unsympathetic to New Deal aims, a removal which the Supreme Court decided was illegal.

In Coolidge's early days as President, he received complaints that members of the Tariff Commission sat in on cases in which they had friendship, business, or even family interests. In a session at the White House, Coolidge scolded the complainers for their prudish attitude and said the connections they were protesting about merely enhanced a member's knowledge of the problems of the industry concerned. Under the Fordney-McCumber Act the commission could raise or lower rates by 50 percent with the concurrence of the President. In March, 1928, Edward P. Costigan resigned from the commission, bitterly protesting that Coolidge had consented to raising rates on a host of items but had permitted lowering on only five items of the most trifling importance, millfeed, bobwhite quail, paintbrush handles, phenol, and cresylic acid. Coolidge packed the commission by putting in high-tariff men. William Culbertson, who was a thorn in his side, was got rid of by being appointed minister to Rumania.

Coolidge wanted the Shipping Board to get out of the business of operating the merchant marine we had built during the war. A Democrat, Bert Haney, was in the way, and so Coolidge found a pretext for getting rid of him. In August, 1925, he wrote to him, "It having come to my attention that you are proposing to remove Admiral Palmer [chairman of the Emergency Fleet Corporation] contrary to the understanding I had with you when I re-appointed you, your resignation is requested." He forced Haney out, and between 1925 and 1929 the board sold 104 vessels which had cost the United States $258,000,000 for $23,000,000.

Senator George W. Norris protested, "Without exception, as far as I know, every appointee of his [Coolidge's] has been someone who has no sympathy for the various acts of Congress. . . .

It is an indirect but positive repeal of Congressional enactments which no administration, however powerful, could bring about by direct means. It is the nullification of federal law by a process of boring from within."

On the day that Coolidge left the White House in 1929, Walter Lippmann wrote, "Surely no one will write of those years since August 1923 that an aggressive President altered the destiny of the Republic. Yet, it is an interesting fact that no one will write of these same years that the Republic wished its destiny to be altered."

In the history of the nation, it is possible to discern a certain rhythm—political action followed by reaction, movement followed by rest. The Coolidge Era was indisputably one of reaction and rest. Liberals in disgust might have applied to the Harding administration the same observation that Henry Adams made of the Grant administration, that "it was the dividing line between what we hoped for and what we got." Yet there is little doubt that the great majority of the American people at that time wanted relief from the effort and tension of striving for higher goals. Americans wanted to enjoy life more fully; they did not want to worry or be worried; they did not want to be worked up about national or international problems.

Coolidge mirrored that popular mood and accentuated it. It is clear that like any astute politician, he swam with the tide. As one example, in 1926 he pushed through the Senate a resolution for our adherence to the World Court, but when, in the Congressional elections that fall, most of those who voted for it lost their seats, Coolidge visibly lost interest in the attempt to get the League of Nations, of which the World Court was a part, to accept the reservations that the Senate had tacked on.

Those who in future years would accuse Coolidge of inertia on legislation would overlook the fact that Congress was enveloped in a lassitude even more profound than the President's. At the start of each session Coolidge regularly deposited a package of legislative proposals before Congress—immigration reforms, federal emergency powers in coal strikes, civil rights reforms, laws to facilitate railroad reorganizations—and Congress consistently ignored them. Hoover later related that as Secretary of Commerce he warned Congress for three years that it must pass a statute for regulating radio communications and channels, but Congress would not act until the patchwork voluntary system broke down.

At the close of 1926 the liberal *Nation* despaired, "The country is politically apathetic. Both Democratic and Republican parties shelter a whole zoo of political specimens, but not within or without them is there a clear-cut issue to fire the country." No one had a plan of action to improve today or tomorrow; no one was sure what needed to be done; no one knew the cause to be served. Richard Washburn Child put it this way, "They say 'We wish the President would do something big.' But what? 'Ah, that is something that requires a good deal of reflection. After all, the responsibility is not ours.' "

The country, lulled into a state of euphoric contentment, was willing to embrace the philosophy so succinctly stated by Coolidge in an annual message to Congress. "What the country requires is not so much new policies as a steady continuity of those which are already crowned with such abundant success." And so politics diminished as a subject of public interest and conversation. F. Scott Fitzgerald in later years wrote, "It was a characteristic of the Jazz Age that it had no interest in politics at all."

The public apathy is forcefully illustrated by the fate of the Child Labor Amendment passed by Congress in 1924 with the strong support of Coolidge and sent to the states for ratification. It stated: "The Congress shall have the power to limit, regulate and prohibit the labor of persons under eighteen years of age." The Child Labor Committee, a nongovernmental group, said in 1924 that 2,000,000 children, fourteen years old and under, were employed in factories, mines, beet fields, and elsewhere. In the six years after the Congressional action, the amendment was ratified by a grand total of six states. It was rejected in Coolidge's home state of Massachusetts, where a referendum in November, 1924, turned it down by a 5 to 2 margin. It was strongly opposed by leading prelates of the Catholic Church, who had great influence with voters of that state.

All sorts of arguments were flung against it. It would render it impossible for boys to sell newspapers and for students to save money for college. It would take away from parents their right to see that their children were engaged in useful, healthful occupations. A minister wrote to the New York *Times,* "More children are ruined by idleness than by labor." It was called an unconscionable trampling upon of states' rights. The Providence *News* commented sarcastically, "When it was an issue involving Prohibition, the righteous people felt that states' rights could be thrown to the winds."

There was propaganda from business sources. The National Association of Manufacturers maintained: "Labor according to the law applies to nearly every form of physical effort which is not recreation or play—all work or chores about the house, sewing, washing, vacation work, selling papers, gardening, driving, etc. How many parents realize this? Has Congress never in the past done foolish things? Can we predict the degree of foolishness of future Congresses?" Moreover, children are not exploited because they cannot be entrusted with adult tasks. "Do we need a law forbidding the average individual to swallow swords?"

I can recall vividly when I was in high school in Reading, Pennsylvania, that a regular occurrence was the sight of a boy or girl going from class to class checking out books. The child was bound for work in the booming hosiery mills or railroad machine shops or perhaps in the Luden's Cough Drop factory. Pennsylvania had a law giving working papers at the age of fourteen but, to salve its conscience, required continuation school for two years—that is, going to a class or two at night. Many were being yanked out of school by their parents to earn needed money. Today the graduating classes in Reading are three times as large even though the city now has a smaller population.

The mood of America was much the same as it had been two decades before when Jane Addams said that Americans had "come to think a bolt of cheap cotton is more to be prized than a child properly nourished, educated and prepared to take his place in life." With the Depression, the entire outlook changed, and the Child Labor Amendment was ratified by twenty-four states before the passage of the Fair Labor Standards Act of 1938 which made the amendment largely academic since it prohibited the employment of children under sixteen years of age in the production of goods in interstate commerce, a law which was declared constitutional by the Supreme Court.

A faction of Republican Senators from regions west of the Mississippi were self-labeled Progressives, though old guard Republican Senator George Moses of New Hampshire thought them more akin to "the sons of the wild jackass." They included George W. Norris of Nebraska, Robert M. La Follette, Jr., of Wisconsin, Hiram Johnson of California, William Borah of Idaho, Edwin F. Ladd and Lynn W. Frazier of North Dakota, and Smith W. Brookhart of Iowa, whose middle name happened to be appropriate, Wildman. They have sometimes been described as precursors of the New Deal, but they actually had no concerted program and were split far apart on farm relief, tariff policy, Prohibition, and public power.

Progressive meant something definite in the Bull Moose days of Theodore Roosevelt. What did it mean when Coolidge was President? A liberal Democrat, Henry T. Rainey of Illinois (who would be House Speaker in 1933), scoffed, "A Progressive is a Republican who thinks his district or state is going Democratic." In a press conference, Coolidge was asked for his opinion and said, "I can't conceive of any party existing for any length of time that wasn't progressive." The debate was in his opinion a useless exercise in semantics and reminded him of the old definitions of orthodoxy and heterodoxy. "I think they used to say that orthodoxy was 'my doxy' and heterodoxy was 'your doxy.' "

Considered the wildest of the "wild jackasses" in the conservative camp was Senator George William Norris of Nebraska. "The only honest man in political life," Lewis Gannett, the literary critic, once said of him, and even cynical Washington newsmen bestowed on him that accolade. Ulric Bell of the Louisville *Courier-Journal* once observed, "Were I Diogenes, I know of no other public man who would come nearer to ending my quest than George Norris." He was born in 1861 in Ohio, the youngest of twelve children. His boyhood was one of hard toil, yet he managed to acquire an education in the law and was elected to the House in 1902. On St. Patrick's Day of 1910 he started the revolt against the czaristic rule of House

Speaker "Uncle Joe" Cannon, which resulted in putting permanent curbs on the power of that position. He was one of the band, called by Wilson "a little group of wilful men," who filibustered in March, 1917, to prevent the arming of our merchant vessels. He was lashed mercilessly as a traitor in the national press and rode out a wave of execration at home. His ordeal is described in *Profiles in Courage* by John F. Kennedy.

Of the Coolidge Era, Norris later said, "In no period of my public life did I feel greater discouragement than during those years." He could not abide Coolidge the man or the Coolidge philosophy or the smug sanctimony with which the President expressed it. He was continuously irked by Coolidge's suspicion that Bolshevism lurked in any measure that Norris considered progressive. He could not understand why the United States recognized Fascist Italy, which oppressed workers, while adamantly refusing to recognize the Soviet Union, which oppressed capitalists.

He and Coolidge clashed head on on the issue of what to do with the Muscle Shoals complex built in Tennessee during the war. At a cost of $200,000,000 the government had constructed Wilson Dam and other facilities to generate electricity for nitrate manufacture for explosives. After the war the huge investment turned into a white elephant. Henry Ford made a bid of $5,000,000 for the nitrate plant and promised to turn out nitrate fertilizer for farmers at not more than 8 percent profit. In March, 1924, the House voted by 227 to 142 to accept the Ford offer, and Coolidge was delighted.

Norris was determined that the government should hold on to Muscle Shoals, and it was due to his determination that it remained to become the core of the Tennessee Valley Authority. "The magic name of Henry Ford," he said, "seems to have dulled the reasoning power of thousands of farmers." In hearings of the Senate Agriculture Committee over which Norris presided as chairman, there was a moment of high levity when a woman witness testified that Norris on a visit to Decatur, Alabama, in 1922, said that he would vote for the Ford offer if he could kiss one of the lovely Southern belles. "You did kiss one of the girls and you are against the Ford offer." Norris rose red with indignation. "I know a blackmail plot when I see it.

I did not kiss that girl. She kissed me." The committee voted against the Ford offer, and Ford, seeing that it would be impossible to overcome Norris' opposition, withdrew his offer.

Coolidge insisted that Muscle Shoals must be sold to a private buyer. "If anything were needed to demonstrate the almost utter incapacity of the national government to deal with an industrial and commercial property, it has been provided by this experience"—but no buyer came along with a bid. Norris became an expert on power costs. He argued voluminously that the plant should be operated by the government to furnish cheap power and as a yardstick for prices charged by other producers. The issue was stalemated for years.

Finally, in 1928 Norris steered a bill through Congress which was watered down to a shadow to get by Coolidge. The government would operate Muscle Shoals to manufacture fertilizer and its ingredients but purely on an experimental basis—none could be sold or even given away to farmers. Surplus power generated in this manufacture might be sold to municipally operated utilities.

Even this was too much for Coolidge to stomach. He pocket vetoed it at the end of the session, and though he was silent publicly, he told members of Congress privately that he feared it was the "opening wedge for Socialism." Norris was infuriated and berated Coolidge for his fear of offending the "power trust" and his fear of "drying up sources of revenues" for the 1928 Presidential campaign. When Democratic candidate Alfred E. Smith made some noises favorable to public power, Norris bolted Hoover to support Smith, despite the fact that the wet and Catholic Smith was anathema to rural Nebraska. Almost the only confrontation between liberals and conservatives that took place in Coolidge's elected term occurred over this paltry bill.

President Edgerton of the NAM declared that if left alone, the working classes hold to "right principles" but that they are "unwittingly susceptible to excitement by agitating exploiters and professional uplifters." In 1925 he said that most horrendous of all was the labor union organizer. "The palatial temples of labor whose golden domes rise in exultant splendor throughout the nation, the millions of dollars extracted by the jewelled hand of greed from the pockets of wage-earners and paid out in lucrative salaries to a ravenous band of pretenders, tell the pitiful story of a slavery such as this country has never known before." He urged the wage earners to "break the shackles that have been forged upon their wrists."

Labor unions withered during the era, declining in number of members, in prestige, and in power. In 1920 the largest union, the AFL (the CIO did not then exist), had 4,178,000 members; in 1929, only 2,993,000. If the membership had been 5,000,000, that would have been only an eighth of the working population. Attempts by the AFL to penetrate the great industries—iron and steel, autos, and rubber products—were miserable failures.

The leadership of Samuel Gompers, who died in 1924 at the age of seventy-four and whose policies were carried on by William Green, lacked fire and acumen. He had been the leading figure of national labor since 1882, when the AFL was formed. For six years afterward he worked as a cigarmaker by day while discharging the business of the embryonic organization at night. By 1904 the union had prospered mightily, and it had 2,000,000 members, two-thirds of what it would have a generation later by the end of the Coolidge Era.

Gompers often boasted of his proletarian background and in fact had been born in squalor in the Whitechapel section of London in 1850. Actually, the aristocratic Jewish-Austrian family Gomperz had furnished the Hapsburg Empire with merchant princes, artists, and scholars, but Samuel's grandfather was shiftless and wandered to Holland and after misfortunes migrated to England. The father brought the family to the United States during the Civil War and followed the trade of cigarmaker, which Samuel adopted.

He was a short man, five feet four inches, verbose and as full of fight as a bantam cock, shrewd in the infighting needed to control an organization which many called a rope of sand. He was sincere and dedicated to the cause. However, his limitations were severe. He was exceedingly egocentric, and it was said of him, "Sam likes to be in the limelight and likes to be played up. In fact, if he were going around the block he would want to be preceded by a brass band." He had no concept of labor as a political force, so labor sat on the sidelines with an occasional jeer or cheer, as he put it, "to punish our enemies, reward our friends." He opposed governmental measures to ameliorate the lot of the workingman because programs such as unemployment insurance, compulsory health insurance, and the like would diminish the interest of workers in union benefit programs.

Benjamin Stolberg wrote of him with affection in the *Atlantic Monthly* after his death, though he recognized his failings. He had a Jewish admiration for learning, but his own knowledge was superficial—he read in the social sciences only to confirm his own prejudices. When he indulged in philosophical speculation, he tended to be sophomoric, such as his remark, "Bolshevism in Russia began in prohibition, since that tends to uproot the habits of a people." He fought intellectuals in the labor movement. The word "intellectuals," Stolberg said, "he rolled off his tongue with the fascination of a deep hatred." He fought bitterly against all radicals, beginning with the anarchists and then Debs and the Socialists and then William Haywood and the IWW and then the Communists, but he knew little or nothing about their ideologies and their aims and purposes.

Most bitter was Gompers' struggle against William Z. Foster and his Communist followers, who had led the great steel strike of 1919. Foster tried to take over the labor movement through his Trade Educational League, and he succeeded in several unions, notably the Furriers' Union and the International Ladies Garment Workers. This limited success had the effect of making Gompers even more rigid in his viewpoints. Gompers and later Green opposed the recognition of Soviet Russia and even urged an embargo on Russian imports as "convict-made" goods. Harold Faulkner wrote, "In the end the chief result of the Communist tactics was to stiffen the conservative leanings of old-line union leaders. Fighting to retain their offices, they prevented a normal replacement by younger men, many of whom had to come to the older leaders to seek aid against the undermining tactics of their Communist foes."

Meanwhile, industry waged a remorseless, unabashed war against unionism. Dr. Gus W. Dyer, professor of economics at Vanderbilt University, addressing the NAM said, "You can hardly conceive of a more un-American, anti-American institution than the closed shop. It is really very remarkable that it is allowed to exist by the sanction of law under the American flag. It tramples under foot the most sacred rights and privileges of the American citizen, and sets itself openly and defiantly against that freedom for which the Anglo-Saxon has been struggling and fighting for centuries."

Industry called its counterattack the American Plan, thus linking it with patriotism. Business looked beneficently on one type of union, the company union, which was to be outlawed in 1935 by the Wagner Act of the New Deal. When a company union was organized by John D. Rockefeller, Jr., in 1916 after the collapse of a bloody strike at the Colorado Fuel and Iron Company, it was something of an innovation; ten years later there were at least 500 such unions with more than 1,500,000 members. Rockefeller, Jr., said, "Unionism benefits only one class of workers, those who belong to the labor union. Our plan takes in all men whether they belong to a union or not," and this was typical of the reasoning used to justify a scheme which was at best a conference-table arrangement for hearing grievances. Some plans were quite elaborate. The Goodyear Company had a plan patterned on the United States government, with a house of representatives and a senate.

The courts badly weakened labor's organizing power. A veteran labor lawyer, Morris Hillquit, commented that while labor had a theoretical right to organize, picket, and boycott, "in practice the rules have been hedged in with so many modifications and departures that they have been reduced to a statement of an abstract social philosophy rather than a statement of positive law." The Supreme Court in the Duplex Printing Company case declared a secondary boycott illegal and in the Hitchman Coal and Coke Company case made it illegal to attempt to organize workers who had signed a yellow dog contract, forbidding membership in a union.

The English observer J. A. Spender wrote of the paradox of a people who craved change but were so Chinese in their worship of the Constitution and their ancestors who devised it that they became immune to progress.

The Coolidge Era is notable for the small number of strikes and the absence of major strikes. The average number per year between 1916 and 1921 was 3,503, compared to an average of 791 between 1926 and 1929. In 1919 the *Literary Digest* said that the great steel strike "aimed at the overthrow of American institutions." In the Coolidge Era, strikes were frowned on by public opinion—they were led by radicals or racketeers; they disrupted the "new partnership" between labor and capital; they raised prices for the consumer. After the anthracite coal strike of 1923 there was no labor trouble of any magnitude until the textile mill strike at Gastonia, North Carolina, in 1929, which riveted attention for the first time in years on the plight of the workingman and community attitudes toward unions.

Throughout the 1920's one sector of industry that had its own depression was the Northern textile industry as one mill after another, lured by starvation wages and a twelve-hour day even for women and minors, departed for the South. Gaston County in North Carolina now had 100 mills. The county seat, Gastonia, had been a hamlet only thirty years before but now, with a population of 32,000, was a symbol of the growth of industry which had made North Carolina one of the richest states in the Union.

The average wage for a twelve-hour day in North Carolina was $12.23, with the most skilled earning as much as $21. The millowners rented houses to workers without water or sanitary facilities for $3.20 a month. Sinclair Lewis reporting from Gastonia said they were packing cases made of the cheapest material. "I have tried to pry the boards of these houses apart, and have found that it could be done with my little finger." Hickman Powell in the New York *World* said, "In the hills the worker had been a gaunt creature, ill-nourished on pork and cornbread." It was now little different. "If you see a husky well-fed man around a mill village, it is a ten to one bet that he is a deputy sheriff." The windows were closed in the hot mills and the air full of lint. One worker was quoted, "I ain't a-feared of Hell. I've spent twenty summers in the mills."

What seems to have triggered the strike was the application of the Bedford Efficiency Plan to the mills, so that a worker who had formerly tended forty-eight looms now had to tend ninety. There were two unions, the United Textile Workers of the AFL and the National Textile Workers, which, it was alleged by the industry, was Communist.

Public sentiment in North Carolina was strongly against the strikers. The *Outlook* quoted a correspondent of a local paper, "To the residents of Gastonia there is but one issue. By all the bugs and beasts of ancient Egypt, he is determined that no organization which denies God, defies the American flag and makes a mockery of marriage shall gain a foothold among 18,000 of the 'most contented' workers in the county. All else about the industrial disagreement is as a snowflake upon the river." The Charlotte *News* denounced the strike leaders as Communists, "despicable curs and snakes from the dives of Hoboken, Passaic and New York." Mary Heaton Vorse reported that it was useless to try to raise a milk fund for babies of striking workers. She was told, "You don't understand. You in the north think of workers as human beings. The folks here think of them as 'hands.' "

The workers on strike were moved out of their company-rented homes and lived in a tent colony outside Gastonia. A picket line was formed one night in June, but it was broken up when it tried to parade to town. Police came to the colony, and a shotgun blast came from union headquarters. Police Chief Orville F. Aderholt lay dead. Sixteen men were indicted and charged with first-degree murder. In September they were put on trial after a change of venue to Charlotte. The prosecution's case was grisly. A plaster of paris effigy of Aderholt in blood-caked, bullet-ridden uniform was carried into the courtroom. One of the jurors lost his mind and was found crawling under beds, asking to be shot and buried face downward. A mistrial was granted.

That night a mob of 500 men attacked union headquarters and destroyed all the literature there. Union organizers were kidnapped, driven to secluded groves, stripped, and larruped on their withers. A truck carrying twenty-two organizers from Bessemer City to South Gastonia for a meeting was forced into a ditch, and in a spray of bullets from a passing car, Mrs. Lucy Perry, a mother of four and the poet laureate of the union, was killed.

In early morning before the gates of a mill at Marion, Sheriff

Oscar F. Adkins was trying to hold at bay a crowd of strikers trying to dissuade workers from going in to replace the departing night shift. Somehow he started grappling with a man over sixty who was armed with a stick. He threw a tear gas bomb, deputies started shooting, and three men were dead. Adkins and his deputies were arrested, but a Charlotte newspaperman told a Northern correspondent, "The people aren't going to tolerate those red bastards, nobody is going to be convicted— and you can run that in your paper."

In mid-October the trial of seven defendants charged with the murder of Sheriff Aderholt took place. Prosecutor John G. Carpenter writhed on the floor while he reenacted Aderholt's death. The organizers were "devils with hoofs and horns who threw away their pitchforks for guns." There were "scenes of debauchery at union headquarters . . . yes, immorality, hugging and kissing in public." In his final appeal to the jury he said, "Do you believe in the flag, do you believe in North Carolina, do you believe in good roads?" The judge sentenced the four Northern defendants to seventeen to twenty years but gave far lesser sentences to the three Southerners on trial.

Finally, the strikers won small concessions, but soon there was the Great Depression, and workers considered themselves fortunate if they had jobs at all.

The Gastonia strife, because it was beclouded by conflicting propaganda and arguments about Communist sponsorship, did not furnish the rallying point for liberals that the Sacco and Vanzetti case did two years before, the one cause of the decade which roused the liberals from their long slumber and fused intellectuals and the left of whatever shade.

On April 15, 1920, in the shoe-manufacturing town of South Braintree, Massachusetts, a paymaster and his guard were walking across a railroad yard. Two men lolling against a fence, one in a cap and another in a felt hat, approached them with drawn guns. There was a struggle, and the paymaster and his guard were shot to death. The assailants escaped with the payroll of $15,000 in a Buick in which there were three other men. On May 5, after a telephone tip, Nicola Sacco and Bartolomeo Vanzetti were arrested on a streetcar in Brockton. They were admitted anarchists who had fled the country to escape the draft; they both were immigrants from Italy who spoke no English; they both carried weapons when arrested, Sacco a .32-caliber Colt automatic, Vanzetti a .38-caliber Harrington and Richardson revolver. They said that they had acquired them years before under assumed names, but at their trial they admitted that they had lied and had acquired them fairly recently.

They were tried at Dedham and convicted and sentenced to die in the electric chair. Slowly public interest started to mount about the two men, who, many thought, were innocent but victims of the "Red scare." It was claimed that the presiding judge, the birdlike Webster Thayer, was hostile to radicals and referred to Sacco and Vanzetti privately in the course of the trial as "those bastards" and said that he would "get those guys hanged." The Communists were the first to find the cause; intellectuals enlisted; contributions poured in. The case was appealed to the highest court in Massachusetts, which rejected the appeal. The Supreme Court of the United States refused to hear it.

The action dragged on for years amid a growing furor and worldwide demonstrations. Governor Alvan Fuller refused to commute the sentence but appointed a blue-ribbon panel headed by President A. Lawrence Lowell of Harvard to review the case. It reported that the men were "guilty beyond a reasonable doubt." They died on August 23, 1927, more than seven years after their arrest. Protest riots and parades took place all over the world. The State Department asked our embassies to explain to the foreign press that the state of Massachusetts and the United States government were totally different entities.

Mencken said that the outcome was Babbitt's saying, "Being Wops [they] got what was coming to them." One of the small army of aroused intellectuals was Heywood Broun, a nationally syndicated columnist. Previously an essayist on light subjects, he now thundered in column after column about this legal lynching. "It is ridiculous to say that Sacco and Vanzetti are being railroaded to the chair. The situation is much worse than that. This is a thing done cold-bloodedly and with deliberation. But care and deliberation do not guarantee justice. Even if every college president in the country tottered forward to say 'guilty' it does not alter the facts. The tragedy of it all lies in the fact that though a southern mountain man may move more quickly to a dirty deed of violence, his feet are set no more firmly in the path of prejudice than a Lowell ambling sedately to a hanging." Then this Harvard alumnus said, "From now on, will the institution of learning at Cambridge which once we called Harvard be known as 'Hangman's House'?"

When the New York *World* refused to run two of Broun's columns and asked him to find something else to write about, Broun resigned. The management ran a statement that it did not want him to leave but that he had expressed himself "with the utmost extravagance."

Though much of the venom was turned against Judge Thayer, it is accepted that his rulings did not constitute reversible error. If the verdict was wrong, then the indictment should have been directed against the system of justice in Massachusetts, one of the more enlightened states of the Union. And indeed, following that course of logic, Broun broadened his attack against law in general. "Scratch through the varnish of any judgment seat, and what will you strike but hate, thick-clotted from centuries of angry verdicts? Did any man ever find power within his hands except to use it as a whip?" Professor Felix Frankfurter of Harvard University who brought substance to the cries of the protesters with his *The Case of Sacco and Vanzetti,* found the case a challenge to the validity of the legal process. "All systems of law, however wise, are administered through men, and therefore may occasionally disclose the frailties of men."

For his book, published in 1962, *Tragedy in Dedham,* Francis Russell compared the two revolvers found on Sacco and Vanzetti when arrested and the bullets in the bodies of the two murdered men. At the time of the trial, the ballistics testimony was a "wilderness of lands and grooves." Russell arranged modern ballistic examinations in the laboratory of the Massachusetts State Police. One of the testers was Colonel Frank Jury, formerly in charge of the New Jersey State Police Firearms Laboratory. Russell himself looked at the striations on bullets fired from the guns and compared them with the original bullets.

In *American Heritage* of June, 1962, he wrote:

79

In the light of the most recent ballistics evidence and after reviewing the inquest and autopsy reports as well as the trial testimony, I felt that I could come to no other conclusion than that the Colt automatic found on Sacco when he was picked up by the police was the one used to murder [the guard] Berardelli three weeks earlier. About the gun found on Vanzetti there is too much uncertainty to come to any conclusion.

Those who defended Sacco and Vanzetti argued that the bloody deed was out of character with the pacifist temperament of both men and certainly could not be reconciled with the movingly eloquent statements of Vanzetti (which were later revealed to have been prepared by fine literary hands). Russell's conclusions were in general agreement with an earlier article by James Grossman in *Commentary* magazine in January, 1962, "Sacco and Vanzetti Reconsidered." Contrary to those who stated that the men were incapable of the deed, wrote Grossman, they were followers of Luigi Galleani, "who approved not only of the traditional propaganda of the deed, killing kings and heads of state, which we associate with some anarchists, but also justified robberies and thefts, if they were committed for the cause." Moreover, in contrast with Vanzetti, Sacco, "in writing to his comrades and friends, publicly or privately, never in any letter that I have seen specifically denied the killing . . . no word of his innocence was spoken at the solemn great moment of his death when he cried out anarchy and bade farewell to his wife, children and friends."

So the haunting question of their guilt remains, as does the further question of whether a later generation was hoaxed by another delusion of the twenties.

Chapter III

THE EXPERIMENT
THAT FAILED

"The Twenties was the decade when America went dry—and more liquor, some said, flowed across the land than ever before." Thus began the treatment of Prohibition in an account of the period which appeared in *American Heritage* magazine. This conforms to a popular impression that Prohibition actually encouraged drinking and that the "noble experiment" broke down in a wild drinking orgy.

What "some said" happens to be arrant nonsense. The amount of liquor consumption was reduced significantly during Prohibition, although drinking did continue on a massive scale. The United States Brewers' Association, which was a legitimate organization since near beer could be produced and sold, repeatedly denounced Prohibition as a failure, but admitted that drinking of hard liquors had been cut by 50 percent. The Anti-Saloon League claimed that drinking had been cut by 95 percent. The truth lies somewhere in between these estimates.

Calvin Coolidge with his Puritanism was far more the avatar of that age than we appreciate today. As myth could construct a false picture of Coolidge, it could construct in retrospect a false picture of an immoral age, the Roaring Twenties. The intellectuals would not have fulminated so strongly against Puritanism if the hold of Puritanism had not been so strong. To be sure, there was some loosening of the bonds, which does not mean a bursting of them. Most obvious was the new freedom for women, who discarded corsets, wore short skirts, and smoked cigarettes in public. As late as 1914 an editor of a paper in Rochester, New York, got a telephone call and heard an excited voice say that if he hurried to the lounge of the Seneca Hotel, he could see the dancer Irene Castle smoking a cigarette in public. In the 1890's, wrote the Lynds in *Middletown*, "A well-brought up boy and girl were commonly forbidden to sit together in the dark." Now they rode across the countryside together in the night, and contraceptives were available in drugstores.

Even so, the English observer Beverley Nichols found life drabber than ever for millions of neglected women, "a neglect born of the unnatural speed of American life—swift wooing, swift passion, and swift oblivion." The flapper, according to F. Scott Fitzgerald, was "lovely, expensive and nineteen."

Greenwich Village standards did spread throughout the country. Malcolm Cowley defined these standards as "the idea of self-expression, the idea of paganism—the body is a temple in which there is nothing unclean . . . the ideal of living for the moment . . . the ideal of feminine equality . . . the idea of psychological adjustment . . . Freudian psychology provided a justification and made it unfashionable to be repressed."

It is hard to measure the extent and impact of this new freedom. Certainly it should have been reflected in the divorce rate. Several histories have pointed out that the rate increased between 1910 to 1930, from .90 per 1,000 population to 1.56. But if the figures are examined more closely, it turns out that the major increase occurred from 1910 to 1920. Except for three years, the rate in the second decade declined below the 1920 level.

Year	Divorce Rate per 1,000
1920	1.60
1921	1.47
1922	1.35

1923	1.48
1924	1.51
1925	1.53
1926	1.55
1927	1.62
1928	1.63
1929	1.66
1930	1.56

The divorce rate today runs about double what it was at the end of the twenties, and after the Second World War it was about three times as high.

Certainly, moral degeneration should have been reflected in declining church membership. However, as Arthur Link showed in his *American Epoch,* church membership increased more rapidly than population, from 43,300,000 to 54,576,000, and church expenditures increased by 149 percent during a decade when national income increased by 98 percent. Said Link:

> These statistics would seem to warrant the conclusion that organized religion not only survived the disillusionment of the 1920's, but also grew to a position of unrivalled pre-eminence among American social institutions. . . . A poll of 250,000 newspaper readers and 36,000 college students taken in 1926 revealed that young people were even more orthodox than their parents. Obviously, the advanced intellectuals in their search for new goals in large measure lost communication with the masses. The deviation from Christian tradition was significant, to be sure, but it was not symptomatic of any mass deviation.

The alleged moral degeneration should have been reflected in an appetite for and an acceptance of erotic literature. On the contrary, although the sex motif is a strong undercurrent in the literature of the age, it is implicit, rather than explicit.

I can recall my mother's reading Dreiser's *An American Tragedy* and her saying to my stepfather in a tone of shock, "No wonder they banned this book in Boston." They left the living room together at that moment, and in adolescent curiosity I looked at the page where she had turned down the book. This is what caused her shock. Roberta Alden, the factory girl, had been going with Clyde Griffiths. The fall weather had been getting chilly, and after a mental conflict that goes on for pages, she finally yields to him and lets him visit her in her room where she gives up her virginity. "The wonder and delight of a new and more intimate form of contact . . . the thing was done, a wild convulsive pleasure motivating both, so much more of a paradise than either might ever know again." Hardly *Lady Chatterley's Lover.*

In a best seller of 1929, *Bad Girl* by Viña Delmar, when the heroine's boyfriend stands her up, she visits him in his room and they start petting.

"Gosh, Dot, I'm a wreck. You see, I ain't used to stopping. Do you get what I mean?"

She said nothing. She was thinking of what it would be like to be a bad girl. "Yes, I'm going to let you." . . .

"Don't you suppose," Dot asked, "that somewhere there are nice people who would think it was all right?"

"Maybe in France," Eddie replied doubtfully.

Dot is so upset that Eddie agrees to marry her. When she returns home and announces her plans for her marriage, her brother suspects that she must have been naughty and orders her to get out. "Dot stifled a sob. She turned to her father appealingly. 'You have heard your brother,' said Mr. Haley. 'If you have sinned, Dorothy, you must take your punishment.'" Her friend, Edna, scoffs, "Why should he marry you? He done his dirty work and is probably laughing a whole string of ha-ha's." But they get married, and she has a baby. And that's the bold book *Bad Girl.*

There was little in print to titillate the prurient. One encounters only references to sex, rather than any spelling out of it. A sensational book, *Flaming Youth* by Warner Fabian, is a wearisome palaver of talk about drinking and petting. In the works of F. Scott Fitzgerald, sex is subordinate to the broad sweep of sentiment, and it has been said that his heroes and heroines carry on their love affairs by talking at each other. The first book about lesbianism, *The Well of Loneliness* by Radclyffe Hall, provoked quite a stir, yet the reader would have had to have some sophistication to realize that the main character had more than a social preference for female over male company.

New York City was regarded throughout the nation as the home of the fleshpots of Babylon. In 1925 the Council of the Methodist Episcopal Church denounced New York as a "foreign city run for foreigners and according to foreign ideas." Yet in this den of iniquity, in March, 1927, the authors and producers of a play, *The Virgin Man,* were sent to jail for ten days after a jury trial for putting on an indecent play. Then Mae West and the producers of her play *Sex* were put on trial. The defense was based on the prior presentation of Shaw's *Mrs. Warren's Profession, La Traviata, Camille,* and Tolstoy's *Resurrection,* and it claimed that the play had no more lascivious element than that it recognized sex as an element in human life. Miss West and the producers were convicted, and she was sent to Welfare Island for ten days. In that same month Governor Alfred E. Smith signed a bill closing for a year a theater or cabaret which put on an indecent show. New York theatrical producer Earl Carroll was sent to a federal penitentiary on a technical charge of perjury, but his real offense had been holding a party in which a showgirl, Joyce Hawley, sat nude in a tub of champagne.

Mrs. Mary Ware Dennett was convicted in a federal court in Brooklyn after a jury trial for using the mails to distribute her pamphlet *The Sex Side of Life, Advice to the Young.* She had written it years before for her children, then fourteen and ten years of age, and parts had been printed in medical reviews. Her defense lawyer, Morris Ernst, pointed out that 30,000 copies had been sold, that it was used at Columbia University and sold in the bookstore of Union Theological Seminary. "If this book is obscene, then life is obscene." His argument was unsuccessful with the jury, although the conviction was reversed by a higher court.

This was an age which retained a great deal of the orthodoxy and stern morality of the nineteenth century—when South Carolina enforced blue laws against playing golf on Sunday and Utah enforced laws prohibiting smoking in public; when the Lutheran Augustan Synod eliminated the word "hell" from the Apostles' Creed in favor of "hades"; when Pennsylvania eliminated all scenes of booze drinking from motion pictures; when the mayor of Detroit ordered Mae West's new show *Diamond Lil* to be shut down because it was "silly, holding no moral and teaching no lesson"; when Abby Rockefeller, daughter of John D. Rockefeller, Jr., hit the front pages by insisting on the elimination of the word "obey" from her marriage ceremony; when Keith's ordered all vaudeville acts to do away with the words "damn" and "hell," use of the word "broad" applied to a woman, the kicking of a man in the trousers or the maneuvering of a girl's skirt, and jokes such as "She thinks that lettuce is a proposition"; when girls wore "two-piece" bathing suits, the second "piece" being a skirt around the thighs; when Ring Lardner waged a campaign in the *New Yorker* against off-color popular songs such as "Tea for Two."

An astute observer of the scene, Raymond Moley, who was a professor of political science at Columbia University and taught at Barnard College, wrote me:

> I joined the faculty of Columbia University in 1923 and lived in New York during the years after that. As a teacher in the University, especially at Barnard College, I knew hundreds of students, both men and women. My friends and acquaintances outside the campus were numerous.
>
> I did not find that during the 1920's the general public morality differed from the years before, when I lived in Cleveland. Contrary to an impression conveyed by later reports, the 1920's were certainly not years of moral decline. Such reports are based upon lurid incidents of some high living in private life. But perhaps because they were more unusual, they were more widely publicized.
>
> So far as drinking was concerned, there was much less than before the enactment of Prohibition and certainly less than since its repeal. The number of patrons of speakeasies and bootleggers was infinitesimal compared with the total population.
>
> Student morality was governed by long-standing middle-class standards.

Moley concluded: "The concept of the Roaring 'Twenties is a myth."

The change that occurred in drinking habits because of Prohibition is indicated in the figures on gallon per capita consumption compiled by the Census Bureau, mostly on the basis of Internal Revenue taxes paid for intoxicating liquors, which necessarily exclude moonshine. The figures are for four years: 1914, when there were no restrictions; 1918, when wartime restrictions were in force; 1935, a year after repeal; 1940, six years after repeal.

Year	Spirits Distilled	Liquors Malt	Wines
1914	1.44	20.69	.53
1918	.85	14.87	.48
1935	.70	10.45	.30
1940	1.02	12.58	.66

Obviously drinking declined during Prohibition, since in 1935, the year after repeal, per capita drinking was far below that of 1914, and even though it picked up five years afterward, except for wine it was still below the 1914 level.

There are commonsense reasons to support this concept of what really went on during Prohibition. An important factor was that the price of liquor—when it was obtainable—increased anywhere from four to ten times over what it had been before. How many could afford to pay $8 to $12 for a quart of gin? Thorstein Veblen commented that drinking had become a sign "of the superior status of those who are able to afford the indulgence." The rich could afford to drink. Al Capone once observed sourly, "When I sell liquor, it's called bootlegging. When my patrons serve it on a silver tray on Lake Shore Drive, it's called hospitality."

Prohibition had little effect on ethnic groups whose diet included spiritous beverages—Germans continued to drink beer, and Italians and French enjoyed wine with their meals. Young people of college age considered liquor fashionable. Formerly a girl would have been horrified at the idea of taking a drink. But as Herbert Asbury relates in his account of Prohibition, "The boy who took a girl out during the 1920's and didn't give her a drink or went to a party without a flask of liquor was considered a poor sport, a clod, or drip." Among this group it can truly be said that Prohibition *did* encourage drinking.

For the large mass of people who could take it or leave it, Prohibition resulted in their leaving it. Social drinking and the cocktail party were largely unknown. Some did not want to break the law on principle, and others did not want to take the risk of breaking the law, however small that risk might be. A very large number were frightened by reports of poisoned liquor, and there was sound reason for such fear. In a period of four days in New York City in 1928, there were thirty-four deaths from wood alcohol.

Most did not want to pay high prices for stuff of uncertain quality. Social service agencies reported that drinking was cut markedly among the poor and that family life was improved, evidence that purchasing power was a most important factor. Sales of milk and ice cream increased by more than half between 1919 and 1925. The growth of the soda counter in the drugstore was attributed to the need for a new place of social congregation to replace the saloon.

There were extravagant claims, of course, made for the blessings of Prohibition. Wayne B. Wheeler, head of the Anti-Saloon League, said that it had eliminated "pauperism and the slums that clustered around their creator, the saloon." Prohibition Commissioner Roy Haynes said that Prohibition was the reason why America was the creditor of "drink-fettered Europe," ignoring the fact that most of the debt was accumulated before the Eighteenth Amendment was enacted. The Republican national chairman in the 1928 Presidential campaign, Hubert Work, said, "Most of the present prosperity is due to Prohibition. There is more money in the savings banks, the children wear better shoes."

The Washington *News* carried an interview with the proprietor of a beauty salon who said, "It is very easy to trace the growth of beauty salons to Prohibition. When men drank, they were not critical. Their wives and sweethearts looked attractive to them without the assistance of beauty parlors. Now men remain clear-eyed at evening and notice wrinkles, pallor, straight hair and unsparkling eyes. As a result, women flock to beauty parlors and we have to turn them away each day."

However small the *ratio* of scofflaws was to the total population, the number in absolute terms was too great for the law to survive. For a law to be effective, the risk of detection must be high and there must be a certain amount of turpitude attached

THE EXPERIMENT THAT FAILED

to the crime; neither factor applied in the case of Prohibition.

By 1924, even with loose enforcement of the Volstead Act, half of all federal prisoners were liquor law violators and 65,000 more had to be boarded out to local jails. "Bargain days" became the practice in federal courts, and offenders were let off with light fines. Juries became more reluctant to convict. In 1929 federal officials announced that they were dropping prosecutions against twenty-nine nightclubs in New York City because juries there would not find a verdict of guilty. Discouragement gave way progressively to demoralization and eventual defeat.

On January 1, 1920, constitutional Prohibition became the law of the land. The drys, led by the Anti-Saloon League, first conquered the state legislatures and then obtained a nationwide outlawing. As Herbert Asbury showed in *The Great Illusion,* the belief that Prohibition came about as a result of the Great War—the hatred of German brewers, the need for grain for bread, that our attention was distracted by the fight for democracy abroad—is not founded in fact. The dry victory was won in the Congressional elections of 1916, five months before we entered the war. Asbury said, "What happened after November 1916 was really a mopping-up operation, the consolidation of a triumph already won."

The spirit of sacrifice in the war did help it along. By 1917 twenty-seven states were already dry, and local option prevailed in many others. The Women's Christian Temperance Union, founded by Frances Willard, had joined with the Anti-Saloon League to distribute millions of pamphlets, flyers and posters stating that drink was responsible for all poverty, disease, crime, and insanity. The crusade against drink was linked to the march of progress. Drunkenness was an anachronism in an age of machinery and was especially dangerous with that new lethal weapon, the motorcar, loose in the streets.

The drys were exultant. Liquor was gone for good, and the millennium had arrived. Proclaimed Billy Sunday, "Goodbye John Barleycorn. You were God's worst enemy. You were Hell's best friend. The reign of tears is over." John F. Kramer, the first chief of the Prohibition Bureau of the Treasury Department, said that his staff of 1,500 agents would be sufficient to enforce the law. "The law says that liquor is not to be used as beverage, must not be manufactured. We shall see that it is not manufactured, nor sold, nor given away, nor hauled in anything on the surface of the earth." The appropriation for 1920 was $2,200,000. Wayne B. Wheeler, of the Anti-Saloon League, said that "Five million dollars a year appropriated to enforce this law will be ample." In 1928 the head of the Prohibition Bureau, Dr. James B. Doran, said that a minimum of $250,000,000 a year was necessary to enforce the law. Congress never appropriated more than $14,000,000.

Fanatics had led the movement and had triumphed over millions who were passive or indifferent. I have a vivid memory of one such zealot. In our junior high school in Reading, Pennsylvania, we had an assembly on Friday mornings, and occasionally an outside speaker would come to address the boys and girls. One morning in 1926 a wizened little man, leaning on crutches and reciting freely from the Bible, described to us in fire and brimstone the gruesome ruin to our lives if we should give way to the wiles of the demon rum. Then he made us all rise and swear an oath that alcohol would never touch our lips.

He was a colorful figure of the era. William G. Upshaw fell off a woodpile on his father's farm in Cobb County, Georgia, when he was seventeen years old and injured his back. For the next seven years he was in a plaster cast and could not take a step. Then he was put into a steel jacket and was able to walk haltingly. He became an evangelist and entered politics, tackling public issues with an evangelistic fervor. He won a seat in Congress as an outspoken advocate of the Ku Klux Klan, probably the first Congressman elected under its banner.

Once in Washington, Upshaw was an implacable foe of the demon rum, constantly offering drastic proposals, such as punishing the drinker, as well as the seller, of liquor. He had crackpot ideas on a lot of other subjects, such as having the members of the President's Cabinet elected by the people. His physical infirmity did not prevent him from traveling far and wide in his battle.

This type of fanaticism continued unabated throughout the life of Prohibition, emanating mostly from the Protestant churches. In January, 1929, a mother of ten children was sentenced to life imprisonment under a Michigan law for her fourth penal offense—selling two pints of liquor. Dr. Clarence True Wilson, of the Board of Temperance, Prohibition and Public Morals of the Methodist Church, said that his only regret was that she had not been put in prison for life before she had had her ten children. "When one has violated the Constitution four times, he or she should be segregated from society to prevent the production of subnormal offspring." Public furor in Michigan forced the repeal of the "life for a pint" ruling.

However, there was too much dissension for even the most stubborn fanaticism to prevail. One problem was that America was surrounded by a wet world eager to relieve its parched throats. There were 18,700 miles of land and sea to patrol, a hopeless task. Ships loaded with liquor left Vancouver in Canada charted for Mexico and returned empty in twenty-four hours, obviously having got rid of their cargo near Seattle or Portland. Detroit faced Canada across the mile-wide Detroit River, and wholesale smuggling by speedboat made it the liquor capital of the world. While customs boats patrolled the surface, an underwater cable towed sledges loaded with liquor from the Canadian shore. Attorney General Daugherty issued a decree in 1922 barring the entry of foreign ships into American ports if they carried liquor, even if the liquor was under seal. There was a strong protest from foreign countries, and the ruling was withdrawn in exchange for agreements enlarging our territorial waters from 3 to 12 miles. So foreign ships now stood in a line 12 miles off our shore, called Rum Row, where they were met at night by speedboats, often 75 feet in length and capable of going 50 miles an hour, enabling them to outrun any Coast Guard boat.

The family doctor was recognized early as the best friend of one who was suffering from thirstitis. Under federal dispensation he was given a pad of 100 blanks that he could use over a ninety-day period to make out prescriptions that could be filled by a druggist. In 1929, 11,000,000 prescriptions were filled. The Prohibition Bureau could not spare the manpower to make even a token inspection of these prescriptions. Concoctions containing alcohol could be bought as easily as chewing gum from the druggist. There were bitters with an alcoholic content double that of champagne, tonics and bracers which stated on the labels that they had 20 percent alcohol, heart cures, lung cures, dandruff cures, and hair tonics.

Denatured alcohol was lawful to manufacture and possess for industrial purposes under federal permit. Alcohol was needed for manufacturing many products—substitutes for German dyes, varnishes and furniture polishes, antifreezing mixtures, rayons, perfumes, smokeless powders. The demand for industrial alcohol quadrupled within a few years after Prohibition went into effect, obviously because much was being diverted into beverages. The denaturant which had been introduced to make it nonpotable, whether it was quinine or brucine, could be eliminated by boiling and condensation, leaving more or less pure grain alcohol. For coloring, caramel could be added to give the brew the appearance of rye or Scotch; charred wood or even fusel oil would lend the Scotch its aged-in-wood flavor. The entire process, including the bottling and shipping, could be accomplished within one night.

It was not difficult to evade the law against brewing beer with an alcoholic content of more than half of 1 percent. For beer of legal content one had first to make beer of from 3 to 8 percent alcohol. The brewer made sure that no federal eye was around and then shipped off the uncut brew. Congressman Fiorello H. LaGuardia demonstrated before movie cameras in front of the Capitol how he could produce beer of 4 percent alcohol quite legally by mixing two parts of malt tonic with one part of near beer.

A commercial still could be bought for $500, and it would produce alcohol at a cost of 50 cents a gallon, which could be sold for $3 or $4 a gallon, thus paying for the still in a few days. It was worth the risk of seizure at these prices. A still for home use could be bought for as little as $6, and stores in many cities openly displayed all the apparatus, ostensibly to enable housewives to make catsup or root beer. The United States Department of Agriculture before Prohibition had published bulletins on how to make alcohol from apples, oats, bananas, pumpkins, and parsnips, and in true bureaucratic fashion, the department continued to distribute them after Prohibition. What went on in a man's home was, of course, his own business. Suppose he permitted grape juice to ferment into wine in his cellar and shared it with his friends—could this be called manufacture for sale?

There were 3,000 Prohibition agents by the end of the decade, and they were earning $3,800 a year, a great advance over their earlier salary of $2,300 but pitifully small in view of the riches of the liquor industry they were pitted against. The result was predictable, widespread corruption. One out of 12 agents hired was fired for suspicion of bribery. Dedicated and fanatically active agents, like the famed Izzie and Moe in New York City, were few and far between. Major Chester P. Mills, New York enforcer, recounted that once a man was recommended by a politician for a job. Mills thought his background was suspicious and asked, "What does a high class man want with a job that pays only $3,000 a year?" and got the reply, "We're all over 21. He wants the job to get his, just the same as the rest of them in this Prohibition racket." Prohibition Commissioner Roy Haynes once complained, "The Prohibition Service proved to be a training school for bootleggers; while in the Service, they naturally learned all the ropes of the underworld as well as the Government's methods in attempting to apprehend and convict violators."

Fervent do-gooders were even less efficient. In an interview in the New York *Times* in 1925, Mrs. Mabel Walker Willebrandt, Assistant Attorney General in charge of Prohibition prosecutions, said, "At present we haven't the right kind of investigators. Many of them are well-meaning sentimentalists and dry, but they can't catch crooks. The sole object of the others has been to appropriate all the graft in sight, and they *won't* catch crooks. These two classes have attained their positions largely because Prohibition agents have been appointed at the instance of senators, congressmen, and political leaders." Not until 1927 were the agents put under civil service.

Throughout the twenties, Mrs. Willebrandt was the sparkplug of the federal enforcement of Prohibition, a remarkable woman who was regarded by the drys as their Joan of Arc. She was relatively young when she was appointed Assistant Attorney General in 1921, only thirty-two, and she continued in that post until 1929. She had been born in the Panhandle district of Kansas, had milked cows on her father's ranch and had set type on a county newspaper he owned. She moved to Southern California, where she married Mr. Willebrandt, from whom she separated. She became principal of a public school in South Pasadena and studied law at night in the University of Southern California. After passing the bar, she rose to prominence in causes advancing women's rights and soon was handling more than 2,000 cases as public defender for Los Angeles County. After she left the government, she was the first woman to head an important committee of the American Bar Association, on aeronautical law.

She always insisted that she was not a crusader for temperance as such, but only, as a lawyer for the government, dedicated to the maintenance of law. "Shall we maintain our institutions, our prestige, and dignity, or become the laughing-stock of the world?" She entered the 1928 Presidential campaign for Hoover and fought with hammer and tongs. A storm arose when, over a nationwide radio hookup before the Ohio Methodist Conference, she urged that the Methodists enter politics as a unit against the wet candidate Alfred E. Smith. The New York *World* said that this was "an experiment in organized sectarian politics which has set a new and sinister precedent," and the Springfield (Massachusetts) *Union* said, "If this speech had been made by a partisan of the Democratic nominee to a gathering of Roman Catholic priests, it would have stirred up popular resentment from coast to coast."

It was Mrs. Willebrandt's belief that enforcement could be effective only if a proper division were made between local and national authorities. "The man who sells drinks in the back room or the one who peddles flasks, even those who bootleg one or two cases to individual customers, should be taken care of by local authorities—the Federal government should take care of the wholesale bootleggers who often work on a gigantic scale. Get the ringleaders and the pocket-flask trade will disappear."

This hope for cooperative enforcement declined steadily. Under pressure from the drys, all the states, with the exception of Maryland, enacted enforcement laws. But with the federal government in the field, their outlook became one of "let

George do it." Coolidge once repeated to his secretary Everett Sanders a joke that Senator James Heflin of Alabama had just told him. An ardent Prohibitionist seemed to cool in ardor, and when asked why, he replied, "I thought that Prohibition was going to be great, but you know it's getting so I can't get liquor for myself anymore." Like many jokes this one had a bedrock of truth. Prior to national Prohibition, state laws had loopholes a mile wide. In Heflin's own state of Alabama, importation of liquor was allowed twice a month. When earnest enforcement began with the Volstead Act, grumbling emanated from even the ultradry areas.

As state interest melted away, New York, Montana, Wisconsin, and Nevada repealed their enforcement laws. By 1927 the total amount spent by states for enforcement was a miserly $689,000. Three states spent less than $1,000, and Utah only $160. Jail sentences meted out by state courts were ridiculously light—in Massachusetts an average of three days and in Kentucky three-tenths of a day.

Instead of granting funds to enforce the laws, Congress stiffened the penalties, which resulted only in greater reluctance of juries to convict. A few days before Coolidge left office, Congress passed the so-called Five and Ten Act, five years in prison and $10,000 fine for the first offense under the Volstead Act. Senator James Reed lashed out at the hypocrisy of Senators who drank but voted dry, and Senator Thaddeus Horatio "Pat" Caraway of Arkansas replied, "I marvel at the motive that makes him seek to lead the people to think that this is a body of sots." However, Mrs. Willebrandt in her *The Inside of Prohibition* wrote, "Bootleggers infest the halls and corridors of Congress and ply their trade there. I have found a curious impression or state of mind among members of Congress, to wit, that they are above and beyond the inhibitions of the Prohibition law."

Coolidge believed in Prohibition; he did not drink and did not serve liquor in the White House, although Harding certainly did. Yet Coolidge abided by the compromise which prevailed in Congress from 1924 on—strong support for the law but not enough money to enforce it. Economy always appealed to him, and anyway he believed in more local and less federal government. In time, the dry groups became exceedingly irked with

Coolidge. "Why does he always talk about *law* enforcement," they would ask, "but never about *Prohibition* enforcement?"

Walter Lippmann wrote that Prohibition was a last-ditch fight by a rural civilization against the "new urban civilization with its irresistible scientific and economic mass power." Mencken always claimed that Prohibition was a conspiracy by the farm folk who were jealous of the good life that the city folk had or that they believed they enjoyed. At any rate, it was in the nation's large cities that the worst flouting of the law occurred.

New York City was close to the top in that respect. At one time the police estimated that there were 20,000 speakeasies in the city. The "nightclub" originated there, and the term survives today as a reminder of Prohibition. The mayor, James "Jimmy" Walker, did not disguise the fact that he was a prominent patron of such establishments. One afternoon there was a rumor that he had been shot. The reporters flocked to his office. "Gentlemen," he said, "at this time of the day I am not even half-shot."

Such places flourished in New York as entertainment for out-of-town buyers and as tourist traps where visitors went so they could report about their adventures when they returned home. Once the federal administrator for Prohibition enforcement in New York sent to Police Commissioner Grover Whalen a list of speakeasies which should be closed as public nuisances. Whalen replied tartly, "If you are unwilling to discharge your sworn obligations or wish to make a confession of your inability to direct the activities of your department, the admission should be made to your superiors in Washington, instead of 'passing the buck' to state law-enforcement officers."

In Philadelphia, General Smedley D. Butler was given a leave of absence from the Marines and made director of public safety. If anything could make Prohibition work, it was the fighting spirit of the Marines. General Butler thus addressed the police on taking office: "Let's go out and clean up the bad spots. We don't want any help from the reformers. We don't want any help from the Marines, or constabulary or anyone else. Good God Almighty, men. Let's do the damned thing ourselves. Hell,

96

we don't want any pussy-footing squads around. Put on your uniforms and go on after them."

In a year in Philadelphia the number of arrests for liquor violations rose from 1,413 to 6,080, but the rate of convictions was less than 4 percent. Butler's efforts were sabotaged at every turn. Speakeasies were warned of impending raids, liquor held for evidence disappeared, and policemen connected with such cases resigned to open speakeasies of their own. After two years Butler had become such a nuisance to Philadelphia that Coolidge acceded to pressure and ordered him back to the Marines. From the front, the general issued his final communiqué, "Trying to enforce the law in Philadelphia was worse than any battle I was ever in."

The attempt by government to enforce abstinence from a liquid which a good part of the population regarded as necessary to their lives or an added joy to it certainly made the national scene more colorful. The English visitor Beverley Nichols wrote:

> Prohibition is a poem because it has added an infinite variety of subtle colors to the canvas of American life. It has sent bands of buccaneers careening down a thousand Main Streets. . . . To the dullest dinner it has added something of the thrill which must have come to all who dined with the Borgias, for who knows what powerful poisons may lurk even in the palest Bronx?

While Nichols exaggerated the number of places infested with "buccaneers," in one city, Chicago, gangsterism did play an important role in civic life.

Before Prohibition, gangsters were not in the liquor trade. As former President William Howard Taft predicted, they would invade it for the profits that could be made from selling illicit liquor.

With the dawn of Prohibition, Chicago hood Johnny Torrio tried to convince his boss and gangland ruler, "Big Jim" Colosimo, that he should enlarge his sights to take in booze, but Colosimo, who had married a brothel madam and had gone on from there to fortune, didn't agree. "Stick to girls," he ordered, "that's where the big money is." So Torrio had him murdered

97

in May, 1920, by a killer imported from New York, Frankie Yale (né Uale).

Torrio brought in an assistant from Brooklyn, Alphonse Capone. His background was none too clear, and Capone provided only misinformation. He claimed that he had been born in Brooklyn in 1899, but it seems that he was born Alfonso Caponi in 1895 in Castellammare, Italy, the son of a shopkeeper, and was brought here by his parents as an infant. He became a thug on the Brooklyn waterfront and in a knife duel acquired two parallel scars, three inches long, on his left cheek, about which he was forever after self-conscious. In 1920 he was working as a bartender and dishwasher at Frankie Yale's Harvard Inn on Coney Island (he was laureled, academically speaking) and wrote to Torrio in Chicago asking for a job. He arrived with his Irish wife, whom he had married when she was fifteen, and his baby girl.

Capone's first job, before his promotion to manage one of Torrio's speakeasies, was as a bouncer in a Torrio brothel. Torrio had gone big time. He had organized the beer and whiskey business, carving it up among fiefs in Chicago and environs. A strong-arm man was valuable to Torrio since gangland was engaging in internecine warfare, trying to muscle in on each other's preserves. Capone, or Scarface Al Brown, as he was known, was moved up again, as a chief on the Chicago South Side.

In 1924 Capone took over the suburb of Cicero with 50,000 population. He elected his own mayor. He had his hoodlums run the polling places and Herbert Asbury recounted, "When Mayor Kenha failed to show him proper respect, Capone shoved him down the steps of City Hall and kicked him when he tried to get up. He lay there until Capone gave him permission to rise." Capone's principality of Cicero became a spa for gangsters from all over the Midwest.

Trouble for Torrio erupted with an outright rebellion by Dion O'Banion, who held the fiefdom of the North Side. Torrio was double-crossed by O'Banion; he was arrested by federal agents and given a short jail term. O'Banion, a former altar boy who had turned bank robber and then bloody executioner, loved nature and indulged himself with the part ownership of a flower shop. One day, according to an eyewitness report, three men walked in, and O'Banion smilingly extended his hand in greeting. The hand was firmly grasped; he was twisted around and shot to death on the spot. He had many flowers at his funeral, the biggest wreath from Capone.

Two weeks after O'Banion's murder, Torrio and his wife were tiptoeing in the darkness across the lawn from their garage to their home when he was spattered with bullets from a touring car. The bullets were tipped with garlic and hence poisonous. He hovered between life and death in a hospital and then served his jail term. Shattered in health, he was whisked from prison in a private car and put on a steamer for Genoa with $1,000,000 in cash to pay for his needs. Al Capone was now the big boss.

The shooting of Torrio was put down to Hymie Weiss, who is said to have originated the practice of "taking for a ride" and who also coined the phrase. In September, 1926, Weiss sent ten cars with guns blazing to rake both Capone's headquarters at the Hawthorne Inn, in Cicero, and an adjoining restaurant, where Capone found refuge by lying prone on the floor during the barrage. Three weeks later Weiss met death from Capone machine guns as he walked around the corner of a cathedral. He was succeeded as head of the North Side boys by "Schemer" Drucci, who died ignominiously, shot by a policeman. He in turn was succeeded by George Clarence "Bugs" Moran.

The civil war continued in gangland, an *imperium in imperio*. Between 1925 and 1929, when Capone was in his heyday, there were 227 killings. Throughout the decade there were only a handful of convictions, and most of those convicted were freed on appeals.

Capone became internationally famous. In the demimonde he was known as the big fellow or simply as the man. In his Chicago headquarters at the Metropole Hotel, politicians came in and out along with uniformed policemen. The Chicago Crime Commission reported that he had given $260,000 to the campaign fund of Mayor "Big Bill" Thompson, who dismissed gang murders during his regime as "only newspaper talk."

A documented study by the United States Attorney in 1926

99

calculated that Capone's income ran to $70,000,000. Capone told Edward D. Sullivan that he paid out $30,000,000 for protection in 1928. Kenneth Allsop in his history of bootlegging stated that it was estimated that at one time 60 percent of Chicago's police force was on his payroll. "There was too much overhead in my business," said Capone in jail.

No swashbuckling great lord had a bigger swagger. With pistols bulging under his armpits, he lolled in his seven-ton, armored, custom-made automobile upholstered in silk, a $50,000 diamond ring sparkling on his finger. When he went out for pleasure, he scattered money like dandruff, a $100 tip to a waiter, $50 to a panhandler. He was generous to charity and sent money to orphanages; in hard winters he distributed groceries, fuel, and clothing to the poor of Cicero. He was a great gambler, shooting craps for $50,000 a throw, but never put any money in stocks, saying, "Wall Street is crooked."

An Internal Revenue officer told author Fred Pasley, "Capone had exceptional business ability, and would have gone far in any legitimate line. If he had only been honest, what a hero he would have made for a Horatio Alger tale." Edward D. Sullivan, who made a study of the man, wrote, "He has concentration and executive ability, which many possessors of better trained minds might envy. He is generous, foolishly so. He is intensely loyal. He has a good memory and is appreciative. He talks little but when he utters a few words, you have heard something."

In an idiosyncratic age, this man who trampled on society's laws, a cheap thug and wholesale murderer (he is said to have killed twenty men personally), was doted on by the public. Newspapers ran fond headlines such as CAPONE GAINS ELEVEN POUNDS. He was cheered when he dropped in on a rally at Northwestern University. The adoration could be explained. He was a self-made success in business in an age which worshiped successful businessmen. Capone described himself in those terms: "I call myself a businessman. I make my money by supplying a demand of the people." Then, too, there is always romance associated with power, particularly with one who is more powerful than the law.

When he appeared at a big prizefight in Miami, Jack Dempsey escorted him to a seat of honor and dusted it off for him.

Poppycock was printed to romanticize him, such as the fact that his scars were the result of machine-gun bullets he had received while fighting as an American soldier in France. He was even given credit for culture. A writer, Jack Bilbo, thus quoted him in 1931: "Sentimentality is the main danger that threatens us in life. One either has to rid oneself of it, or one is entirely within its power." When he was in prison in Philadelphia in 1929, a newspaper ran a story that he was reading Shaw and Shakespeare.

Bugs Moran was as unruly as his predecessors on the North Side. He hijacked Capone's trucks and tried to take over his territory. The edict went out from Capone that Moran must go. This set the stage for the famous St. Valentine's Day Massacre on February 14, 1929.

It turned out to be a slight case of misdirected murder, since the intended victim didn't show up. Moran was elusive and well protected. Moreover, he did not operate on any fixed schedule, which always presents a problem for would-be assassins. From time to time he would drop in on a Moran hangout, the S.M.C. Cartage Company in the 2100 block of North Clark Street, but his visits were unpredictable.

The Capone mob worked out a plan. They arranged for a fake hijacking of one of their trucks by a man named Sorello, who delivered the cargo to the Moran gang at the S.M.C. Cartage Company, where he was treated brusquely. On February 11 he managed to get Moran on the phone. He complained that the boys had pushed him around and had taken some of the money due him as commission. He had hijacked another truck, but this time he would do business only with Moran, not with his boys. Moran said good-humoredly that he would be at the Cartage Company on Thursday morning, February 14, at ten thirty. Sorello could rely on it, and so he could bring in the truck cargo.

Upon hearing the news at his Palm Island estate outside Miami, Capone was overjoyed, and ordered his gang to make sure that Moran received "a great, big valentine."

Two men rented a front room opposite the S.M.C. Cartage Company, where they took up observation posts on the morning of the fourteenth. They were to telephone the main force as soon as Moran arrived. Six men entered the garage; one of them was an optometrist who got a big kick from fraternizing with gangsters. Another was not a gunman but a father of seven, who supplemented his income by doing odd jobs for Moran; he was there that day to repair a truck.

The men at the observation post were wondering if Moran would show up. Then a seventh man stepped out of the car and briskly entered. The men had been warned that they might have no chance to see Moran's face, but they had studied photographs, knew his age, build, height, weight, and gait, and also were told that he customarily wore brown clothes. This man answered the description. They called in that Moran had arrived and the party could begin.

The man was not Moran. He was Morris Weinshank, a member of the gang who was breaking away from Moran and may have dropped in to say good-bye to him.

It was 10:30 A.M. A newly bought Cadillac, equipped with a siren and other paraphernalia to make it look like a police car, drove up from a nearby garage. Two men in police uniforms entered and snarled, "Hands up." Six men were waiting for their morning coffee to brew; a seventh was ordered to get out from the wheeled platform under a truck he was repairing. The seven doomed men were lined up facing the wall and frisked for weapons. Two killers in civilian clothes moved out from behind a truck and took out submachine guns carried in harnesses under their overcoats. A hundred .45-caliber bullets ripped into the victims. Two shotgun blasts finished off two men who were crawling away. The assassins, covered by the ersatz police officers, were seen leaving the garage. A man in plain clothes had been at the wheel of the Cadillac letting the engine idle. Now it melted away in the traffic. The whole thing had taken two minutes.

The whining and barking of a dog attracted neighbors, who walked in and discovered the bodies. Moran had been delayed by a phone call as he left his hotel. He was having a doughnut and coffee in a nearby café when he heard the news. He immediately took refuge in a private room of a hospital to receive treatment for a bad cold. When he was interviewed by reporters, he said that he didn't know anything about gangs; he was in the real estate business. A reporter asked him if he believed that the police killed the men. "You must be new around here, mister, only Capone kills like that." When interviewed on his Miami estate and asked about Moran's comment, Capone replied, "Say, they don't call that guy 'Bugs' for nothing."

It was the beginning of the end for Capone. The massacre aroused public indignation about anarchy within the walls of a civilized community. Capone was arrested in Philadelphia in May on a charge of carrying concealed weapons and sentenced to a year in jail. His arrest was at 8:15 P.M., his indictment was handed down at 10:25 A.M. the next day, his trial started at 11:30 A.M., his plea of guilty was entered at 12:15 P.M., and his incarceration began at 12:50 P.M. Said Capone in awe, "They work fast here." It was believed that Capone may have maneuvered himself into being jailed as a refuge from Moran's vengeance. A week before, two of the St. Valentine's Day assassins had been found murdered in a ditched car on the outskirts of Hammond, Indiana.

Capone had been treated as a celebrity. Now the realization dawned that he was a common criminal and a menace to society. The Chicago Crime Commission used an effective publicity device, putting on Capone the label of Public Enemy Number One. Like a noisome animal, he was kicked out of one place after another and even had to get a court order to remain on his Miami estate. In 1931 he was sentenced to ten years for evasion of federal income taxes. He announced, "This is a low blow below the belt. But what can you expect when the whole country is prejudiced against you?" In the federal penitentiary he was almost killed when brutally beaten by a fellow prisoner. He died in 1947 of paresis on his Florida estate. Capone lived on in the mythology of the Depression. He was personified in W. R. Burnett's *Little Caesar* and again in *Scarface, Shame of a Nation*, which brought cinematic fame to Paul Muni.

In the days of wine and roses, illusions gave added richness to daily living. In the succeeding grim days of the Depression, they were luxuries which had to be dispensed with. Capone's rapid fall owed much to the different temper of the times. Prohibition itself was a casualty of the Depression. Despite all its failures,

103

it might have survived years longer, but in the cold, gray morning after of hard times, when things had to be assessed in dollar-and-cent terms, it was clearly absurd for the community to subsidize a gangster world while depriving the government of needed revenue from the sale of liquor.

Chapter IV

A-U-T-O

The passion of the American for the gas buggy transformed the face of America in the time of Coolidge. In 1912 there had been only 1 car for every 114 persons; in 1920 there was 1 for every 13 persons. A contributing factor was that mass-production techniques had enabled the prices of cars to fall sharply. Between 1913 and 1923 the cost of the same model of Ford had fallen from $600 to $398, a Studebaker from $1,550 to $1,275, a Chevrolet from $1,200 to $425 and a Packard from $4,150 to $2,885. A standard tire had fallen from $28 to $15.50 and a storage battery from $22.50 to $15.85.

Even after the auto had clearly become a fixture of American life, observers consistently underestimated the future demand. The magazines of the early twenties were filled with discussions of the question "Is the Auto Market Saturated?" In 1921 there were 9,340,000 cars registered, and a highly respected economist for the Cleveland Trust Company, Leonard Ayres, opined, "Very nearly all Americans who can afford to have cars now own them." The New York *Times* said that demand would expand over the years, but: "The use in the near future of anything like twice the present number of cars seems most unlikely. Another consideration of no small importance is that if the number of cars is doubled in the near future some other motive power than gasoline will have to be developed to propel them." These calculations were based on the expectation that few Negroes would

105

ever own cars, and women were excluded if their husbands had them.

The number continued to climb, helped by the demand for the new closed sedans which were replacing the touring car, the convertible of that day. In 1926 the *New Republic,* commenting on the registration figure of 17,500,000, said that surely the saturation point was near—there were only 7,000,000 people with incomes of more than $2,000, and if that number were multiplied by three, that would be the wildest limit. Leonard Ayres now said that although an outside figure could not be set, saturation would come suddenly "like a thief in the night." He pointed out that the entire population of California and a few other states could be transported in cars if they were filled.

The infatuation of Americans for the automobile is a fascinating sociological phenomenon. (Today there are about 81,-000,000 passenger cars in the United States.) There was no correlation between the demand and financial capacity. People would go into debt and stay broke in order to have a car. Some people preferred a car to a home. In the West there were gas gypsies without homes who moved from one farm to another for work. Oswald Garrison Villard wrote after a tour of America that the slogan of the "full dinner pail" had been supplanted by the "full gasoline tank." The Dallas *News* commented, "Home is where the garage is."

In August, 1925, the White House forwarded to D. R. Crissinger, governor of the Federal Reserve Board, a letter from a citizen to Coolidge in which the writer warned that a mountain of installment debt was piling up to buy autos. Crissinger replied to Sanders, Coolidge's secretary, that such promissory notes were not normally financed by Federal Reserve Banks since there were auto discount companies doing this. He was aware, however, that the situation had an impact on all industry. "People will have an automobile and sacrifice paying their doctor bill, the grocery bill and clothing bill. The discount companies find it extremely profitable because they have learned that the family will sacrifice every other convenience, every other luxury and often necessities rather than give up the auto."

One of Herbert Hoover's favorite stories was about a debate held in a small town in Iowa between Senator Smith W. Brookhart and a Congressman Cole. There was a large crowd, and many cars were parked around the speaker's platform. The debate was broadcast, and each speaker had been allotted fifteen minutes. However, Brookhart took up twenty-seven minutes in a ranting speech in which he said that because of government policies, the farmers were surely on the road to bankruptcy and the poorhouse. Congressman Cole got up and said, "Senator Brookhart was supposed to leave me fifteen minutes. He has left me only three. But that's more than I need for what I have to say, which is only this—if we are on the road to the poorhouse, at least we have the consolation that each one of us will be able to get there in his own car."

Where are the cars of yesterday? Boys in the twenties played a game to see who could identify the make of a car from afar. In addition to the brands known today (the latest was the Chrysler introduced in 1924), there were the Anderson, Case, Davis, Daniels, Elcar, Flint, Franklin, Gardner, Gray, Haynes, Jewett, Essex, McFarlane, Moon, Overland (later renamed Pontiac), Peerless, Reo, Rollin, Paige, Rickenbacker, Stutz, Velie. And who can remember cars of an even earlier vintage? Kisselcar, Lozier, Flanders, Apperson, Jack Rabbit, Brush Runabout, Penn Thirty, White Steamer, Dorris, Spaulding.

In 1929 there were more autos than radios or telephones, despite the great usefulness of the radio and telephone and their relative cheapness: 10,000,000 radios and 18,520,000 telephones compared to 24,500,000 autos. As late as 1935 the National Resources Planning Board reported to President Roosevelt that while only 12 percent of farms had water piped to them, 60 percent had cars. In a well-publicized interview, a farmer's wife was asked why she had a car while she had no bathtub. After pondering, she replied, "Well, you can't get to town in a bathtub."

When Coolidge, in a conversation with the president of AT&T, congratulated him on the growth of the telephone industry and the executive replied that he could not understand why the telephone lagged behind the auto in use, Coolidge said, "Well, no one can show himself off in a phone booth." There was more than utilitarianism to account for the passion for the auto. Utilitarianism was, however, one of the reasons for the success of the Model T Ford. A current joke asked why it was like a bathtub, to which the response was, "Because you hate to be seen in one." But eventually, even Ford had to respond to the demand that his auto be something of a showpiece.

Sinclair Lewis wrote, "To George F. Babbitt, as to most prosperous citizens of Zenith, his motor car was poetry and tragedy, love and heroism." It became the family pet, toy, dream, and adventure. The English observer C. E. M. Joad wrote in *The Babbitt Warren,* "It is the attribute that modern civilized man finds the most complete expression of his worship of machinery. It is for him the supreme symbol of his power over nature, the *deus in machina* of the progress age."

The revolution in society wrought by the motorcar was clearly evident in Middletown, the sociological study of a typical American city (actually Muncie, Indiana) by Robert S. and Helen Merrell Lynd, published in 1929. An auto financing company estimated that 75 to 90 percent of the cars were bought with time payments. Homes were mortgaged to buy cars. A working-class wife told the Lynds, "We'd rather go without clothes than give up the car." A member of the Trades' Council, when asked by the Lynds what the men were working for, replied that 65 percent were working to buy cars, as against 10 percent who were working to buy homes.

Walking for pleasure in Middletown had gone out of fashion. A high school boy who couldn't take a girl to a dance in a car was as socially undesirable as one without ears. The make of one's car rivaled the appearance of one's home as evidence of status. House architecture had to conform to the needs of the car. "Houses are crowded closer to the paving line, and shrubbery and flowers must give way as the lawn shrinks to allow a driveway to the garage."

The revolution spread in every direction. At the beginning of the century a trip of fifty miles was a major one and required long preparation; now it could be made in an hour. The cleavage between city and country tended to disappear as cities sprawled into suburbs. Life took on a different form as distant vacations were possible, and camping out, which was formerly a recreation confined to safaris for the rich, became practicable for the masses. New words came into everyday language: "joyride," "flat tire," "sparkplug," and from the underworld, "taking for a ride."

The nation was transformed economically. By 1929 the auto industry was the greatest in America, and $1 out of every $5 spent by the consumer, excluding rent and insurance, went for automobiles, including garage rent and repairs. By 1929 there were 121,500 filling stations. For years gasoline had been considered the offal of the oil industry, since there was little known use for it; now gasoline filled the gap for oil producers left by the diminishing demand for kerosene as electric lights came into use. Trucks, 3,400,000 in 1929, displaced other forms of transportation, supplanting coastal steamers and freighters. A new industry, road building, came into being, a pork barrel for the politician, necessitating a whole new framework of heavier taxation.

In 1906 Woodrow Wilson, then president of Princeton University, said, "Nothing has spread socialistic feeling in this country more than the automobile. To the country man they are a picture of the arrogance of wealth with all its independence and carelessness." That was before the era of the cheap car. In the twenties the Englishman A. G. Gardiner could write that the motorcar, instead of a symbol of social inequality, was "a powerful influence for allaying social unrest by making power universally accessible and a new interest common to all."

The advent of Henry Ford's Model T revolutionized the car for the common man. "So good luck, Mr. Ford," said Will Rogers. "It will take a hundred years to tell us whether you have helped us or hurt us, but you certainly didn't leave us like you found us."

The first patent notice on a gasoline engine was filed here by George Selden in 1879, but changes in specifications were continually filed, and the patent was not actually taken out until 1895. The first gasoline car was built by Charles E. Duryea in 1892 in Massachusetts, and by 1896 he was making ten a year. The magazine *Horseless Age* was first published in 1894 and attained a circulation of 50,000. In 1895 it listed seventy-three manufacturers experimenting with cars. The fever was on.

The French were far ahead of us in the nineteenth-century

109

development of what they called the automobile (it was the gas buggy here). They were mad about automobile races, and in the first major race between Paris and Bordeaux and back in June, 1895, the winning car averaged 15 miles an hour in a journey lasting two days and nights. Gas cars were also popularized in America by races. One of the early daredevil drivers was a mechanic named Henry Ford who won a big race at Grosse Pointe, Michigan, in 1901 and then turned his car, the 999, over to Barney Oldfield. This car could hit the fantastic speed of 70 miles an hour. In 1904, Ford himself set the American record by driving a mile in 39.4 seconds.

In 1900 the automobile was looked on as a curiosity. America had only 4,000 cars in use, most of them imported from Europe. The War Department purchased three and issued a communiqué, "Three automobiles have been purchased by the War Department for the use of officers. Each is equipped so that a mule may be hitched to it should it refuse to run." The *Literary Digest* said in 1900, "The ordinary horseless carriage is at present a luxury for the wealthy, and although its price will probably fall in the future, it will never, of course, come into common use like the bicycle." The gas buggies were regarded as dangerous instruments, and drivers had to appear before municipal inspectors of boilers to obtain an engineer's license.

Auto travel for any great distance was impracticable away from cities because of lack of roads. As described by David L. Cohn, "The roads of the land, where there were roads, were mule-belly deep in winter mud, and axle-deep in summer dust." In 1900 Roy Chapin performed the sensational feat of driving from Detroit to New York in eight days, but because the highways were impossible to traverse, he used the towpath of the Erie Canal, competing for space with the mules pulling barges. Few realize how recent in our history are good roads. Harry Truman related that when he was an official of Jackson County, Missouri, in 1920, he had to ballast his Dodge with concrete blocks on his rounds of duty to avoid being capsized by potholes in the roads.

Autos were seen more often after 1900, but they were still expensive, particularly the imports from Europe which ranged up to $10,000 in price. A typical American auto, the Welch of

1907, cost $5,500, which would be the equivalent of more than $20,000 today. It boasted an overhead camshaft. Gear changing was a terrifying experience in those days when gears were constantly being stripped, but the Welch had a complex transmission in which the gears were constantly meshed and the car could go, the company advertised, "instantly from one speed to another, even from direct drive to reverse, without shock or damage." Its top speed was 55 miles per hour.

At the start of the century Ransom E. Olds, head of the Olds Motor Vehicle Company, turned out in Detroit a cheap car, a curved-dash runabout mostly for sports use priced at $650, and by 1904 he was producing 5,000 a year. A Gus Edwards song, "In My Merry Oldsmobile," helped the public become conscious of the car.

A frequent visitor at the Olds shop, hungry with curiosity, was Ford, who in 1900 was thirty-six years old. Born on a farm in Dearborn, Michigan, he had early shown a profound disinterest in farming and a rapt interest in mechanics. One of his early obsessions was the taking apart and putting together of watches. At the age of twenty-seven he left the farm for good for a job as engineer and machinist for the Detroit Electric Company, where he rose to the post of chief engineer. In his free time in a woodshed back of his home he worked on a horseless carriage, and one spring in 1896 at 4 A.M. he drove it out and around the block. It had bicycle wheels, no brakes, no reverse gear, and the transmission was a belt from the motor to the rear wheels.

His fame grew as a racing driver. He was the mechanical brain of two auto companies which were failures, the Detroit Automobile Company and the Henry Ford Automobile Company. Then in June, 1903, one of the great success stories of America and indeed of the world began when the Ford Motor Company was formed. It was capitalized for only $100,000, and of that only $28,500 in cash was paid in. Ford contributed no money at all, but for his services he became vice-president, received 25.5 percent of the stock and a salary of $3,000 a year. Together with A. Y. Malcolmson, a wealthy coal dealer who was the guiding financial brain, he would have majority control. James Couzens, who was a checker in Malcolmson's coal yards and destined to become a prominent United States Senator, put up $2,500, of which $1,500 was in the form of a note. When he sold out his interest to Ford in 1919, aside from huge dividends along the way, he received $29,308,858. Others besides Ford put up no money for stock. The Dodge brothers received 10 percent of the stock for agreeing to make the engine and parts. Another man received a block of stock for donating the shop.

The popular belief that Ford entered the auto business with a vision of a cheap car for the masses is without merit. The Model T did not come along until 1909, or six years after the Ford Motor Company was founded. *T* is the twentieth letter in the alphabet, and so the Model T advertises the fact that it was not built until Ford had made an even score of experiments. The Model A of 1903 cranked on the side, had a detachable tonneau, and was advertised "built for business, and for pleasure . . . and also for the good of your health." It sold for $900. The Model B of 1905 sold for $2,000; the Model C for $950; the Model F for $1,200.

The first autos built by Ford were almost handmade. In Allan Nevins' words: "Ford's small working force dealt with four cars in a group; when they were finished, the group moved on to another four cars. Two or three men usually worked on each car." By 1907 standardization and interchangeability of parts were possible. By then Malcolmson, who favored the higher-priced cars, was out, and Ford had control with 58 percent of the stock. The cars bought by Americans, whether domestic or imported, were becoming land battleships, and their increasing price made them status symbols. Undoubtedly the thought was germinating in Ford's mind that there was a market for a cheap car and that the industrial methods for producing a lower-priced car were almost within reach. After the expensive Model K at $2,500, which was a sales dud, Ford in his models N, R, and S turned out cars below $1,000. The cheap car was an idea whose time had come.

By 1908 there were 200,000 autos in America. In that year Ford announced that he would put Model T on the market: "It will be so low in price that no man making a good salary will be unable to own one, and enjoy with his family the blessings of hours of pleasure in God's open spaces."

There would hereafter be only one model Ford, and before the T was abandoned in 1927, there would be 15,000,000 of them. Ford's statement became classic: "A customer can have his car painted any color he chooses—as long as it is black." Actually, some early Fords were Brewster green with red striping or all red, but soon they were all black. The first Model T with 40 horsepower was seven feet high with the driver enthroned over the gasoline tank. The engine, influenced by the newest European cars, had moved from the rear to under the hood.

What were the advantages of the Model T? For one thing its lightness made it possible to travel 25 miles on a gallon of gasoline, instead of the 10 miles customary for heavy cars. The gas pump was eliminated by a splash-and-gravity oiling system; batteries were eliminated by a magneto which provided spark and lights. On the bad roads the transverse springs and planetary gears provided traction where other cars bucked. Instead of separate castings for each cylinder block, a single block was made for the four cylinders. Instead of having to lie on the ground to make repairs, one could stand up, the detachable cylinder permitting easy access to the engine. It was made of strong chrome-vanadium steel, which Ford had experts perfect after picking up a strip from a sturdy French racing auto that he saw wrecked at Palm Beach in Florida in 1905. Thus, his car was really not a "Tin Lizzie" but a "Vanadium Lizzie."

Running this car was quite an art, as described by Ralph Stein:

> The T of course had no hand gearshift. Its two speeds and reverse were controlled by means of three foot pedals, which tightened the brake bands of the planetary transmission and that of the foot brake inside the gearbox. A hand lever operated the tiny brakes on the rear wheels. There was no accelerator. To vary speed, you diddled with a lever on the steering column, where also lived the spark-control lever. Once the engine was started—until 1919 by hand cranking—you pressed the left-hand pedal halfway down, which put the gears in neutral. Then you released the handbrake, which had kept the gears in neutral while you cranked. To get moving, you tramped all the way down on the same left-hand pedal, meanwhile opening the hand throttle. You

113

were now in low. At about eight miles an hour you eased the throttle a bit and took your foot off the right pedal. With a neck-snapping bound and a mournful howl from the transmission the flivver catapulted ahead. You were now in high, in which speed you could do 40 m.p.h. if all was well with the engine.

Because of chronically worn bands, small hills were sometimes unclimbable, even in low, forcing undaunted drivers to go up backward.

David L. Cohn wrote:

> The time would come when skeptical man would have no faith except in the infallibility of machinery. Model T kept its devotees from sinking to this low, spiritual estate, however, for by a process that can only be described as mystical, they acquired a belief in things they could not see and powers they could not comprehend. Mr. Ford supplied instructions for setting his car in motion, but its owners found that it did not move in accord with physical laws but only to certain incantations and feats and sleight of hand . . . no man could pass on to his brother the secret of his success because success was a combination of constantly varying proportions of prayer, prestidigitation and intuition.

The first Model T was not dramatically cheap, $950. By 1913 the price had dropped to $550 and by 1916 to $365. Only 10,607 cars were sold in 1909, but by 1912 Ford's output was 15,000 a month. The Model T was a very durable car. It kept running at a time when crankshafts snapped, bearings melted, and axles collapsed. A study of 1923 showed that it lasted an average of eight years compared to six and one-half years for all other makes. Ford was always proud of the technical perfection of his car and in post-Model T days treasured a letter, an unsolicited testimonial, from the notorious gangster John Dillinger: "I want to thank you for making an excellent car. If I am ever captured, it will have to be by someone in another Ford."

Tin Lizzies filled the land and were especially prized by farmers. Ford had the farmer very much in mind when he designed the car. When asked how far the back seats should be from the front, he said, "Far enough for a farmer to get his milk cans on the floor." The Model T was as unadorned and as utilitarian as a plow. With a pickup truck attachment, it could take crops to market. It was a peripatetic power plant. The wheels could be jacked up, and by the attachment of a pulley it could be a churn in the dairy, a cider press in the orchard, saw wood, fill a silo, bale hay in the fields—do everything, it was said, but wash the dishes.

It was celebrated in humor which was as authentically American as Paul Bunyan and Johnny Appleseed. It was called a "rattling good car." Ford was hailed as a better evangelist than Billy Sunday, "because he has shaken hell out of far more people than Billy Sunday ever did."

A joke for which Ford claimed credit concerned the farmer who on his deathbed requested that his Ford be buried with him. "I've never been in a hole yet where my Ford didn't get me out."

As customer tastes became more sophisticated in the twenties, the Ford became simpler and simpler. Esteeming his car for its utility, Ford refused to make concessions. Owners of Fords had to paint them colors other than black and equip them with gadgets and obtain embellishments from suppliers, some of whose entire business consisted of serving owners of Fords.

The winds of change finally caught up with the Model T. It was clear that Americans wanted more from their car. Arthur Brisbane wrote to Ford, "These are days of big wages and extravagance. The average American thinks more of the paint on the outside than of the engine under the hood or the steel in the axles." Another friend wrote to him, "Amid prosperity even the plumber and the carpenter want a car which looks and handles a little more like his rich neighbor's."

Obsolescence by change of style became a powerful factor in promoting yearly sales of cars. Some slight alteration would make last year's models immediately worth less by 25 percent or more. Style often supplanted wear as a reason for buying the new model. One could hold one's head high when facing his neighbor only if one had the latest. This psychological motivation of keeping up with the Joneses became a major prop to the economy. However, in the case of the Ford, which was the same from year to year, there was no such compulsion to buy the latest model. And so Ford's share of the market started to decline. Always hovering over 40 percent, it slipped to 33 percent.

Ford cut the prices of the Model T for 1926—a runabout cost $360 and a touring car $380—but the sales decline continued.

His associates argued with Ford that the T was now obsolete. Smooth roads no longer demanded the planetary gears. The cooling system, shock absorbers, and magnetos were superior on other cars. A Buick with a little wear cost only slightly more than a Ford in the secondhand market. Ford long resisted. Some executives who pressed him too far found it advisable to work elsewhere. He was willing to offer Fords in colors other than black. He made experimental models of other types of cars which were foredoomed to failure.

Finally, he capitulated. In May, 1926, it was announced that there would be a new Ford to supplant the Model T.

The Ford plant was shut down for months in 1927 while the new machine progressed from conception to cocoon to chrysalis and then to the creature on wheels. Sight unseen, 500,000 advance orders were filed by customers with Ford dealers. The nation rocked with excitement when it was unveiled on December 2 to the accompaniment of full-page advertisements which ran for five consecutive days in 200 papers from coast to coast. Millions mobbed the showrooms. The New York *Sun* said, "Henry Ford invited the public in to see his new car. It was exactly as if Secretary of the Treasury Mellon had thrown open the doors of the sub-Treasury and invited the public in to help him count the gold reserve."

Ford had given the public a totally new car with four-wheel brakes, standard transmission, and hydraulic shock absorbers for $100 less than his nearest competitor in the low-priced market, the Chevrolet. However, there were many laments for the Model T and with it the passing of an era. The Detroit *News* said, "Is there another single thing produced by man that did so much for so many? To millions it was the first tangible evidence of a modest place on Easy Street. To millions more it was the sole extravagance in a life otherwise drab and dull."

The New York *Evening Post* said:

> The old Ford dripped oil into our faces as we lay under it on country roads at midnight. The new Ford is shown off like a modiste's mannikin to a generation which has lost the joy of getting its hands dirty. It is a remarkable piece of machinery but it

isn't a Ford because the Ford was an educational institution as well as a machine. The old Ford, the old, black, cantankerous, obstinate, puttering Ford brought wisdom to many fools and made many men go raving, tearing mad. This new lily of the valley isn't going to teach us anything. It looks as if it would run indefinitely without complaint, which is all wrong. It is made for serenity and comfort, which is all wrong. Where is the gas tank? Out in front where it can be reached. Where is the timer? Up on top where it can no longer bark your knuckles. Where are the brake bands? In a ridiculously exposed position where their value as trainers of character and refined language are completely lost. We are degenerating. We are entering a period of Roman luxury. Ford is a garage car. Back to the pioneer days when we threw sand under the fan belt and tightened the hose with a dime.

Ford's mechanical genius brought into being modern mass production. "Fordism" or "Fordismus" became an international word, used even in the Soviet Union. Basic to his scheme was the conveyor belt. The work was brought to the man, not the man to the work, and it was brought waist-high so that he would not have to stoop, even to attach a screw. He started this process in 1910 in his new Highland Park plant with the production of the flywheel magneto, cutting manufacturing time from twenty minutes per man to four minutes by splitting the operation into twenty-nine different operations. The method was by degrees applied to the making of the entire car.

Now men would not run the machines; the machines would run the men, who had to keep up with the inexorable pace of the conveyor belt. In the minute division of labor in his plants, Ford boasted that any job could be learned within a short time and that 43 percent of the jobs could be learned in less than a day.

He organized his production vertically, much as Rockefeller did in oil. He bought up an iron range and coal mines and a fleet of steamers to carry Superior ore to his mills; he built a steel mill at his River Rouge plant; he bought a railroad, the Detroit, Toledo and Ironton; he bought 70,000 acres of timberland; he bought or built factories to make his parts, and his tools were custom-made, by himself. He boasted that iron ore on his River Rouge docks at eight o'clock on Monday morning could be marketed on Wednesday noon as a car, reserving fifteen hours for shipment, literally *deus ex machina.*

The jobs on the assembly line were repetitive and monotonous. "Ford employees are not really alive—they are half dead," a labor official in Detroit said. Ford conceded that there were many dropouts but said that in the mass, men actually dreaded responsibility of any kind and were content to have repetitive jobs as long as their bellies were full.

In January, 1914, Ford had made a startling announcement. His workers were to be paid $5 a day for a nine-hour day, this at a time when the prevailing wage was only $2.34. The New York *Times* saw it as utopian, based on a vision of "universal human uplift through a single venture in the field of beneficence." But was it all philanthropy? The turnover of labor on the assembly line had been prodigious, and after the raise in pay the assembly line was speeded up and the men were given only fifteen minutes for lunch and three for going to the toilet.

Ford changed the philosophy of American industry. No longer was hope of maximum profits based on low wages. The greatest reliance was on attaining the widest market by low prices and trying to keep prices down by volume and efficiency.

In a celebrated court case in 1927, Henry Ford was sued by Aaron Sapiro for $1,000,000 for libeling him, Sapiro, and the Jewish race at large. Sapiro was a gifted, if somewhat egotistical, Chicago lawyer, who was a leading figure in the farm cooperative movement, which many, including Calvin Coolidge, looked on as the salvation of the farmer's ills. Sapiro had drafted the contract uniting the citrus fruit farmers of California under the name of Sunkist, and he then turned to a drive to form cooperatives for Midwestern farmers. Bernard Baruch, Julius Rosenwald, and many gentiles contributed financially to the movement. The Dearborn *Independent,* a publication owned by Ford, attacked the Jews—Otto Kahn, Albert Lasker, Rosenwald, and Sapiro—for a conspiracy "to control the food markets of the world . . . between the lines one read the story of the Jewish Communist movement in America which seeks to make the United States what it has already made of Russia." Then the libel suit was filed.

When the trial began, Ford was chagrined to find that Sapiro
was not represented by a Jew, but by a prominent Irish lawyer,
William J. Gallagher. Ford muttered darkly that the "Catholics
are tools of the Jews." While Sapiro posed as the champion of
the Jews and did so long after the trial, at the very outset the
presiding judge threw out part of the grounds of the suit by
saying that no one Jew could sue in behalf of an entire people
and pocket the damages for himself. Then the testimony cen-
tered on whether Ford was actually aware of what was carried
in his paper. Its editor, William J. Cameron, testified that, "I
run the paper and use my own judgment," although it was well
known within the organization that Ford visited Cameron every
day of the week.

Sapiro was anxious to get Ford on the witness stand, a prospect which the auto magnate viewed with alarm. Shortly before
he was scheduled to testify, according to a company spokesman,
he was sideswiped while driving near Dearborn, and his car
plunged down an embankment, causing physical injuries to
Ford. Three weeks afterward the Detroit *Times* reported that
a woman on the jury had accepted a package from a stranger,
and she gave an interview to the *Times*. The resulting publicity
forced the judge to declare a mistrial.

Harry H. Bennett, Ford's strong-arm man, in a later account
said that he visited Ford in his home soon after the news of the
accident and that he found Ford normal and without outer injury. Bennett said, "Mr. Ford, I'm going to find out who
dropped you into the river if it takes the rest of my life." Ford
replied, "No, drop it, Harry, it was probably just a bunch of
kids." When Bennett persisted, Ford said, "Well, I wasn't in
the car when it went down the river. I don't know how it got
down there. But now we've got a chance to settle that thing."

To the surprise of all, including Cameron and Ford's son,
Edsel, Ford apologized to the Jews through his close friend
Arthur Brisbane, retracting all the charges he had ever made
against the race, and said he would close down the Dearborn
Independent. He gave Sapiro a cash settlement for legal expenses rumored to be $144,000. He had the effrontery to say
that he had been unaware of what the *Independent* had been
publishing for years, but now that he had learned about it, the

material "justifies the righteous indignation entertained by Jews everywhere toward me because of the mental anguish occasioned by the unprovoked reflections made upon them." He concluded, "Had I appreciated even the general nature, to say nothing of the detail of these utterances, I would have forbidden their circulation without a moment's hesitation."

His change of heart was ascribed by many observers to his desire to end the Jewish boycott of Fords while he was in the course of scrapping the Model T for his new Model A. The Chicago *Tribune* said, "Mr. Ford advances an empty head to explain his cold feet." The Richmond *Times-Dispatch* said, "In denying knowledge of the anti-semitic policy he has set himself up as a target for ridicule." The New York *Daily News* made this interesting suggestion: "We respectfully suggest that the last sweet dose of love and kisses be ladled out to Mr. Ford's new-found friends by leaving the name Ford off the new car. Let it be called instead, let us say, the Solomon Six or the Abraham Eight." Yet it was a notable victory for the Jews. The *American Hebrew* said, "He is the first man in history beguiled by anti-semitism who has made a public recantation."

Ford, in private, was not cured at all. After a talk he had with President Roosevelt, he said, "He took up five minutes telling me of his ancestry. He wanted to prove to me that he had no Jewish blood." Republican fund raisers could always strike oil with him when they recited names of Jews who surrounded Roosevelt, their Jewishness often fictionalized. According to Bennett, Wendell Willkie in 1940 tried to get $500,000 out of him by using this gambit. Ford hated to be taken for a sucker, and in time he became aware of the fact that he was being conned. Finally, he rocked some Republican solicitors on their heels when they tried this approach. He said, "That's all right. If they weren't around Roosevelt to handle the money, this country would go broke in a hurry."

The origins of his anti-Semitism are not clear. Allan Nevins and Frank Ernest Hill in their extensive study of the man and his vast industrial enterprise say, "Ford's spasm of violent anti-semitism grew more out of ignorance and misinformation than out of deep-seated bigotry or vein of malice. It had more of loutishness in it." They speculate that it may have sprung into being in early life, when the only Jew in the countryside was the roving peddler and the Jew was regarded in rural areas as a Fagin or Shylock. It may have been fed by ideas relayed to him by Thomas Edison, who told him that Jewish capitalists were responsible for German militarism. He may have been influenced by Cameron, who was a member of a sect, called the British Israelites, who believed themselves the descendants of the ten lost tribes of Israel, having only scorn for other Israelites.

His anti-Semitism seemed to grow more virulent after the fiasco of his peace ship venture in 1915. In some flash of mystical thought, he had conceived the idea of serving as a mediator between the opposing sides in the Great War, hoping to "get the boys out of the trenches by Christmas." When he got to Europe along with his shipload of necromancers, dreamy idealists, frauds, and freeloaders, he found that no government representative had any interest whatever in him, and he said in Sweden, "I guess I'd better get home to momma." It was reported that he had heaped his resentment for his failure on Rosika Schwimmer, a Hungarian Jewess who was a sponsor of the idea, and that this fiasco fostered his anti-Semitism. However, Mme. Schwimmer said that in a conversation with her in 1914 Ford said, "I know who started this war, the German-Jewish bankers," and slapping his coat pocket, he added, "I have the evidence here, the facts." In a later year, Ford said that on board the peace ship a Jewish journalist, Herman Bernstein, had confessed to him that the cause of the war lay in the skulduggery of the "International Jew." Bernstein denied this.

At any rate, beginning in 1920, the Dearborn *Independent* launched an intensive campaign designed to prove that the Jews were engaged in an international campaign aimed at the destruction of gentile life. As usual the charges adopted the contradictory lines that the Jews were arch-capitalists and arch-Communists. The paper revived the long-discredited forgery the *Protocols of the Learned Elders of Zion*. Ford ordered the anti-Jewish campaign to cease in December, 1921, when he reportedly was bitten by the Presidential bug, but it was later revived. The *Independent* ran articles such as "The Jewish Associates of Benedict Arnold," "The Gentle Art of Changing

Jewish Names," "The All-Jewish Mark of Red Russia," etc. Meanwhile Ford was spouting anti-Semitic gems in private, such as, "We'll show indisputably that one of the factors that brought on the Civil War, and made settlement of the issues impossible, was the Jew." To an editor of *Collier's* magazine he once said, "Unions are organized by Jewish financiers. They are a scheme to interrupt work. A union is a neat trick for a Jew to have in hand when he wants to get a clutch on industry."

The noted editor William Allen White, who fought the Ku Klux Klan and bigotry in general during the twenties, wrote after the Ford apology, "Ford has one talent in his little bag of tricks. That talent is a certain knack of industrial organization. His ideas and opinions on ethics, politics and literature are silly and insignificant. It is a sad commentary on humanity that Ford's great wealth has concealed his mental sloth and his incapacity to think."

There were few who realized how stupid and uninformed Ford was away from his work. In 1915 he sued the Chicago *Tribune* for libel after it had called him an anarchist for denouncing preparedness for war and calling soldiers "murderers." In the trial at Mount Clemens, Michigan, he had an agonizing time on the witness stand. He was asked if he knew who Benedict Arnold was and replied that he had heard of him. When asked for an identification, he said, "I have forgotten just who he is. He is a writer, I think." He could not say what the causes of the Spanish-American War were and could not distinguish between the Revolutionary War and the War of 1812.

He often said that "history is bunk." He never read books, because "books muddle me." He refused to let Edsel go to college and distrusted all academically trained men. Experts had to be used in his plants, but in his presence they had to pretend that they were trial-and-error men. As far as he was concerned, his employees could be graduates of Harvard or Sing Sing, and as a matter of fact, he hired more ex-convicts than any other industrialist. He liked to talk to them when they were hired, his favorite question being: "Now, tell me how you got into it. I'll bet a woman got you into it, wasn't it?"

When he talked to the press, there was always someone like
Cameron or Bennett by his side to interrupt with, "What Mr.
Ford means is this . . ." or "Mr. Ford likes to talk in parables."
Ford would spout mumbo jumbo about some world problems
and wrap it all up with, "Well, there is only one cure for all
that and that is Hard Work."

In 1926 during the British general strike he said to a newsman, "The British people don't know it, but the strike was
jockeyed by the very same people—the people who are back of
the statesmen who manufacture war." Or, "I think the Klan,
the Knights of Columbus and the Masons can be traced back to
Wall Street. Yes, sir, now you have it." With his typically inconsistent outlook, his chief architect was Jewish, and he was
bewildered when a Detroit rabbi whom he admired sent back
a gift of an auto. The Jewish bogey was different from the Jew
he knew in the flesh.

Despite his ignorance, Ford's activities, hobbies, and pet beliefs filled the papers. He was an extremely popular figure, particularly in rural areas, and was seriously considered for the
Presidency in 1922 and 1923. One of his beliefs was in reincarnation, proof of which he constantly cited. One day, while
riding on a country road, he said, "When the auto was new, a
chicken got scared, ran for home and would get killed by the
car. Look at that chicken run for safety to the nearest side of
the road. That chicken has been hit in the ass in a previous life."

He spent little on advertising the Model T and was aware of
the fact that he himself was his auto's best advertisement—and
best of all, it was all free. He was present at Harding's funeral
service at Marion, Ohio, causing Chief Justice Taft to write to
his wife, "Of course, Ford came to advertise himself. A joke
book and a funeral are all the same to him." As a genuine character, he knew instinctively what was good copy for papers and
catered to that need. William C. Richards, who has collected
Fordiana in his book *The Last Billionaire,* gives some instances.
At seventy-one, when he had a bandage on his foot to cover a
blister, he told the reporters that he had got it from playing
football with his grandchildren. Once when he was wearing
mismatched shoes, he claimed he did that every birthday to re-
mind himself that he had once been poor. The billionaire would

often borrow a nickel from a newsman. After spending a week-end at the home of the Morgan partner Edward E. Stotesbury in Philadelphia, he said, "The Stotesburys are charming and delightful people. Yes, indeed, it was a great experience to see how the rich live." That was on the front pages.

He was always doing the original and the unexpected. He tried to buy the Muscle Shoals, Tennessee, complex of dams and electric generating plants from the United States government. He was one of the earliest manufacturers of airplanes. He reconstructed the little schoolhouse at Sterling, Massachusetts, where the lamb was supposed to have followed Mary. He developed a hobby of collecting antiques and became one of the largest buyers; he had one of the finest collections of old violins in America. The papers continually printed speculations about what Ford would do next. Was it true that he was bringing out a new auto horn that would sound like the human voice? Would he try to raise the birthrate by offering a free Ford to all women who bore nine children?

He was a bug on the subject of good health. Until the age of seventy-seven (he died at eighty-three) he would sprint around his plant, often in a turtleneck sweater, and would sometimes challenge newsmen to a footrace. He was a "grasshopper in loco-motion" and would enter and leave his car with a jackknife motion. He detested tobacco and liquor. "Study the history of any criminal," he said, "and you will find an inveterate smoker." A notice was posted in his factories in 1922: "It will cost a man his job to have the odor of beer, wine or liquor on his breath or have any of these intoxicants in his home."

He had his own ideas about food. His fundamental tenet was that overeating was suicidal and that sparse eating led to long life. "I always leave the dinner table hungry." Orange juice caused arthritis; milk was unfit for anyone over the age of eight. Bennett related that he once took sugar to the plant chemist and asked him to examine the sharp edges of the crystals under the microscope to confirm that they were "daggers" in the body. He remained unconvinced even when the chemist dissolved the crystals in water. He was crazy for a while about carrots as the secret of longevity and then shifted to soybeans, growing acres of them on his farms. He served a meal of fourteen courses of soybeans, and he became so enthusiastic about them that he made enamel knobs for his cars and even a suit out of them.

Edsel was a problem for his father, who wanted his son to be a carbon copy of himself—but Edsel was made of a different mold. Edsel was amiable and self-effacing, in contrast with the rambunctious, abrasive old man. He was a democrat while Henry was an autocrat. Edsel did not believe in brass-knuckle labor relations; he was intellectually inclined, an omnivorous reader. His viewpoint on the future of the car market was different, too. While the father thought engineering was the keystone, the son believed that styling would be paramount.

The father tried to dominate the son. One afternoon he rode with Bennett to Edsel's estate on Lake St. Clair, barged in, and destroyed the liquor supply. Although he named Edsel the company president when he was twenty-six, he made life a trial for him, countermanding his orders and rehiring fired men. The sensitive young man in frustration and suppressed fury often threw up in nausea. He died in 1943, predeceasing his father by four years. The blow to Henry was softened by his faith in reincarnation. His mind was often haunted by memories of his conflicts with his son. Once he asked Bennett whether he thought he had been cruel to him. "I didn't want to be cruel—I only wanted to get him mad."

Until he began sliding downhill at eighty, Ford shared authority with no one. He was an absolute dictator and knew all that was going on in the plants. Bennett said that when he arrived to head the secret police after the war, he found that every fourth man on the assembly line was a spy. One man followed another to the summit by Ford's side. "Power ran in cycles," said Richards. "None found it safe to walk with his chest too far out. Even if the chest remained normal, its owner might find himself impaled." William S. Knudsen left to join General Motors, which he eventually headed. Among other casualties were James Couzens, Charles E. Sorenson, and Ernest G. Liebold. The steel king Charles M. Schwab once said, "I hire men to tell me what to do. Ford hires them so he can tell THEM what to do."

The contribution of the man is far easier to assess than his complex character. He never gave anything to philanthropy, and it is ironic that Rockefeller, who gave hundreds of millions away, was abominated while Ford was loved by the public. But he did have generous impulses. Apparently he believed that in setting the $5 a day wage, he was sharing his profits with the workers. He regularly picked up strays on his ride to work and gave them jobs. He led the way in the twenties by ordaining the five-day workweek, of which the president of the National Association of Manufacturers said, "Ford may try to amend the Decalogue, but any general acceptance of the five-day week means a surrender to easy and loose living." After the stock market crash of 1929, when President Hoover asked business to hold the line on wages, Ford actually raised the minimum wage from $6 to $7 a day and maintained it at great competitive cost to the company for two years.

Yet his attitude toward his workers as individuals was scornful. His was the sternest kind of paternalism, and he held hard-fisted antiunion beliefs. Bennett stated that if he had been on the other side of the fence, he would have sympathized with the United Auto Workers' organizing drive in the thirties.

When the auto companies shut down for new models and then reopened, men were rehired like new employees and lost their seniority. Although Ford seemed sincere when he opposed preparedness and militarism, he made Eagle motors and Liberty ships during World War I. He said that he would return the profits he had made to the government, but there is no record that he ever did so. There were always conflicting motivations in Ford's mind.

Ford did not dominate autos as Rockefeller did oil. He was one of a trio of remarkable personalities in the field. The second, a whirlwind of energy, a man of fire and vision, was William C. (for Crapo) Durant, who built General Motors. Durant was born in Boston at the outbreak of the Civil War. He went to the Midwest, and by the time he was twenty-one years old he owned an insurance company. Before he was forty, he had become a millionaire in Flint, Michigan, by manufacturing road carts. One David D. Buick was making cars in Flint, and in 1903 his company was foundering. Durant returned from Wall Street and became a local hero by rescuing the company, ousting Buick, who thereupon slipped into limbo but left behind a famous auto name.

Durant thought big. At a time when there were only 200,000 autos in the nation, he roused laughter with his prediction that the industry would in a few years be able to sell 500,000 cars a year. While Ford, the utilitarian, concentrated on one model, Durant was more accurate in his judgment that the best hope for a prosperous company lay in diversification. Companies were falling fast by the wayside because customers were shifting their preferences from one car to another; thus, the soundest basis for a company was to sell several lines.

He first attempted to merge Buick with Ford, Reo, and Maxwell, a project which never got off the ground. He telephoned Ford in a hotel room in New York. It was a year before the Model T, and while the company was prospering, its outlook was shaky because of a patent suit against Ford brought by George Selden. Ford would have been willing to sell out if the price were right. Durant made an offer of $8,000,000. Ford said to Couzens, who was on the phone with Durant, "Tell him he can have it if the money is all in cash, and I'll throw in my lumbago." Durant did not have the cash, Ford would not take securities, and so the deal fell through.

Durant formed the General Motors Company and acquired twelve auto producers, including Oldsmobile, Cadillac, and Overland. He made a disastrous mistake when he gave up a fourth of his stock to the Heney Lamp Company for an electric lamp that proved worthless, and he had to go for help to New York bankers, who no sooner got a substantial stock interest than they ousted Durant. Under the Boston banker James J. Storrow, General Motors sold off unprofitable cars—such as the Rainier, Reliance, and Ewing—and kept the core of cars we know today in the GM line, along with the General Motors Truck Company.

Durant made a strong comeback with the car named for the famed Frenchman Louis Chevrolet and managed to regain control of GM in 1916. In five years of hectic activity he added Frigidaire, Fisher Body Corporation, and General Motors Acceptance Corporation to finance installment purchases. In the recession of 1921 he again ran into stormy weather, and this time the Du Ponts came to the rescue. Again the price of outside help was his ouster, and again he launched a comeback with Durant Motors, which fell apart after the Crash.

In February, 1936, when he was seventy-five, Durant filed a notice of bankruptcy, and later that year the indomitable fighter appeared in photographs sweeping the floor of a supermarket he was opening in Asbury Park, New Jersey, in a former GM auto showroom. Durant announced this would be the first of a chain, and then he disappeared from the news for good.

The third of the trio was Walter P. Chrysler, who was born in Kansas in 1875, the son of an engineer for the Union Pacific Railroad. As a boy, he swept floors in a roundhouse of the UP for ten cents an hour, then took a pay cut of 50 percent when he became an apprentice machinist in the railroad shops. At the age of twenty-one he had finished his apprenticeship and started vagabonding around the country, playing the tuba for a living and working on every type of machine he came across. In 1908, when he was thirty-three years old, he was superintendent for motive power for the Great Western Railroad and known far and wide as W.P., the mechanical genius. That year he attended an auto show in Chicago, where he had planned to stay for one day. He stayed four. He bought an ivory-white Locomobile touring car and had it transported to Oelwein, Iowa, where he took it apart and put it together again eight times. Only after that did he take his first drive in it.

Autos would be his career. He left a job at $12,000 a year as head mechanic for the American Locomotive Company to take another 50 percent pay cut for a job offered by Charles W. Nash as works manager for Buick. Soon he was making $25,000 a year, and the rewards were so great from General Motors that he retired at forty-five. He was offered $1,000,000 a year for two years to redesign the Willys-Overland and later was persuaded to put the Maxwell back on its feet. He bought out the Maxwell Company to found Chrysler. The feature of the first Chrysler of 1924 was a high-compression engine which racing-car designers had used and which everyone had believed impossible to make for an inexpensive car. Chrysler developed it, and it was an immediate sensation.

In 1928, Chrysler added the Plymouth and De Soto to his

line, bought out Dodge, and announced plans to erect the nation's highest building in midtown Manhattan. It was to be surmounted by a shimmering Cleopatra's needle; today it is still a feature of the New York skyline. The competition between Ford and General Motors was now widened to include Chrysler as a member of the Big Three. The market, declared Chrysler, was infinite. "It devolves upon the United States to motorize the world."

The automobile had become institutionalized during the Coolidge Era. Herbert Hoover and the Republican Party could not define this side of paradise better in the 1928 Presidential campaign than by promising "two cars in every garage."

Calvin Coolidge never owned an automobile until after his Presidency and in the early years of the century had taken a dim view of the prospect that the auto would ever supplant the horse. Now, during his Presidency, the industry bulwarked his philosophy of government. It demonstrated the vigor of the free enterprise system and proved that its spirit of innovation brought more jobs to men and women in all walks of life. The widening ownership of autos showed that his economic policies brought about a more abundant life and a greater participation in prosperity for the common man.

Chapter V

PERSONALITY CRAZE

Absorption with personality was so much a hallmark of the age that even Calvin Coolidge became a personality that fascinated the public. Walter Lippmann, in an article he wrote in 1926, conjectured that in Coolidge the public was rediscovering rugged virtues of our past that it feared we had lost. Americans now craved luxury and were buying it furiously, largely on the installment plan, but they liked the idea of having a simple, frugal man as their symbol in the White House.

> They are delighted with the oil lamps in the farmhouse at Plymouth, and with fine, old Colonel Coolidge and his chores and his antique grandeur . . . they are delighted that the President comes of such stock, and they even feel, I think, that they are stern, ascetic and devoted to plain living because they vote for a man who is. . . . Thus we have attained a Puritanism de luxe in which it is possible to praise the classic virtues, while continuing to enjoy all the modern conveniences.

Certainly, if the American press and public could find glamor in a drab personality like that of Coolidge, it could become ecstatic about personalities with some flair. It would be futile to explore the rationality of it all. There was an exuberance in the air, a *joie de vivre* that found expression in identification with other human beings. Most ambrosial was the delight of sharing vicariously in the experience of superior human beings, those who stood above the mass.

After the dramatic solo flight of Charles A. Lindbergh across the Atlantic Ocean in May, 1927, the mail that poured in to President Coolidge reflected the thrill America felt at the feat. Among the requests made to the President were the following:

1. That he forbid Lindbergh to fly back home across the Atlantic (a project that had undoubtedly never occurred to Lindbergh).
2. That the day of the flight, May 21, be a legal holiday, Lindbergh Day.
3. That Lindbergh be declared exempt from federal income taxes.
4. That he be appointed Secretary of Aviation in the Cabinet (a post that did not exist).
5. That he be appointed an ambassador-at-large, with the portfolio of ambassador of goodwill.
6. That his portrait be put beside that of George Washington on the three-cent stamp.
7. That the name of a bright star in the heavens be renamed Lindbergh.

As always, Coolidge was matter of fact and coldly logical. He addressed an inquiry to the Department of Commerce. Should not a medal be given to the designer of Lindbergh's plane, the *Spirit of St. Louis?* A letter to him from William P. MacCracken, Assistant Secretary of Commerce, replied that this did not seem practical. If the designer of the plane were thus honored, then the inventor of the earth inductor compass that Lindbergh used should also be honored, and if that were done, the inventors of other gadgets would have to be recognized. (The earth inductor compass, a new device, enabled Lindbergh to steer a straight line through fog or dark since its coil, rotating on a vertical axis, showed any deviation in relation to the lines of force around the globe.)

Coolidge arranged Lindbergh's return to Washington. He was to arrive immediately after noon on a Saturday when government offices let out, thus making it unnecessary to declare a holiday. The President had sent the cruiser *Memphis* to carry him and his plane home from Europe. The ship was met 100 miles at sea by four destroyers and was escorted up Chesapeake Bay by two Army blimps and forty airplanes. At the Navy Yard pier he was greeted by three members of the Cabinet and former Secretary of State Charles Evans Hughes, top Army and Navy brass, including the Chiefs of the Army and Navy Air Forces, his mother, and Commander Richard E. Byrd. There was a parade to the Washington Monument, and Coolidge in a long speech hailed our "ambassador without portfolio," voiced "the gratitude of the Republic," awarded him the Distinguished Flying Cross, and made him a colonel in the Army Reserve Corps. In a press conference in Washington's largest auditorium, he was presented by Postmaster General New with the Lindbergh airmail stamp, the first living man so honored.

He was a weekend guest at the temporary White House on Dupont Circle. (The White House was undergoing repairs, and the Coolidges were occupying "Cissy" Patterson's mansion.) At the dinner there on Saturday night, one of the guests, Coolidge's friend Dwight Morrow, father of Anne Morrow, met Lindbergh, thereby enabling Coolidge unwittingly to play Cupid to one of the most famous love matches of the era. The next morning Lindbergh went to church with the Coolidges. When he appeared in a light suit, the President discreetly hinted that darker clothes might be more appropriate, and Lindbergh reluctantly changed. He invariably accepted suggestions with the word "check."

The next morning he flew an Army pursuit plane to Mitchell Field in New York. (The *Spirit of St. Louis* had been damaged by salt air on the ocean trip.) The trip to New York took two hours and four minutes; this conveys an idea of the primitiveness of the planes of that day. From there he went by amphibious plane to the Narrows, where he transferred to the municipal welcoming boat, the *Macom,* and with Grover Whalen, the city's official greeter, he proceeded up the harbor with an escort of 400 ships, with every whistle screeching. "My mind is ablaze with noise, terrible noise," wrote Lindbergh of the welcome. Then up Broadway he rode, showered with ticker tape and confetti, to City Hall, where he received the State Medal of Valor from Mayor Jimmy Walker.

The outpouring of praise from the press could hardly be surpassed. The Baltimore *Sun* said, "He has exulted the race of men." The Minneapolis *Star* said, "This was heroism worthy of the greatest that has ever entered Valhalla." The New York *Post* said, "He has flown like a poem into the heart of America. Romance lived again in him." At a dinner in New York for him, former Secretary of State Hughes said, "He has lifted us into the freer and upper air that is his home. He has displaced everything that is petty, that is sordid, that is vulgar. What is money in the presence of Charles A. Lindbergh, what is . . . etc.?" Even a worldly cynic like Heywood Broun wrote, "We came up out of slumps and slouches. There was more brotherhood in being than I have ever seen here since the Armistice."

Of the wild adulation, Lindbergh said over and over again, "Do I deserve all this?" As summarized in *The Great American Bandwagon,* by Charles Merz, in six days Lindbergh had received fifteen medals; a song, "When Lindbergh Came Home," had been written by George M. Cohan; a new dance, the Lindbergh Hop, had been invented; the Pennsylvania Railroad had named a Pullman car for him; eleven laundries in New York had sought to incorporate with his name; he had been tendered the largest dinner ever given an individual in New York at the Hotel Commodore, where 36,000 cups and plates had been used, 12,000 pieces of cake eaten, and 300 pounds of butter consumed.

In his book about Lindbergh, Kenneth Davis quotes Joseph Campbell's *The Hero with a Thousand Faces* concerning the constant factors that go into the making of a hero, "a magnification in the formula represented in the rites of passage: separation, initiation, return." In the "monomyth," a "hero ventures forth from the world of common day into a region of supernatural wonder; fabulous forces are there encountered and a decisive victory is won; the hero comes back from this mysterious venture with the power to bestow boons on his fellow men." Certainly the Lindbergh feat embodied all those elements.

Immediately after the war, a Frenchman, Raymond Orteig, had offered $25,000 for the first nonstop flight between New York and Paris in the next five years, and when there were no attempts during that time, he renewed his offer. The first efforts failed. In 1926 René Fonck's plane crashed and exploded into flames when he took off from Roosevelt Field in New York. Two of the crew perished, making a spectacular newsreel. In the spring of 1927 two French airmen, Charles Nungesser and François Coli, disappeared and presumably died after taking off from Paris. There were two pilots now waiting on Roosevelt Field for good weather: Commander Richard E. Byrd, in a plane with the most modern equipment and with a crew of three other specialists; and a longtime air barnstormer, Clarence Chamberlin, who would take along as a passenger Charles Levine, president of Columbia Aircraft Corporation.

Before they decided to leave, the lone twenty-five-year-old former Army mail pilot, after a record transcontinental flight of twenty-one hours and twenty minutes in his *Spirit of St. Louis,* beat them to it. On a murky morning, taking a risk on the weather, he flew off from a rain-soaked field, saying, "So long," as casually as if he were setting off on an automobile trip. It was problematical whether the plane, heavily loaded as it was with fuel, would get off the ground or become a fiery wreck like Fonck's aircraft. Steadily the plane ascended, and the New York *Times* report said, "The wheels of the plane cleared by a bare ten feet a tractor which lay directly in its path. A gully was ahead into which he might have plunged but which he safely left below. Over the telephone lines he passed with a scant twenty feet to spare."

The "separation" phase was over, and the "initiation" phase began when the plane headed east into the Atlantic Ocean from Newfoundland. That night during the broadcast of the Jack Sharkey-Jim Maloney fight from Yankee Stadium the voice of announcer Joe Humphries asked the crowd to stand for a minute of silent prayer. There were songs of prayer sung on the radio that night. Will Rogers' column read, "No attempt at jokes today. A slim, tall, bashful, smiling American boy is somewhere over the middle of the Atlantic Ocean, where no lone human being has ever ventured before."

Then the news came of the landing at Le Bourget airfield! He had flown the 3,610 miles to Paris in thirty-three hours and twenty-nine minutes, a record for distance in nonstop flight. It was a triumph of personal courage and a triumph, too, of unpremeditated art in the display of personal modesty. His personal belongings on the flight were only a razor, passport, and six letters of introduction, apparently in the belief that after tidying up, he would have to make acquaintances. Then there were his frequent references, before and after the flight, to himself and the plane as "We."

What "boons to his fellow men" did this hero confer on his "return" from the mysterious venture? John W. Ward, writing in 1958 of "The Meaning of Lindbergh's Flight," said, "From the moment of success there were two Lindberghs, the private Lindbergh and the public Lindbergh. The latter was the construction of the imagination of Lindbergh's time fastened to an unwilling object." A nation which had cherished moral absolutes was uneasy in an age of relativism. Lindbergh "gave the American people a glimpse of what they liked to think themselves to be at a time when they feared they had deserted their own vision of themselves . . . the response to Lindbergh involved a mass ritual in which America celebrated itself more than it celebrated Lindbergh." (This is similar to Lippmann's explanation of the Coolidge worship.)

He was the lone pioneer figure who had moved the American frontier ever westward. His feat, said Dean Howard Chandler of the Cathedral of St. John the Divine, required the "self-discipline of years," which stands out in the present age of "revolt against discipline" and the tendency to "uninhibited self-expression." He has revealed the true American, misrepresented in the newspapers, said former Secretary Hughes. "He has driven the sensation-mongerers out of the temples of our thought. He has kindled anew the fires on the eight ancient altars of that temple. Where are the stories of crime, of divorce, of the triangles that are never equilateral?"

The flight was symbolic in another sense. It was a victory for the modern machine, to be worshiped as an instrument to lead us all to a new paradise, instead of a devilish device which would enthrall mankind. There can be no doubt that the flight was the catalyst responsible for the great leap forward that aviation took in the next five years. Interest in planes had lagged. The government inaugurated airmail flight in 1918, a bomber carrying a bag of mail once a day between New York and Washington. Not until 1924 was the first airmail flight inaugurated across the continent; it took thirty-two hours and the airmail stamp cost twenty-four cents. There were many who believed that the greatest potential for the nation's defense lay in dirigibles, which could be the mother ship for planes, rather than in long-distance aircraft. After the Lindbergh flight, everybody was talking about the feasibility of networks for carrying passengers commercially. In the succeeding year and a half after the flight, the price of Wright Aeronautical Company stock soared from $25 to $245. There was even discussion about the possibility of transoceanic service, although it was the prevailing opinion that this would not be possible until there were floating airports stationed in the Atlantic Ocean.

It was natural that royalty should be the object of special attention. In 1924 the nation was agog about the prospective visit of Edward Albert Christian George Andrew Patrick David Windsor, who would be traveling incognito as Lord Renfrew, but who, everybody knew, was the Prince of Wales. Because his worldwide travels helped promote British goods, he had been dubbed the Prince of Sales. This was a Prince Charming out of *Grimm's Fairy Tales,* thirty years old, unmarried, under middle height but handsome, with the round face of a Kewpie doll.

Preceded by the shipment of eight of his polo ponies he arrived on the *Berengaria* at the end of August and managed to elude any official welcome. Then he went to pay a visit on President Coolidge, stopping off at Baltimore to visit a crippled child, while attended by the press. After alighting at Union Station in Washington, he was driven to the White House.

The prince was quite nervous. He fidgeted, standing first on one foot and then the other, his hands continually darting in and out of his pockets, smoking cigarettes one after another. He had lunch with the President, his wife and son John. Coolidge saw the nervousness of his guest and tried to make him comfortable, working to make conversation as the White House staff had never seen him work before. While the President dug deeper and deeper into his store of recollections of history, the prince merely smiled. No doubt Coolidge was relieved when the meal was finished, and he could turn the prince over to the wives of Washington officialdom who were eager to curtsy before him.

Going from Washington to Long Island, the prince embarked on a mad social whirl on the estates of the Morgans, the Vanderbilts, and the Phippses. He was a marathon dancer, driving from one party to another as the women lined up for his attentions. Once he took the place of a drummer in the band. He played polo with a patch on one eye because a pony had hoofed a clod of earth into it, went on a fox hunt, rode the steeplechase, and raced in a speedboat. All this the press reported avidly. Will Rogers accompanied him and told America, "All kidding aside, the Kid is there. He is a Regular Guy."

Was the prince fittingly called the Playboy of the Western World? The kind of publicity he was receiving so disturbed his entourage that his aide, Captain Lascelles, confided to the press that the prince was an avid reader, who was now making his way through *The Life and Letters of Walter H. Page*. Many wondered when the prince had any time for reading. One afternoon he drove in from Long Island and visited Julia Richman High School, the Museum of Natural History, and two printing plants of newspapers, again attended by the press. So much for culture!

The Reverend Thomas Kirkwood of Syracuse assailed the voguish aping of the prince: "It is a sad commentary on our democracy to see the way so many of our youths are spoiling their good hats by turning down the brim in front because the Prince does so." When he visited the International Polo Cup matches at Meadow Brook, according to the New York *Times,* "The whole stand was a fogbank from thousands and thousands of hats worn in the Prince's style. Gray hats were so numerous that even the special police could not identify him."

The prince was highly sensitive on one subject. He had fallen off his horse on at least fourteen occasions in the last two years while hunting or steeplechasing. As the great British sportsman John Jorrocks, MFH, had said, "There is no young man wot will not rather 'ave a himputation on his morality than 'is 'ossmanship." The prince explained to the press that he had never fallen "off" a horse but rather "with" his horse. If the horse falls, how could he be expected to stay upright?

In late September he departed for his ranch in Alberta, Canada, and returned briefly on his way home a month later. He visited the Ford plant in Detroit to see autos assembled, and Ford showed the prince a new electric motor which would be capable of drawing 150 coal cars at forty miles an hour. "Well, sir, it wasn't two seconds before he was asking me questions about it I couldn't answer." When Ford expressed his surprise at his technical knowledge, he said that the prince replied, "You may not know that I took four years of electrical engineering."

The greatest concern of the Empire about the prince was: When would he marry? His American trip had resulted in no progress in that direction. Cosmo Hamilton, the British playwright, in a speech to the English-Speaking Union in Philadelphia explained that the trouble was Socialism, which had infected his companions in the gay clubs of London. "One can't be smart unless one is a Socialist. It is like the cross-word puzzle here. The Prince is up against it. He doesn't marry because there has been injected into him from all sides the virus of Socialism." The connection was not clear, since Socialists do marry.

For the remainder of the decade the prince was featured in our papers, though he never returned here. His tours over the world, to South Africa, South America, to Canada, were fully reported; so, too, were his falls from horses. Regularly photos appeared in the papers of a cut and bruised young man walking forlornly from a horse. In November, 1925, he fell twice in one week. In 1928 he hit a new record, six tumbles in five days, and a week later he fell off a horse twice in the same race. It was now abundantly clear that he was the worst horseman in the British royal line. The Empire was filled with dread when it was announced in 1929 that he had learned to fly, but was reassured when the prince promised that he would not be at the controls unless he had an experienced pilot by his side.

The years went on, and despair grew as the prince remained single. There were bubbles about Princess Astrid of Sweden, then Princess Ingrid of Sweden, Lady Curzon, Princess Beatrice of Spain. By the end of the decade he was thirty-six years old and without a permanent love interest. Mrs. Simpson was yet to appear on the scene.

A royal visitor of 1926 made a good deal more of a stir. This was Queen Marie of Rumania. At the time she was over fifty and had lost her beauty, but bejeweled photographs of her at an earlier age filled the newspapers, dazzling the viewer. Actually little of her could be seen since her neck was enclosed in strings of pearls and she wore a jeweled headdress that resembled a football helmet.

She was a granddaughter of Queen Victoria, her father having been Victoria's second son, the Duke of Edinburgh, and she was also descended from Czar Alexander II of Russia. Her husband, King Ferdinand, had equally little Rumanian blood. He was a German Hohenzollern prince, having been nominated for the job of heir apparent of Rumania because his predecessor, King Carol, had no heir. The queen had early shown her affinity for the press. When she arrived for the Versailles Peace Conference, her first words were: "Where is the press?" The Versailles Treaty almost doubled the territory of Rumania, giving it control of Bessarabia and shoving into its borders many minority groups. It was a backward country of 18,000,000 people, and the regime survived by brute force. Peasants were shot down in Bessarabia by the hundreds, freedom of speech was gone, the jails were packed with political prisoners, and the government was openly anti-Semitic.

All this was forgotten by the American public, if it had ever been known, in the ocean of publicity for the queen who for years had waged an unflagging campaign for the limelight. Her picture had long been in the newspapers, and she had written articles for the Hearst press on subjects such as "My Experience with Men," "Clothes and the Woman," "Dreams Do Come True" and "Making Marriage Durable." And now in the fall of 1926 she would be here in the flesh with an entourage of twenty—a genuine live queen! All America was excited. The New York *World* said that this was an extraordinary event "because it brings together the world's first ultra-modern publicity engine and the world's first ultra-modern Queen. When the modern publicity engine which dotes on motion-picture Queens

139

is actually confronted by a Queen who of her own accord has become a motion-picture version Queen because she dotes on publicity, the lid is off and almost anything can happen. Applesauce flows fast and loose."

Her reception in England was disappointing, but then the English have a queen of their own. On the ocean liner *Leviathan* she announced that she was getting ready for America. She would not touch liquor; she refused to have French soup; she insisted on eating American apple pie and American oysters. She issued statements that America was "marvellously efficient," "terribly sincere," "gloriously generous" (it was rumored that the real purpose of her visit was to get a loan of $100,000,000). In New York she received the deluxe treatment from Grover Whalen and Mayor Walker, though heavy rains held down the size of the crowds. Her stay in Manhattan was a round of receptions, dinners, and press conferences, at each of which she made profound statements such as, "Women have done so much for peace. Some day women will end war—that is if they don't start fighting among themselves." When she visited the jeweler Cartier, a plaque was set up commemorating her visit.

The queen arrived in Washington on October 18 and was driven immediately to the Rumanian Legation. Mrs. Coolidge sent flowers with her card. The next day a car drew up to the White House with an acknowledgment written by a lady-in-waiting and not by the queen, a breach of etiquette. On the twentieth the queen and her party visited the White House.

She was the first queen to visit a President, and there had been some speculation on how the Vermont farmboy would greet her. Would he bow low and kiss her hand? What happened was that she said, "I am pleased to meet you, Mr. President," and he replied, "I am pleased to meet you." (Contrary to report, he did not say "Howdy, Queen.") It had been planned that she and the President would sit on one sofa and Secretary of State Kellogg would sit on another facing them, but Marie upset plans by choosing to sit on an overstuffed chair facing the fireplace. The President had no choice but to take a small cane-seat affair next to her on which he had to sit sideways.

The President, having been coached, asked if he could see her children, Prince Nicholas and Princess Ileana, and they were produced. The queen, so the schedule read, would then take her departure, but to the surprise of all she sat down again as if prepared for a long stay. After an interval, Coolidge rose and walked off with his wife.

Following Marie's return to her legation, the Coolidges reciprocated her call. Only one photograph had been allowed in the White House, but when the Presidential party was seated in the legation, a horde of photographers emerged from behind a curtain, forcing the Coolidges to submit to endless photos. The next night there was a state dinner at the White House for forty guests. The queen, more bejeweled and beplumed than ever, sat next to Coolidge and tried to draw him out in conversation, with the usual result.

There is a story that after she left, Mrs. Coolidge saw the President staring out the window. She asked what he was looking at, and he replied, "I just wanted to be sure that she's gone." Fictional or not as this may be, he had undoubtedly found the whole thing a crashing bore. He had to put up with protocol since he had no choice. White House chief usher Ike Hoover, listing the attitude toward protocol of the various Presidents he had known, said that Coolidge regarded it all as "comedy."

As for the queen, she made a transcontinental tour in which she received an ecstatic welcome everywhere. In Kansas City, Mayor Beach said, "This is the greatest day in the history of Kansas City." When she arrived at Denver the Denver *Post* had the greeting AS ONE QUEEN TO ANOTHER across its front page. The main streets were hung with bunting of red, blue, and yellow, the Rumanian national colors. Everywhere, Marie spouted talk, despite the pleas of the syndicate which sold her column that she reserve her thoughts for her readers.

It all became very tiresome. F.P.A. (Franklin P. Adams) wrote in his diary (a column of his thoughts in the New York *World*, outwardly modeled on Pepys):

> Queen Marie is travelling about in great luxury and a vast amount of money is being expended by somebody and there are tayles of the Queen's great candor and frankness, and I think it would be a good idea to say to her "All right. How much does your country want?" and say either Yes or No. For it seems to me that the money spent on silk hats by members of the reception

141

committees here and there would keep Rumania in funds for years.

Soon afterward Coolidge entertained another celebrity at a White House meal, the new American operatic sensation Marion N. (for Nevada) Talley, who was in Washington to give a concert. Miss Talley, only nineteen, was seated at the right of Coolidge, who characteristically attacked his food without a word and without any sign that he was conscious of her presence. His guest of honor was frozen in shyness. William Allen White was at the luncheon, and Mrs. Coolidge whispered to him, "For heaven's sake, stir up those two at the head of the table." And so White told Coolidge that Miss Talley was going to purchase a farm in western Kansas. Mrs. Talley, Marion's mother, joined in. The silence was at last broken, and Coolidge made a quip or two.

As an operatic star, Marion Talley was synthetic, as genuine as a cultured pearl is to a real one. She was created by ballyhoo and sold as many another product was sold in that age. During the twenties, amid growing chauvinism, resentment was often expressed that in the field of music, particularly opera, America was dependent on foreigners. It was therefore satisfying to native pride when Lawrence Tibbett, a Californian who had never studied abroad, made a sensationally successful debut as Ford in *Falstaff* in 1925. In 1927 an American opera, *The King's Henchman,* music by Deems Taylor and book by Edna St. Vincent Millay, was hailed as the precursor of a new national art.

During 1925 word spread of a great new operatic soprano who had been discovered in Kansas City, Missouri, the daughter of a railroad telegrapher. Her talent had been brought to light when she was fifteen, at which time Kansas City had taken her under its wing; thus, she became a community project who might have been named the Spirit of Kansas City. A benefit concert was held to raise money to give her the best training and wealthy patrons made contributions. She had an audition at the Metropolitan in New York at seventeen and then was sent abroad to study.

She made her debut at the Metropolitan in February, 1926, after tons of publicity. She had never sung in opera before except for two small roles in a civic opera company in Kansas City.

However the house was sold out well in advance, and there were offers of $100 to $150 for a seat. Five thousand were turned away. Taxiloads of flowers were already at the door. She appeared as Gilda in *Rigoletto,* a large, unpretty girl who scampered on stage in the second act with a nervous, awkward run to thunderous applause. After "Caro Nome," she received a deafening ovation, plus twelve curtain calls after the act and twenty after the final curtain. Asked if he was pleased, manager Giulio Gatti-Casazza said over and over again, *"Sì, sì magnifico."*

The critics however were not enthusiastic. Olin Downes of the New York *Times* said, "Miss Talley, precipitated at the age of 19 and with virtually no experience upon one of the most famous operatic stages in the world, has not at present the artistic knowledge to make the most of her gifts. The wisdom of the aforesaid precipitation may be better discussed on another occasion, and after Miss Talley has appeared a second time in a second role." Olga Samaroff of the New York *Post* said, "Miss Talley's voice with all its natural beauty, sweetness and extended range is not powerful . . . the long melodic lines last night were tremulous and lacking in the sustained power which in early youth can be achieved through real mastery."

While the critics emphasized her tender years, the fact remained that operatic stars had made successful debuts at younger ages than nineteen. Adelina Patti sang Lucia at the Brooklyn Academy of Music when she was sixteen, and Schumann-Heink and Lilli Lehmann made their debuts at seventeen.

Miss Talley appeared in other roles, and the audiences were less enthusiastic. Kansas City could not be there in force as it had been on the first night. As Eastern critics became more critical, the Midwest became more critical of the Eastern critics. The Kansas City (Missouri) *Star* said editorially, "This city is blamed for the unprecedented publicity preceding the debate. There is no reason for this. Kansas City has been altogether rational about its discovery. It has found her most interesting and promising and has done what was needed to supplement her efforts to get proper training and finally an advantageous appearance. It is quite within reason to believe that Miss Talley would have fared even better at the hands of the critics in one of the greater European capitals. New York critics evinced a timidity, due perhaps to their inexperience in judging voices which are wholly natural." The Wichita *Beacon* said, "We have been told very often that the prairie country is hopeless from the standpoint of beauty. How can anything good come out of Nazareth?" The Jefferson City *Capital News* said, "Kansas City has faith and believes that Marion will easily become one of the famous singers of the generation. Therefore Kansas City boosts and even the people of New York respond to the spirit while Marion delivers the goods. So to hell with the critics!"

In 1928 she broke with her manager, who revealed that in two years, entirely apart from her earnings at the Metropolitan Opera, she had taken in $334,894 from concerts. In 1929 Marion Talley retired at the age of twenty-two. She became a farmer and was photographed on her tractor wearing a sombrero. She admitted frankly that she was glad to be away from singing, which she found drudgery. There was a general concession, even in Kansas City, that her voice, while sweet and lovely, was no better than that of hundreds of female church choir singers throughout the country.

Marion Talley is now over sixty. *Eheu, fugaces . . . anni. . . .*

When celebrities arrived at New York, they were given a lavish welcome. Even Charles Levine who was merely a passenger on Clarence Chamberlin's transatlantic flight received a ticker-tape welcome. The city's official greeter, Grover A. (for Aloysius) Whalen, was actually the general manager of Wanamaker's Department Store who took time off for this duty. He regarded the job seriously. When Queen Marie arrived, he issued a bulletin for the official party on proper costume: "Frock coats, striped trousers, gray cravats, black shoes, silk hats and lacquer canes."

In "Grover the Magnificent," Henry F. Pringle wrote, "Some men achieve greatness by cunning or industry or by engaging press agents. Grover Whalen rode to fame on a winning smile, irreproachable manners and a meticulous attention to his wardrobe. A lesser man would have failed. He would have been called a dude, an inconsequential clothes-horse." He was a remnant of the dear, dear days beyond recall when "the dull, plumaged male bird of today wore bright feathers, when the burgomaster sported elaborate stocks, frilled shirts, brocaded waistcoats, silken pantaloons and stockings."

After being doused by ticker tape and confetti of shredded paper from office wastebaskets before the gaze of the lunch-hour crowds lined along Broadway, the celebrity of the day was lauded in front of City Hall by the mayor, James J. "Jimmy" Walker, slim, dapper and verbally facile, who had just risen from bed for the occasion.

Walker was himself a political phenomenon of the times. This scintillating figure of lighthearted charm belonged on the stage, rather than in one of the most important jobs in the nation. The *Outlook* once said, "Jimmy translated the problems of municipal government, a series of headaches to the average citizen, into simple musical comedy terms that the average person understands. In his hands they became problems that can be solved with a jig and a jest."

When he ran for reelection in 1929 against Fiorello H. LaGuardia and won by a record majority, the *New Yorker* magazine said that while Walker himself did nothing, others, his civil service engineers, for example, accomplished such duties as paving the streets and building tunnels:

> The city struggles on. Meanwhile Walker does things of infinitely greater importance. He lives. He is carefree, obviously happy. He makes whoopee, stays up late, rises late. He dresses snappy and talks snappy. He dines with the Biddles and is photographed with Coleen Moore. Thus he becomes a symbol for some odd-million starved souls numbly seeking escape from reality. In importance he ranks ahead of Roxy's, Babe Ruth's home run score, Ziegfeld's chorus, the tabloids, the Snooks case or Lindbergh's private life. He is five hundred years ahead of his time, or maybe only one hundred at the rate we're going.

Meanwhile, New York City was being wretchedly and corruptly misgoverned. But in the halcyon years of the twenties, Walker lived a charmed life. Gene Fowler wrote, "When Walker had become the John Barrymore of the political stage, most people looked with lenient eyes upon the foibles of the city's darling, for Jim was created in New York's own image."

He was born in Greenwich Village in 1881, the son of a carpenter who went into Tammany politics. Under his father's pressure he attended New York Law School, and after interrupting his studies to play semiprofessional baseball, he managed to graduate. Having no interest in the law but great ambitions as a songwriter, he did not take the bar examinations, preferring to hang out his shingle in Tin Pan Alley. He wrote lyrics for songs such as "Goodbye Eyes of Blue," "After They Gather the Hay," and "There's Music in the Rustle of a Skirt." Then in 1908 came his smash hit, "Will You Love Me in December as You Do in May?"

His subsequent songs were flops, and to please his father, now a big wheel in Tammany circles, he entered politics. In the State Assembly he finally, at the age of thirty-one, took the bar examination and married a former actress he had known for several years. His debonair charm and wit endeared him to Charles F. Murphy, leader of Tammany Hall. He entered the State Senate and became Democratic floor leader where his best-known accomplishment was his sponsorship of the bill to legalize boxing in New York, the Walker Law.

In 1925 he ran in the Democratic primary against the incumbent mayor, John F. Hylan, who was too stuffy for New York's taste. Walker was the Broadway show business candidate. The first nominating speech for him was made by Georgie Jessel, and the demonstration that followed was led by George M. Cohan. Irving Berlin wrote a song, "We'll Walk In with Walker." To get the support of Governor Alfred E. Smith, who was a good family man, the candidate exiled his current sweetheart, actress Vonnie Shelton. He won easily.

During his first two years as mayor, Walker took seven vacations for a total of 150 days, visiting London, Paris, Berlin, Rome, Houston, Hollywood, San Francisco, Atlanta, Bermuda, Canada, Havana, and Florida. His working day did not start until noon, and he was notoriously late for appointments, once keeping President Coolidge waiting for forty minutes. Governor "Al" Smith paid a visit to City Hall in vain and said wryly, "If you make a date with Jimmy in December, he'll keep it in May." He conducted meetings of the Board of Estimate, which were public, like a stage performance. Once a heckler shouted at him, "Liar," and Walker replied, "Now that you have identified yourself, we shall proceed."

146

He popped up at all kinds of gatherings and was always ready with a speech, often a marvel of impromptu oratory. After his Presidency, Coolidge told an associate, "Walker has the Celtic ability to put all his goods in the front window and leave none in reserve—the kind of man who, if you wake him from a sound sleep to make a speech, is able to start right in speaking. But if you examine the speech later, you will find he has said nothing worth while."

The popinjay mayor was the life of the party wherever he appeared. He took as his new sweetheart actress Betty Compton, whom he eventually married after getting a divorce. He changed clothes at least three times a day and had wardrobes in several places around town for his convenience. He pranced as thousands cheered. A New York journalist wrote, "New York wore James J. Walker in its lapel and he returned the compliment."

In the Depression, New York taxpayers took a less indulgent attitude toward the song and dance man who played mayor. Hearings before the Hofstadter committee of the state legislature revealed that he had received gifts of hundreds of thousands of dollars, and he resigned in 1932 to escape removal from office by Governor Franklin D. Roosevelt.

On August 15, 1926, Rudolph Valentino, Hollywood's greatest screen lover, was in his suite at the Ambassador Hotel in New York with his valet. Suddenly he gasped, put his hand to his body, and fainted. He was rushed to the Polyclinic Hospital, where he was operated on for a gastric ulcer and appendicitis. When he woke from the anesthetic, he asked the doctor, "Am I a pink puff?" to which the reply was, "No, indeed, you have been very brave."

His condition was serious. The hospital was inundated with telephone calls from women, and a special information booth was established on the ground floor. A bulletin was issued that he had passed the crisis, that his temperature was normal, and that he felt so strong that he was eager to leave. Then pleurisy developed, and on August 23 he was dead. He was thirty-one years of age.

Rodolpho Alfonzo Raffaelo Pierre Filibert Guglielmi di Valentina d'Antonguolla was born in 1895 in the small Italian town of Castellaneta, the son of a veterinarian. Presumably he had attended the Royal School of Agriculture in Genoa. He arrived in this country in 1913 intending to become a gardener. He worked for a while on the Long Island estate of Cornelius Bliss, Jr. Then there followed a period of penury, in which he was reduced to odd jobs in order to eat, shining the brass of autos and sweeping floors of office buildings. The headwaiter of Maxim's restaurant hired him as a dancer, part of whose job was to dance with lonely women diners. He joined a musical comedy troupe and was left stranded in San Francisco. A chance friend who was then a leading movie actor, Norman Kerry, got him a small film part playing a tough guy, and this led to minor roles on the New York stage. There he caught the eye of a woman writer who had just adapted Vicente Blasco-Ibáñez's *The Four Horsemen of the Apocalypse* for the screen, and he was given the role of Julio Desmoyers in which he scored a great success, a highlight of the film being his dancing of the tango.

He was given larger roles and scored in *Blood and Sand,* about the life and death of a toreador, and in *The Sheik,* which made "sheik" the male counterpart to "flapper" in the everyday vocabulary. There was a popular song "The Sheik of Araby." The new film idol far outsoared the late Wallace Reid, who had died suddenly in 1923. When *Son of the Sheik* opened on Broadway, a month before Valentino's death, he was mobbed by screeching females, one of whom tackled him at the ankles and tried to unlace his shoelaces for a souvenir.

Valentino was an excited, as well as an exciting, lover, as I discovered when I re-viewed *The Sheik* in my adult life.

> AGNES AYRES: Why have you abducted me?
> VALENTINO (chest madly heaving and nostrils dilating): Can't you guess?

His film producer, Adolph Zukor, wrote in a later year that his acting "was largely confined to protruding his large, almost occult eyes, until the vast areas of white were visible, drawing back the lips of his wide, sensuous mouth to bare his gleaming teeth and flaring his nostrils."

H. L. Mencken, "by one of the chances that relieve the dullness of life and make it instructive," had had a private dinner with Valentino only a week before his fatal illness. Valentino had asked for the meeting through an actress who acted as intermediary since he wanted the famous man's advice. An editorial writer for the Chicago *Tribune* had found in the men's room of a hotel a talcum powder which was colored pink, and he had written an editorial entitled "Pink Powder Puff," in which he suggested getting rid of Rudy "before the younger generation of American males replaces razors with depilatories and the ancient caveman virtues of their forefathers are replaced by cosmetics, flopping pants and slave bracelets."

Valentino arrived in Chicago at the time of publication, and, enraged about the aspersion on his manhood, challenged the writer to a duel and then to a fistfight, but in vain.

At first, Mencken advised him to forget the whole thing. Then Mencken, who had regarded the dinner as the lightest of capers, looked more closely at Valentino and discovered "what is commonly called for want of a better name, a gentleman. In brief, Valentino's agony was the agony of a man of relatively civilized feelings thrown into a situation of intolerable vulgarity." With some touch of fineness in him, "Valentino was only the hero of the rabble. Imbeciles surrounded him in a dense herd. He was pursued by women—but what women! . . . in those last days, unless I am a worse psychologist than even the professors of psychology, it was revolting him. Worse, it was making him afraid." The inscrutable gods were kind in bringing his life to a swift close. If he had lived, he would have enclosed himself in a web of deception, "of increasing pretension, of solemn artiness, of hollow hocus-pocus, deceptive only to himself."

His funeral was given over to the *vulgus ignobile*. His body was taken to Campbell's Funeral Parlor at 66th Street and Broadway, and he lay in state on a draped catafalque, surrounded by candles. When the home opened the next morning, the queue stretched eight blocks north to 74th Street, made up mostly of weeping women and girls. Forty patrolmen and six mounted police had to control the crowds. The plate-glass windows of the parlor were broken, and three persons fell through them. The casualty toll of the day was 100. At 11:40 P.M. the police cut off the line, preventing thousands from going in. That night ten black-

149

shirted men came to the funeral home and said that as members of the Fascist League of America they would guard the body through the night. A wreath was laid by them upon instructions from Premier Benito Mussolini. The next morning the mounted police again had to hold back the mob. Finally, when a fracas between Fascists and anti-Fascists seemed inevitable, the doors were closed to the public.

A New York mother found the grief too great to bear and shot herself, a sheaf of Valentino photographs in her hand. In London a dancer did away with herself and left a note, "It is heartbreaking to live in the past when the future is hopeless. Please look after Rudolph's pictures."

The Polish actress Pola Negri announced that she had been his fiancée; this was a surprise to Valentino's closest associates since he had had such a host of marital troubles with two wives that it seemed unlikely that he would let himself in for more agony with the tempestuous Miss Negri. She arrived from Hollywood on August 29. At the coffin she conveniently swooned for the photographers. The next day a cortege of twelve cars carried the corpse to St. Malachy's Church on West 49th Street. Sobbing and wailing, Miss Negri had to be supported going into and leaving the church. During the service her baying rose higher than the notes of the pipe organ and ceased only when the reporters and photographers were requested to leave. Not until three days later was the body, accompanied by the inconsolable Miss Negri, transported to a train for the trip across the continent to Hollywood for burial.

M. M. Marberry in his article "The Overloved One," in *American Heritage,* August, 1965, described how later research found that genuine shock over the death had been artificially magnified. Much of the ballyhoo was staged by a movie studio press agent, named Oscar Dobb, since the studio wanted the interment to be made memorable in order to protect its investment in *Son of the Sheik.* Dobb revealed to the press that Rudy's last words had been, "Let the tent be struck," which had a fine, classic ring and the additional merit of linking it with the love-making sequences of the film. When it was discovered that they had also been the last words of General Robert E. Lee, they were amended to, "I want the sunlight to greet me." The second publicity source was the press agent for Campbell's, who initially hired thirty persons at a dollar a head to stand outside the funeral home. The third source was Valentino's own publicity manager who was involved in several books, one by himself, *As I Knew Him;* another by the film star, *How to Keep Fit;* and a third of poetry, in which Valentino, thanks to his ghostwriter, showed signs of budding into a second Shelley. Miss Negri's agent did his part, claiming that Valentino's last words were in fact, "Pola, I love you and will love you in eternity." Miss Negri announced she would enter a convent but not, of course, until after she had fulfilled her movie contract commitments.

Press agentry brought results. Valentino was in debt at the time of his death, but his heirs got $600,000 from *Son of the Sheik.* Campbell's had been a struggling funeral parlor, but now it climbed to the top. Miss Negri had a splurge in popularity until the talkies plunged her into obscurity. She married Prince Serge Mdivani a few months later and wound up suing the Valentino estate for $15,000 she alleged that she had lent her fiancé. As for Valentino himself, his second wife, Natacha Rambova, said she had a message from him in the spirit world. "I have many valuable friends up here and am happy. Caruso likes me. So does Wally Reid and Sarah Bernhardt. These spirits do the same thing as they did on earth, but of course in a different way. They act with more soul now."

Leisure time grew, and sports came into their own. A marked difference in the newspaper of the beginning of the twenties and the end is in the development of the sports section. One figure dominated each sport, Red Grange in football, Babe Ruth in baseball, Bobby Jones in golf, Bill Tilden in tennis. Huge growds gaped at these heroes with what former sports reporter Ring Lardner called, "an excess of anile idolatry."

Some were personalities who would have enriched any age, such as Tilden who was the monarch of the courts. He had been stagestruck as a child, and his interest in the theater continued as an adult, when he invested a good deal of money in stage ventures. Once he walked up and down the aisle of a theater holding aloft a finger which he had injured in a tournament. The tennis court was his personal stage. To win support from the gallery, he would go to absurd lengths. His opponent was always the underdog, but Tilden would let him get so far ahead that defeat seemed inevitable. Seemingly he was a man crushed by despair. Then with full histrionics he would rise, straighten his sagging shoulders, slowly strip off his sweater, douse his head in ice water, and stage a spectacular come-from-behind drive that would blast his opponent off the court.

On September 22, 1927, an event occurred that wiped out of national consciousness all other issues or problems—the so-called Battle of the Century, between Gene Tunney and Jack Dempsey, for the world's heavyweight boxing championship.

In September, 1923, Dempsey had knocked out Luis Angel Firpo of Argentina in two rounds of what is regarded as the most exciting bout in boxing history. After that Dempsey had been inactive, dodging a fight against the man considered the leading contender, Harry Wills. Dempsey had the support of most of the public since Wills was a Negro and the public did not relish the possibility of another Jack Johnson as champion. Finally a fight was arranged for September 23, 1926, between Dempsey and former Marine James "Gene" Tunney in the Sesqui-Centennial Stadium in Philadelphia.

Dempsey was the 3 to 1 favorite, even though at thirty-one he was three years older than Tunney and had not been in the ring for three long years. Tunney, a good puncher and fast on his feet, had a fetish about keeping fit while Dempsey had whiled away many evenings in nightclub life with his new movie-actress wife, Estelle Taylor. The overestimation of Dempsey at this time is curious. It was probably a reflection of the period's exaltation of public personalities, which in the case of athletes gave rise to such titles as the King of Swat, the Four Horsemen, the Flying Finn. Sportswriter Grantland Rice once wrote a story commencing, "Once or twice within the course of a century a prodigy comes along to ride the crest of the world. He may be a Rembrandt or a Galileo or a Shakespeare. He may be a Da Vinci or a Milton. But there is about him an indefinable mastery that lifts him far above the puny achievements of the near great." Of what gift from heaven was he writing? "Golf has contributed this to the galaxy of masters in the person of Robert Tyre Jones who today won his third amateur championship."

Because of this superman worship and the recollection of the Firpo fight, Dempsey was regarded as the "untamed savage," the brute latent in civilized man who was sure to massacre an ordinary human in fistic combat. In training for the fight, Dempsey looked far from impressive, and it was evident to boxing writers that age and inactivity had taken their toll—he was woefully slow afoot, and his formerly sharp reflexes were dulled. Yet in spite of the testimony of their eyes, the odds were not affected, and an overwhelming majority of the boxing writers predicted a victory for him.

The fight was held before a mammoth crowd of 121,000, who paid a record gate of $1,895,000. Dempsey proved to be a shell of his old self and was almost helpless in facing the ring craft of Tunney. In a driving rain he was battered into helplessness. The judges gave only a decision, but he probably lost every round.

The public, refusing to be disillusioned, retained its fixation about Dempsey. Promoter Tex Rickard set up an elimination tournament and Jack Sharkey emerged as the leading contender to fight it out with Dempsey for the right to face Tunney. The fight took place before 80,000 in Yankee Stadium on July 22, 1927. By the seventh round, Dempsey was groggy from the rain of blows from the faster Sharkey; he swung wildly and hit Sharkey four times below the belt. If Sharkey had sunk to the floor, he would probably have been declared the winner on a foul. Instead, he clutched his midsection and turned complainingly to the referee, whereupon Dempsey, having a clear field, leaned back, clouted Sharkey on the jaw, and floored him. The referee, showing some doubt, counted Sharkey out, thus saving the big fight for Rickard. (Since that time, referees in New York give the familiar injunction to fighters before hostilities begin, "Protect yourself at all times.")

So the buildup was ready for the Battle of the Century to be fought on September 22 at Soldier Field, Chicago. By clear logic there should have been no doubt of the outcome. Tunney had given Dempsey a bad beating, and a year would have passed. Tunney would be a year older, too, but it was Dempsey who was obviously sliding downhill. Nonetheless, there was a surge of sentiment toward Dempsey, and enough people believed that he could win so that he entered the ring only a 7 to 5 underdog. On paper it should have been 5 to 1.

The nation was agog. The fight was the coast-to-coast topic of conversation to an extent that is impossible to convey to a later generation.

The VIP list to attend included ten governors, several United States Senators, and mayors without number. This was a far cry from the time not too far in the past when John L. Sullivan fought James J. Corbett for the championship before a few thousand in New Orleans for a side bet of $10,000; when Corbett fought Joe Choynski on a barge off San Francisco, and they cut each other to pieces for fifty rounds for a few hundred dollars; when Tex Rickard had to move the Jeffries-Johnson fight from place to place before finding a haven in Reno, Nevada. A minister brought a suit in federal court to bar the Dempsey-Tunney fight on the ground that it was "degraded and brutal." The Albany *Knickerbocker News* denounced it as a "public debauch, a Neronic monstrosity." The St. Louis *Globe-Democrat* commented:

> It is one of the amazing social phenomena of modern times that this form of combat which has become the accepted form of fighting supremacy has risen from the lowest dregs of society to a position where it is recognized, approved and supported by the great majority of all classes of society. Once, not so long ago, utterly condemned by the law, it is now not only sanctioned by the law but even gladly attended by the highest officers of the law.

The fight was covered by 1,200 reporters. The AP and UP leased 245,000 miles of wire. The result was reported the next day by the New York *Times* in three-line banner headlines and four columns on the right-hand side of the front page. There were twenty-four special trains run to Chicago; the Twentieth Century Limited, the day before, was run in seven sections with seventy-seven Pullman cars. Two airplanes carried passengers from New York to Chicago, making the trip in twelve hours, which was eight hours faster than the train. In a record-breaking radio hookup eighty stations broadcast the fight to an audience estimated as the greatest in history, 60,000,000. Warden Lewis

Lawes of Sing Sing gave special permission to the inmates to stay up to hear the fight.

Seats cost $5 to $40, and even the $40 seats were forty rows away, back of the reporters and the VIP's. The cheaper seats were two blocks away. Most seats were sold without a seat plan on a take-it-or-leave-it basis. To those in the faraway hills of the stadium, the ring looked like a distant spot in which marionettes danced around. The crowd did not measure up to Rickard's hopes. The paid attendance was 104,000, but at the higher prices the gate was $2,658,000, a record which still stands. Tunney received (aside from radio and movie revenues) about $900,000 and Dempsey half as much.

Millions gathered around the radios. The *Life* magazine of that time ran a satiric cartoon captioned "Battle of the Century," depicting crippled war veterans listening to the fight. The result should have been cut-and-dried, and it appeared that it would go that way as Tunney pummeled Dempsey about the ring. Then came the unexpected, which H. L. Mencken once wrote was the only thing that makes life worth living. In the seventh round Graham McNamee, the announcer, was saying, "Tunney shot a hard left to Dempsey's face which he follows up with two mean lefts and as the left is in Dempsey's face, he lands a right."

There was a huge roar through which McNamee's voice could hardly be heard, "And then Dempsey comes back. Tunney is down from a barrage of lefts and rights to the face." No more could be heard for many seconds—and then McNamee's voice faintly, "The fight is going on." Ten listeners, according to the AP, died of heart failure during the fight, and seven succumbed in that round. Tunney weathered the storm and backpedaled while Dempsey motioned to him to come in and fight. In the eighth round Tunney did wade in and knocked Dempsey to the floor for a count of one. At the end of the fight McNamee said that Dempsey was out on his feet. Tunney was without doubt the winner, and he was so declared. On the radio Tunney greeted "my friends in Connecticut," by which he meant "Polly" Lauder, a wealthy young lady whom he thereafter married.

And so the Battle of the Century was over, but the rhubarb

lingered on. Dempsey officially protested the fight on the ground that Tunney was on the canvas for at least fifteen seconds since the referee, Dave Barry, did not begin the count of nine until he had returned from escorting Dempsey to a neutral corner. The Illinois Boxing Commission overruled the "long count" protest. It stated that to prevent a repetition of what had happened in the Firpo fight, when Dempsey stood over Firpo and clubbed him down every time he got up, the fighters had been told before the bout that the count would not start until whoever scored a knockdown went to the farthest neutral corner.

Tunney was an unpopular champion with the public, an antihero. In the public mind of the twenties a sports hero must regard his sport as a religion; he must be proud of the role he plays. Tunney had only scorn for the base degrees by which he climbed. As described by the New York *Times* on the eve of the big fight, "Tunney thoroughly dislikes the ring but, being in it, he is imbued with the idea that he can elevate it." To the public, which saw no need of elevation, this was heresy. Then, too, the sports king must be completely democratic. Babe Ruth played sandlot ball with the boys, and Bobby Jones was buddy-buddy with his caddie. Tunney scorned contact with ring *hoi polloi* in favor of social climbing. He was a cynic who refused to join in the acclaim for Lindbergh, saying, "He had a wonderful motor."

And then the unforgivable! On April 23, 1928, Tunney appeared before the literature class of his fishing companion, Professor William Lyon Phelps of Yale, to lecture on Shakespeare. The young man who had started out as a teamster in Greenwich Village opened his lecture by quoting Carlyle and paraphrasing Spencer. He disclosed that his acquaintance with Shakespeare began when, as a Marine, he had run across *A Winter's Tale,* which he had read ten times before he got the hang of it.

"Shakespeare was a sport," he said. He discussed *Troilus and Cressida* and combat in the Trojan War. Ajax, he said, was "a great, big, ambitious fellow like Jack Sharkey who didn't have the stuff." Of a speech by Achilles to Ulysses he said that it meant "cash in when you can," because the public memory of heroes is short.

When asked by a reporter afterward how it went, Tunney

replied, "I felt a little nervous. You see it is not my métier."
Those who knew Tunney well said that while he was a nice
fellow, he was singularly devoid of a sense of humor.

Heywood Broun wrote sourly:

> Tunney did better against Shakespeare than anyone had a right
> to expect. My own student days came before the Jazz Age, and I
> have a residue of resentment against prize-fighters, trained seals
> and motion-picture stars in the classroom. The world has gone
> beyond the notions of us veteran classical scholars. Go-getters sit
> in the seats of the mighty. Harvard, I trust, will counter by asking
> Babe Ruth to tell the boys at Cambridge just what Milton has
> meant to him.

Dempsey, who was appearing in court in one of his perennial
legal battles with his former manager, Jack Kearns, was asked
by a reporter what he thought of Tunney's appearance at Yale.

"I got a big kick out of it," he replied.

"What do you think of Gene as a lecturer?"

"Oh, if it helps his racket, I guess it's O.K."

"How are you getting on with Shakespeare, Jack?"

"Sorry, never had the pleasure."

The Dempsey versus Tunney argument raged on in the press.
John Kieran, erudite sports columnist for the New York *Times*,
wrote, "As soon as it is apparent that the letter concerns the
merits or demerits of either Dempsey or Tunney, the missive
should be immersed in a bucket of water, dissected at least six
inches below the surface and only the lightest part allowed to
float to the top." He quoted from the placid letter of one old
lady who refused to haul up the white flag of surrender: "Permit
me to say that Jack Dempsey's knowledge of literature, music
and the arts is quite as extensive as Mr. Tunney's although not
so persistently advertised."

Chapter VI

CULTURE—HIGHBROW

In the *North American Review* for July, 1928, an article by Catherine Beach Ely entitled "Hokum of the Intelligentsia" listed ten highbrow maxims:

1) The middle class is thick-headed and hard-hearted.
2) The New has value merely because it is new and the Old is worthless because it is old.
3) Pessimism is more artistic than optimism.
4) The mental faddist is an original genius.
5) Realism consists in details of unchastity.
6) Degeneracy is piquant.
7) The Puritan complex excludes art and beauty.
8) The Victorians were fussy idiots.
9) Protestant ministers are pretentious hypocrites.
10) Slander of the dead is clever biography.

The article reflected the exasperation many felt for the hauteur of the intellectuals, their supercilious disdain for the mob. In no other era of our history was their estrangement from the masses so great. Never was there such revulsion for their environment by the intellectuals, a bitter indictment which offered no cure and no alternatives. The bridges of communication were blown up.

In 1922 Harold Stearns edited a collection of essays by thirty eminent contributors, *Civilization in the United States*. After reviewing the proofs, Stearns left the country to join the growing

American colony of self-exiled artists on Paris' Left Bank. In his introduction to the book, Stearns wrote, "The most moving and pathetic fact in the social life of America today is emotional and esthetic starvation. . . . We have no heritage or tradition to which to cling, except those that have already withered in our hands and turned to dust."

In his contribution George Jean Nathan said, "In no civilized country in the world today is there among playwrights so little fervor for sound drama as in the United States." Van Wyck Brooks said, "Our writers all but universally lack the power of growth, the endurance that enables one to continue to produce personal work after the freshness of youth has gone. Weeds and wild flowers! Weeds without beauty and fragrance, wild flowers that cannot survive the heat of day."

It was not the writers who were most culpable, however, but the stifling life about them. How can art flourish in materialistic America? Lewis Mumford saw the spiritual failure manifested in the industrialized city life. Garet Garrett looked on modern business as a thoroughfare for "man's acquisitive instincts." Mencken regarded politics as a display of "cowardice and venality." J. E. Spingarn believed our universities eviscerated personality and intellect.

"You are all a lost generation," said Gertrude Stein to Ernest Hemingway in Paris. Never was there so much self-lamentation. George Santayana wrote:

> My heart rebels against my generation
> That talks of freedom and is slave to riches,
> And toiling 'neath each day's burden
> Boasts of to-morrow.

What were the influences responsible for this spiritual malaise? One was the impact of modern industry and science. Walter Lippmann said that the acids of modernity had eaten away the structures that had been the foundations of our previous values. Joseph Wood Krutch in *The Modern Temper* maintained that the new world of relentless science was one in which the human spirit could no longer be free. Ezra Pound saw the tragedy in the "Fordian" thrust of American life.

159

Ford's world is the world of the hired man. Ford himself is the hired man raised to the thousandth degree, a titanic but by no means gargantuan figure, a revolutionist to such a degree that the bickering of impotent reds about him is almost comic. . . . But where does this get us? For everything above comfortable brute existence there is a vacuum.

Another factor was undoubtedly the disillusion and cynicism bred by the war and its aftermath. Pound wrote in his "Hugh Selwyn Mauberley":

> Died some pro patria
> non dulce, non et decor
> walked eye-deep in hell
> believing in old men's lies.

The war had been a monstrous hoax. What further trust could be put in authority of any kind? The intellectuals reacted with a sense of outrage. Antiwar messages were contained in many works—in John Dos Passos' *Three Soldiers* and Ernest Hemingway's *Farewell to Arms,* in *What Price Glory?* by Laurence Stallings and the international sensation *All Quiet on the Western Front,* by Erich Maria Remarque.

A novelist of gentler temperament, Willa Cather in her *One of Ours,* combined the two themes of the futility of the war and the ravaged state of postwar society. A Nebraska farmboy who is frustrated in civilian life finds his cause fighting in France and dies there. His mother thinks about the commercialization and ugliness of the America that followed in the war's wake. "It seems as if the flood of meanness and greed had been held back just long enough for the boys to go over and then swept down and engulfed everything that was left at home." She sees nothing but evil that came from it all, and she rereads his letters. "He died believing his country better than it is and France better than any country can be . . . for him the cause was clear, the cause was glorious. . . . Perhaps it was as well to see that vision and then to see no more."

T. S. Eliot's "The Waste Land" appeared in 1922, and the title was picked up by others to symbolize the postwar world of sterility. Writers overtly attempted to convey the mood of a

Two portraits of the same man. President Calvin Coolidge would smile for photographers, but at right we see the grim countenance of the true Coolidge. Below, a studio photograph that smoothed out the rough edges of his face.

Coolidge was always willing to pose for photographers. Above, he is shown becoming an Indian Chief, to the delight of the nation, in August, 1927, while he was on vacation in the Black Hills of South Dakota. Below, he donned clothes as if for farm chores. However, Coolidge *could* milk a cow.

Four idols in the time of Silent Cal. Upper left, Charles A. Lindbergh, the "Lone Eagle," beside his plane, *The Spirit of St. Louis*, after his spectacular flight across the Atlantic Ocean in May, 1927. Upper right, Rudolph Valentino, the screen star, whose death in August, 1926, when he was thirty-one years old, set off a hysterical wave of national grief. Lower left, H. L. Mencken, the darling of the intellectuals, who delighted and shocked the twenties with his unconventional views. And lower right, the operatic sensation of 1926, nineteen-year-old soprano Marion Talley, as she appeared as Gilda in *Rigoletto*, her triumph at the Metropolitan Opera House.

Andrew W. Mellon, Coolidge's Secretary of the Treasury and the nation's third richest man, whose probusiness philosophy dominated government in the twenties.

Grace Goodhue Coolidge, the President's wife, painted in the White House by Howard Chandler Christy.

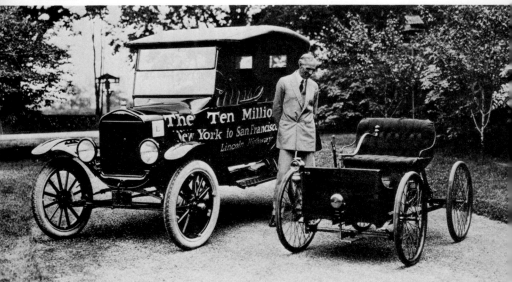

Henry Ford, the headline-grabbing automobile manufacturer who revolutionized American life, posing in June, 1924, between his first and his ten millionth car.

Visiting royalty was the object of endless interest to the American public. Above, Queen Marie of Rumania arriving in New York aboard the *Leviathan*. Her daughter, Princess Ileana, stands on the left. Below, the Prince of Wales at the time of his visit to the States in 1924.

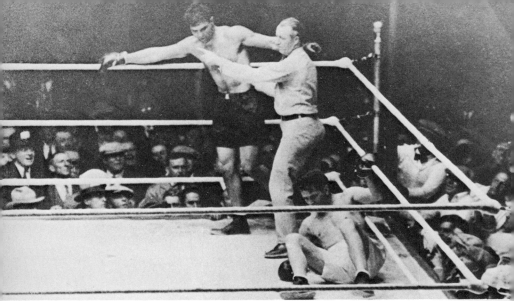

The famous long count during the Battle of the Century in Chicago in 1927. After Jack Dempsey knocked Gene Tunney down during their heavyweight championship fight, he went to his own corner. Referee Dave Barry walked over and escorted Dempsey to a neutral corner. It was claimed this gave Tunney eighteen seconds before he had to rise again.

Al Capone, king of the Chicago underworld, who became enormously rich from bootlegging during Prohibition.

Jimmy Walker, New York City's colorful mayor (second from left), waits for the arrival of distinguished visitors at Mitchell Field, along with the city's official greeter, Grover Whelan (far right), and two other gentlemen.

Shadows on the 1920's. Above, the Ku Klux Klan marches down Pennsylvania Avenue toward the White House in August, 1925; and below, Chicago's gangland slaying, the St. Valentine's Day Massacre, in which seven underworld members were executed in a garage by machine-gun fire.

Crowds gathered in Wall Street on Black Thursday in October, 1929, as the stock market crash brought the era to a dramatic close.

"waste land" in their works. *The Great Gatsby*, by F. Scott Fitzgerald, obligingly identified as a "waste land" a "valley of ashes" halfway between West Egg, Long Island, and Manhattan and used it as a grimy backdrop for part of the story.

Eliot himself was not referring to contemporary society in the title of the poem. "I dislike the word 'generation.' When I wrote the poem called 'The Waste Land' some of the more approving critics said that I had expressed the 'disillusionment of the generation,' which is nonsense. I may have expressed for them their own illusion of being disillusioned, but that did not form part of my intention." He was concerned with the immemorial antiquity of the search for union with a source of inner vitality, and he was inspired by Jessie L. Weston's book on the Grail legend and Sir James Frazer's *The Golden Bough*—but Eliot notwithstanding, the title of his poem became the voguish catchphrase.

In *The Twenties* Frederick J. Hoffman says of American writing in the postwar decade:

> Perhaps the most striking quality of the post-war intellectual was his attitude of refusal—refusal of the comfortable platitudes of the middle class, refusal of the desperate assurances of liberal tacticians, and finally refusal of the suggestion that the war had provided an opportunity for renewing tradition, reviving it, or changing it without destroying it.

Our sacred literary gods were rejected. Emerson and Thoreau were no longer revered; Longfellow and Whittier were ridiculed. Whitman was accepted with the qualification that poets must go beyond his "barbaric yawp." Melville, on the other hand, gained newfound acclaim. The Puritan bore the main onus of guilt, as Hoffman says, for having overrated morality and suppressing art, for having exalted ambition above a normal life, and, like the modern businessman, for having made morality and art the servants of financial success.

Wesley Bagby wrote in his *The Road to Normalcy*, "Realism before the war had been an agent of social protest, but after the war there was a note of hopelessness—society was not just criticized but ridiculed and rejected." Malcolm Cowley expatriating himself to France in 1929 said that in the absurd world of Coolidge, "Society was regarded either as a sort of self-operating, self-repairing, self-perpetuating machine, or it was not regarded. The political rebels had no place in it."

Rejection of society was manifested by the overt physical act of uprooting oneself and relocating in haunts where there were other tortured souls, far removed from the madding crowd of *hoi polloi*. Refuge could be found in this country in Greenwich Village, whose inhabitants prompted John Reed to write:

> Inglorious Miltons by the score,
> And Rodins, one to every floor,
> In short, those unknown men of genius
> Who dwell in third-floor-rears gangrenous,
> Reft of their rightful heritage
> By a commercial, soulless age,
> Unwept, I might add—and unsung,
> Insolvent, but entirely young.

The Village on a larger scale was *la rive gauche* of Paris, where American expatriates escaped to gather in the cafés or the salons in self-communion. The *sine qua non* was a little money from their families, assisted by a favorable rate of exchange of francs for dollars, and they could pick up some money on the side from one of the many literary journals. They were not bothered here by Prohibition and could pursue their love affairs free from prying eyes.

Why live abroad? In his *Portrait of the Artist as American,* Matthew Josephson has his artist exclaim:

> We're the *disinherited* of art! The soil of American perception is a poor, little barren artificial deposit. . . . An American to excel has ten times as much to learn as a European. We lack the deeper sense. We have neither taste nor force. How should we have them? Our crude and garish climate, our silent past, our deafening present, the constant pressure about us of unlovely conditions are as void of all that nourishes and prompts and inspires an artist as my sad heart is in saying so! We poor aspirants must live in perpetual exile!

For many the Paris experience was not useful, unless having a good time might be considered useful. But there were exceptions. The young newspaper correspondent Ernest Hemingway, out of Kansas City by way of the Italian battlefront where he served as an ambulance driver, came to the Left Bank to learn to write fiction. He lived at the top of five flights of winding stairs on the Rue Cardinal Lemoine and turned out his stories while lying on a bed in a room which had sheltered the poet Verlaine in his last decrepit and drunken years. He followed Gertrude Stein's precept that the writer should focus on the immediate present, which was the valid and exciting element to report. As she put it in Steinese, "The thing seen by everyone living in the living they are doing."

Hemingway epitomized and blazed the way for the new spirit, as Robert O. Stephens pointed out in his essay "The Rhetoric of Escape." The rejection theme: "His people live in a pragmatic world where independently existing values no longer prevail." Sensation seeking: "His characters occupy themselves with concrete details of moment to moment living. Their futures they make by sensation, syllable by syllable." Escape: Each character "carries out a cycle of the escape pattern and in his quest for new values goes on to another predicament which he rejects and avoids in order to turn to another situation."

Hemingway's style of writing, short, crisp, action-charged sentences, reporting vividly the experience of the present, deeply influenced a whole generation, as did his hedonistic concept of immediate sensation. Young men got drunk and girls of good family doggedly took on a succession of lovers in order to be fashionable. Edna St. Vincent Millay wrote:

> My candle burns at both ends;
>   It will not last the night;
> But, ah, my foes, and, oh, my friends—
>   It gives a lovely light.

The ultimate social rebel was H. L. Mencken, the darling of the intellectuals, who delighted and shocked his generation with his ribaldry, his impudent wit, and his hyperbolic expression, all set forth with a wondrous command of words to which his monumental *American Language* bears testimony.

Henry Louis Mencken was born in Baltimore in 1880 to a family of Germans who had sought haven here from the political upheavals of 1848. As a boy of nine he had discovered *Huckleberry Finn*, an event he termed the "most stupendous of my whole life," which turned him into a bookworm. At the

163

age of nineteen he wangled a job on the Baltimore *Morning Herald* and six years later shifted to the Baltimore *Sun,* for which he wrote to the end of his career. In that paper he conducted a column of Menckeniana in which he ripped into well-hallowed institutions. He launched a magazine, *Smart Set,* with George Jean Nathan and later he published the famous *American Mercury* which became a brand name for Mencken.

He reached a height of cynicism that was tantamount to nihilism. Nothing was sacred. The only organized movement he ever endorsed was woman suffrage, on the ground that it would make democracy even more absurd than it was. He suggested that the United States needed a wave of suicides among college presidents, and he volunteered to provide the weapons.

As for sex—the woman a man loves is "simply the first girl to sneak over what may be called the threshold of his disgusts." Once he referred to the "labial infamy." Moreover, "the satisfaction of a man with an attractive wife is to show her off. Her beauty sets off the assumption that she was sought after eagerly by other men, and that it took a lot of money or a lot of skill to obtain a monopoly of her." Even Veblen was not that utilitarian. Of procreation, Mencken said, "It is no more creditable or discreditable than to have rheumatism. Ethically it is absolutely meaningless, and practically it is a matter of chance."

A genuine scholar, as well as a polemicist, Mencken wrote one of the first and best books about the German philosopher Friedrich Nietzsche in English in 1908, and it was from Nietzsche that he drew many of his attitudes, inveighing against the illiterate mass—the "booboisie," the swinish herd—who seek to fasten its petty beliefs, the "herden-moral," on the small band of those with superior minds and tastes. It was his conviction that "the American people constitute the most timorous, snivelling, poltroonish, ignominious mob of serfs and goosesteppers ever gathered under one flag in Christendom since the end of the Middle Ages. . . . It is difficult even for an American to contemplate the American without yielding to something hard to distinguish from moral indignation." The mass "is inert and moves ahead only when it is dragged or driven."

The most horrendous enemy of the superior man is the "husbandman," the farmer. "No more grasping, selfish and dishonest mammal indeed is known to students of the anthropoidea . . . there has never been a time in good seasons or bad when his hands were not itching for more; there has never been a time when he was not ready to support any charlatan, however grotesque, who promised to get it for him." The intelligentsia are beleaguered in a few walled towns by these Fundamentalists armed with dung forks. Their animus against the city folk was responsible for Prohibition, the Mann Act, and the ban on smoking cigarettes in many small towns, but not against chewing tobacco since farmers chew. "If he does [win out] then Eoanthropus will triumph finally over Homo Sapiens. If he does, then the humble swineherd will drive us all into a pen."

Democracy, he said, is "grounded upon so childish a complex of fallacies that they must be protected by a rigid system of taboos, else even half wits would argue it to pieces." Politics is purged "of all genuine significance and stuffed with such gorgeous humors, such inordinate farce that one comes to the end of a campaign with one's ribs loose." All Presidents in his time were frauds or nincompoops. In 1948, reporting on his last Presidential campaign for the Baltimore *Sun,* he said, "It is my firm conviction reached after long experience, profound pondering, and incessant prayer, that no man who is worth a hoot will ever be President of the United States hereafter—until, that is, the Republic blows itself up."

Mencken revived interest in authors long since gone such as Bierce and Maeterlinck, and sponsored budding authors such as Fitzgerald, Lewis and Dreiser. He quickened the blood and thinking of his generation. William Goldhurst in his book *Fitzgerald and His Contemporaries* shows his influence on Fitzgerald, whose viewpoint of society was a parochial one. In his essay "On Being an American," Mencken said, "Here is a country in which it is an axiom that a businessman should be a member of the Chamber of Commerce, an admirer of Charles M. Schwab, a reader of the *Saturday Evening Post,* a golfer—in brief, a vegetable." Fitzgerald's play of 1923, *The Vegetable,* in which the critics recognized Mencken's influence, starts with the hero, a clerk in a railroad office, yelling for his copy of the *Saturday Evening Post.*

Another acerb critic of the social scene, one who used satirical fiction rather than outright invective, was Ring Lardner. Maxwell Geismar has written, "To a small circle of intellectuals Lardner is known as one of the most savage and merciless satirists and social critics of his time, who dissected Babbitt before Babbitt was born, who created a new American language which made Hemingway's look like parlor conversation."

Ringgold Wilmer Lardner was born in Niles, Michigan, in 1885. He barely got through high school and spent a few months in a business school. He got a job on the Chicago *Tribune* as a sportswriter in 1909, and his talent became evident in his highly popular column "In the Wake of the News." In 1919 he moved to the East, where he became a syndicated columnist and a freelance short-story writer. He bought a house at Great Neck, Long Island, where he was a neighbor of Fitzgerald, with whom he often sat up through the night, drinking and talking. "He was a disillusioned idealist," recalled Fitzgerald. On Fitzgerald's recommendation he collected his stories into his first book, *How to Write Short Stories.*

Despite being a name writer, making $60,000 a year, with a fine family and a luxurious home with many servants, Lardner was prey to monumental binges. The life of a professional funnyman, said Mark Twain, is no fun at all. In 1929 Lardner celebrated his Broadway success *June Moon,* written with George S. Kaufman, by going off on a mammoth spree, which was followed by months of recuperation in a hospital.

He rode the wave of the boom and sank steadily after the Crash. He suffered from tuberculosis and heart trouble. His money faded away, and so did the Muse. Alternating between caffeine and morphine he wept and laughed over his typewriter. He died in a hospital in 1933 at the age of forty-eight while playing bridge with his wife and the Grantland Rices.

His short stories reveal facets of the moral decadence and emptiness of values of his time. "The Love Nest" deals with the unhappiness behind the façade of outer success. A movie producer takes a writer, Bartlett, to his home to meet his wife, a former movie star, to whom he has been wed for ten years. During the drive the host says, "I mean she still likes a good time but her home and kiddies come first. I mean her home and kiddies come first." The house at Ardsley-on-Hudson might have been mistaken for the Yale Bowl. "It insures me of a happy wife and family. And what more can a man ask?"

The couple exchange fond "sweethearts," and she says to Bartlett, "I call it our love nest. Quite a big nest, don't you think?" Husband wonders what happened to the Bourbon, since the bottle is half-empty. She says he must have forgotten to lock the cupboard. He goes off on an errand, and the writer discovers she is a secret boozer. "Did you fall for all that applesauce about the happy home and the contented wife? Listen, Barker [sic], I'd give anything in the world to be out of this mess. I'd give anything never to see him again. I'd change places with the scum of the earth just to be free." She had not needed him to become a success as a film star. "I could be a Swanson and get myself a marquis, maybe a prince. And look what I did get."

"A Caddy's Diary" is a biting commentary on moral standards, a dissection of prevailing dishonesty as reflected in the microcosm of the golf course. The caddies have to lie about the scores of their golfers in order to collect tips. The ladies, who use foul language which the men would be surprised to hear, are the worst in this respect. In a ladies' tournament, "I guess if they had kept the score right, the total for the 4 of them would of run well over a 1000." The caddies spend more time in the woods than on the course, and a caddie says it was not fair to charge the ladies regular dues "as they hardly ever used the course."

The narrator caddie says to his pal, Joe, about one golfer, "Well, Crane is all right, only he has just got no money." Joe replied, "He ain't all right, no more than the rest of them." "Well, at least he don't cheat on his score." Joe says, "And you know why that is. Neither does Jack Andrews cheat on his score, but that is because they play too good." A crowd watches them play, so they can't cheat. "But that is one of the penalties for being a good player. You can't cheat." Crane springs a scandalous surprise; he runs off with $8,000 from the bank where he works and takes along his girl friend. The diarist tells Joe, "It seems to me that these people have got a lot of nerve to pan Mr. Crane and call him a sucker for doing what he done, it seems to me like $8000 and a swell dame is a pretty fair reward compared with what some of these other people sells their soul for." He

feels like saying so to some of the members, but Joe tells him
he is in no position to do so. "When Mr. Thomas asks you how
many shots he has had and you say 4 when you know it is 5, you
are selling your soul for a $10.00 tip."

In "Champion" which, in the late forties, was expanded into
a memorable motion picture starring Kirk Douglas, the boxer
at the age of seventeen beats up his crippled brother and knocks
down his mother. After leaving home, he is forced into a shotgun marriage. He rises in the boxing world, and his wife sends
him a letter begging for $36 which she lent him, explaining
that their baby is ill. His mother writes for money, too, asking
him at least to contact his brother who has been bedridden for
three years. He tears up their letters but pours money on his
girl. He throws out his manager, who had picked him up from
the gutter, then steals away the wife of his new manager. The
sports editor of a paper rejects a story which conveys something of the truth and prints, instead, a glorifying picture of
him. "The people don't want to see him knocked. He's the
champion."

Warren G. Harding once discoursed, "What is the greatest
thing in life, my countrymen? Happiness. And there is more
happiness in the American village than in any place on earth."
In many of his stories Lardner showed that he disagreed. So did
Sherwood Anderson, who in *Winesburg, Ohio* and *Poor White*
unmasked the tortured lives in American small towns, in what
was termed a new realism. Anderson, who was born in a small
Ohio town, was a stableboy, a newsboy, a worker in cabbage
fields, and a soldier in the Spanish-American War, before turning into a successful advertising man and manufacturer in
Elyria, Ohio. Then, at the age of forty, he left his business to
pursue a career as a writer, specializing in the life of the small
town he knew so well.

In *Poor White* a character says, "All men lead their lives
behind a wall of misunderstanding they themselves have built
and most men die in silence and unnoticed behind the walls."
In *Winesburg* a character says that "everyone is a Christ and
they are all crucified." Irving Howe wrote of the book, "In
rather shy, lyrical outbursts the book conveys a vision of American life in depressed landscapes cluttered with dead stumps,

twisted oddities and pitiful wrecks." The lesions of the psyche are due to a failure of love, and a visitor to Winesburg finds the common theme. "I am a lover and have not found anything to love."

A world-famous figure in literature created by Sinclair Lewis was Babbitt, who was the living embodiment of the "booboisie" businessman derided by Mencken.

Lewis was born in Sauk Centre, Minnesota, in 1885, and the flavor of life in the Midwest obsessed him. His novel *Main Street*, published in 1920, gave the feeling of stultification in a small Midwestern town, Gopher Prairie, Minnesota, and was a smash success. Two years later came *Babbitt*, which was set in the fairly large city of Zenith and told of George F. Babbitt, a real estate salesman.

Babbitt was less an individual than a standardized commodity with standardized values. His treasures in life were material—his motorcar and his possession of standard advertised wares, which gave him self-respect and drew respect from the community. He lived in the ethic of "gotta hustle, gotta hustle," a voice of febrile intensity which he heard everywhere. "Men who had made five thousand the year before last and ten thousand last year were urging on nerve-yelping bodies and parched brains so that they might make twenty thousand this year and the men who had broken down immediately after their twenty thousand dollars were hustling to catch trains to hustle through their vacations which the hustling doctors had ordered."

The novel did not purport to transcribe life in the manner of *The Great Gatsby* or *An American Tragedy*. It was satire, but so scathing was the portrait that *Nation's Business* printed a series of "Babbitt Ballads" in defense of the American small businessman, of which this is an example:

> Babbitts—though we jeer and flout them,
> We could never do without them.
> Artists all—we would be beggars,
> Were it not for Butter 'n Eggers.

> For though Art is very swell, it
> Hardly pays unless you sell it.
> And the artist—ain't it funny,
> Like the Babbitt, values money.

Lewis looked and acted like a fury, with his red hair, acne-pitted face, tall, gangling figure, and volcanic temperament. In April, 1926, he created a sensation in the Linwood Boulevard Church in Kansas City when he ridiculed Fundamentalist doctrines, damned the Christian religion, and then dramatically placed his watch on the pulpit and challenged God to strike him dead in ten minutes. "Here is a lovely chance for God to show what he can do if he is a Fundamentalist God." Weeks later he rocked the public when he refused to accept the Pulitzer Prize for *Arrowsmith*, saying that the prize tends to make writers "safe, obedient, puerile and sterile." Lewis was a vital force in personal contact, remarkable for his ability to characterize types by reproducing their conversation. "Remembering Lewis, one always felt after we parted that there had been a dozen men in the room," a friend recalled.

F. Scott Fitzgerald, eponymous in letters with the decade, was born in St. Paul, Minnesota, in 1896. His father had been unsuccessful in business, but he enjoyed the advantages of some money because his mother had rich relatives. Among the younger set in the Twin Cities he was known as a dining-out, dancing-out, country-club boy. He attended prep school and in 1913 entered Princeton, where he was a classmate of the critic Edmund Wilson. He took part aggressively in the social life of an institution of learning then inhabited by patricians. He spent a good part of his freshman year writing the *Triangle Show*. After graduation in the war year of 1917, he attended officers' training school where his platoon commander was Captain Dwight D. Eisenhower. He became an aide-de-camp to a general and to his chagrin did not go overseas.

He had met Zelda Sayre of Birmingham, Alabama, fell in love, and determined to marry her. After the war he got a job in an advertising agency in New York, and life was full of beauty and promise. Youth had excitement for him. Of his last days at Princeton he wrote, "Some of us wept because we knew we'd never be quite as young any more." He started in the advertising business with a sense of expectancy. "Everything is possible. I am in the land of ambition and success."

However, life was difficult on a subsistence wage, living in a

170

small room. When he traveled to see Zelda, he had to sleep in a day coach. His Princeton friends whom he saw were rich while he wore a shabby suit and had to pawn his field glasses for extra dollars. He began writing short stories and in his first winter in New York received 122 rejection slips, selling only one story for $30.

He threw up his job, went back to St. Paul, and wrote a book entitled *This Side of Paradise,* which was accepted by Scribner's and published when he was twenty-three. It was a success. Its main character, flippant Amory Blaine, lived hedonistically in the best lost generation style. At the end Fitzgerald wrote the theme plain—his generation had "grown up to find all Gods dead, all wars fought, all faiths in men shaken."

He married Zelda. Even before *This Side* appeared in print, he sold fifteen short stories with fees ranging to $2,000 per story. In the exuberance of youth and newfound money the Fitzgeralds jumped together into the fountain in front of the Plaza and drove down Broadway on top of a taxicab. *The Beautiful and Damned* appeared in 1922 and his play *The Vegetable* in 1923. Two years later came his masterpiece, *The Great Gatsby,* not about flaming youth but a mature critique of the values men lived by in contemporary American civilization.

Though he was under thirty, his creative life was almost over. He left his fine home in Great Neck and his gay friends to expatriate himself in Europe with Zelda and his daughter, "Scottie." He felt free to live and write for fun. They partied *sans souci,* kidnapped orchestras to play for them, inscribed unprintable graffiti on the walls of Grace Moore's villa. Zelda was a beauty, and he looked like the perpetual undergraduate. In 1926 John Chapin Mosher wrote, "That the Fitzgeralds are the best looking couple in modern literary society doesn't do them justice."

His personal story duplicated the boom and Crash. The family returned to the States in 1931 and settled in Baltimore. Life became increasingly difficult as his fortunes dissolved. Zelda became an inmate of a mental institution. *Tender Is the Night* published in 1934, a full nine years after *Gatsby,* was neither a critical nor a public success. He became an alcoholic. In an interview in 1960, Hemingway said, "Fitzgerald was soft. He dis-

171

solved at the least touch of alcohol." He himself had no patience with writers who operated only "in saucedom."

Fitzgerald drifted to Hollywood, where he became a scenario writer, turning out mostly salami but working on some better than average scripts, such as *Gone with the Wind* and *Madame Curie*. Budd Schulberg, who in later years wrote a successful novel based on Fitzgerald's disintegration, *The Disenchanted*, said that when he first heard his name from a producer, he responded, "I thought he was dead." Fitzgerald himself told him that someone hearing his name said, "Fitzgerald? I know the name, he's a character in a Katherine Brush novel." He who had started his meteoric career with *This Side of Paradise* finished on its "far side," as Arthur Mizener fittingly entitled his book. He died in 1939 at the age of forty-four, leaving the unfinished manuscript of *The Last Tycoon*, which showed a remnant of his fine talent.

The Great Gatsby will endure, if only as a social document of the times. The story narrated by Nick Carraway in the first person takes place in 1922. A bachelor, he lives in a modest home in West Egg across Long Island Sound from posh East Egg. Next to him lives a mysterious Jay Gatsby on a forty-acre estate and in a home that is "a factual imitation of some Hotel de Ville." Gatsby holds fabulous parties with a mob of guests. Carraway is invited to a party and meets Gatsby, "an elegant young roughneck, a year or two over thirty, whose elaborate formality of speech just missed being absurd."

Gatsby first gives him a yarn about being a rich man's son who has led an exotic life, but later admits that he is a nobody, James Gatz from North Dakota, without education, who became a bodyguard to a rich man and who himself had somehow become rich and assumed a new identity, "a Platonic conception of himself" erected out of half-truths and falsehoods. Five years before, when he was an Army officer before going overseas, he had had a brief affair with Daisy Fay, a rich girl in Louisville, but she had wed a rich man, Tom Buchanan, who had given her a $350,000 necklace as a wedding gift. Daisy, who is Nick's cousin, lives in East Egg with Tom, and Gatsby wants to meet her again through Nick and revive the romance, regaining her now that he is rich. "Can't repeat the past?" he cried incredulously. "Of course you can."

Gatsby does meet Daisy again, and somehow the embers of the dead romance are rekindled. One Saturday afternoon, in a suite at the Plaza, Gatsby informs Buchanan and the much-wavering Daisy that Daisy loves him and he is going to take her away. Tom then tells Daisy that he has investigated and found that the source of Gatsby's money is a bootlegging operation. Daisy visibly wilts, retreating to the security of Buchanan's money. They drive back to Long Island, the distraught Daisy at the wheel of Gatsby's car. Buchanan has been having a sordid love affair with Myrtle Wilson, the wife of a garage owner, who has finally learned that she has been carrying on with someone and has locked her up. As chance would have it, Myrtle breaks out of the house, runs onto the road, and is run over and killed by Daisy, who drives on. Though knowing that Daisy was the guilty party, Buchanan, probably with Daisy's connivance, lets the half-crazed Wilson learn that the murder car belonged to Gatsby. Wilson, believing that Gatsby was his wife's lover, shoots him to death by the side of the pool on his estate.

In a naïve way, Gatsby aspired to recapture a vision of lost grace and beauty. The novel has been interpreted as a kind of allegory of the conflict in America between idealism and materialism, but on a less abstract plane is it not an essay on the emphasis on money and the uses of money in our society? In an early magazine version of "The Snows of Kilimanjaro," Hemingway had written, "He remembered poor Scott Fitzgerald and his romantic awe of [the rich] and how he had started a story once 'The very rich are different from you and me,' and how someone said to Scott, yes, they have more money. But that was not humorous to Scott. He thought they were a special glamorous race and when he found out that they weren't it wrecked him as much as any other thing that wrecked him."

The ring of verity in the plot may be due to the fact that it sprang from Fitzgerald's own experience. He is said to have been rejected by the daughter of a Chicago broker because he had no money, and he admitted that he feared that he might likewise lose Zelda. "In the years since I have never ceased wondering where my friends' money came from, nor to stop thinking that a sort of *droit du seigneur* might have been exercised to give one of them my girl."

The plot jingles to the tune of money. In the materialistic society in which he lives, Gatsby believes that money buys anything. Since he lost Daisy to money, he thinks that money will bring her back, and perhaps, perhaps, it might have done so, if his money had been as safe and respectable as Buchanan's was. Of Daisy herself, Gatsby tells Nick, "Her voice is full of money." Gatsby cannot conceive of Nick's doing him the slight favor of inviting him to tea with Daisy without offering to reward him by a deal. The richest irony comes after Gatsby's death, when his father, brought East by Nick, is less grief-stricken than excited about the money his son had made.

In the end the book is an indictment of money power and class snobbery. Gatsby, says Nick, had been enslaved by "a vast, vulgar, meretricious beauty." As foolish as he was, Gatsby had been noble in his dream. He told Nick that he intended to take the blame for the hit-and-run murder at the same time that Tom and Daisy were putting their heads together to do him in. Nick's last words to him were the shout, "They're a rotten crowd. You're worth the whole damn bunch put together."

Tom and Daisy promptly forget about Gatsby and do not bother to attend the funeral. The rich were content to trample heedlessly on those who stood in their way. "They were careless people, they smashed up things and creatures and then retreated back into their money or vast carelessness or whatever it was that kept them together and let other people clean up the mess they had made." Yet weeks later, on meeting Tom Buchanan, Nick shakes hands with him because it would have been silly not to have done so. In a childlike way Buchanan believed it natural that Gatsby should die so that he and Daisy could live.

With one exception, none of the hundreds who feasted on Gatsby, none of his business associates, attend his funeral. No character in the novel has the instinct and will for the decent thing to do, save Gatsby and Nick, and the latter confides to the reader at the outset, "I am one of the few honest people I have ever known."

There is a similarity of theme in Dreiser's *An American Tragedy*, which also appeared in 1925. Clyde Griffiths, the son

CULTURE—HIGHBROW

of impoverished Salvation Army parents, noneducated, who learned about and envied the rich as a hotel bellhop, aspires to the love of a girl of social refinement and riches, and the result is fatal since he has to do away with his pregnant sweetheart. Certainly, the attainment of love, money, beauty, and social position all rolled into one is the summit of the "American dream."

Despite all the dirges for the lost generation, this was an interesting period for writers. Margaret Marshall wrote, "The 'disillusion' of the Twenties on which we wasted so much gin and eloquence seems poignantly youthful, romantic and affirmative . . . we have only to remember the joy with which the 'lost generation' battered down the standards of its ancestors, immediate and remote, to recognize that not believing was a driving faith."

In the same vein, John K. Hutchens wrote:

> It seems incontestable that 1918–1929 really was a good time for the American writer. If his post-war disillusion was bitter, it was a creative disillusion, as witness the uses to which it was put by Hemingway, Fitzgerald, E. E. Cummings and T. S. Eliot. If the civilization of the country was materialistic, it was an ugly fact against which writers could and did react with brilliant intensity in satire and realism. The revolution in manners, morals and thinking, for which the Jazz Age is so foolishly inadequate a label, was in short profound and challenging. It inspired and liberated some artists, it destroyed others. Historically, the important fact about it was that it was personal and individualistic. . . . The rebels, sometimes called "nihilists," have endured longer than the dreams of eternal prosperity widely held in the best circles of the time.

It was a period of youthful romanticism. Love was both rhapsodized and scoffed at, as in Dorothy Parker's short poem:

> By the time you swear you're his,
> Shivering and sighing,
> And he vows his passion is
> Infinite and undying—
> Lady, make a note of this;
> One of you is lying.

175

There was a more realistic interpretation of history, which on the whole represented a salutary trend toward balance and truth. Charles A. Beard, for example, showed that individual property interest played as much a part in the birth and formation of our new nation as did love of country. William E. Woodward in 1923 wrote a novel *Bunk,* and the term "debunk" came into usage. Almost simultaneously in 1926, Woodward and Rupert Hughes came out with biographies of George Washington debunking him and raising a furor among professional patriots. Woodward said of Washington, "His inner life was faint." He was "vain, fond of adulation and power." His preoccupations were those of the average American of the twenties, "with material success, with practical details, with money, land, authority." This is quite plausible, but some of Woodward's conclusions were extreme, including his statement that if Washington had shouldered a musket instead of staying in the rear lines, "such a gesture would have brought the Revolution to a successful conclusion within one year." Hughes reprinted in full Washington's letter to married Sally Fairfax, showing that the general's mind was not all on Martha, and said, "The true moral, if any, to be drawn from his life is that one should dress as magnificently as possible, and indulge in every luxury available, including the dance, the theatre, the ballroom, hunting, fishing, racing, drinking and gambling. . . ."

In a press conference, Coolidge was asked about his reaction to these books. He merely pointed out the window and said, "His monument is still out there."

From Europe flowed a new movement called Expressionism, seeded mostly in Germany, where it influenced the imaginative film *The Cabinet of Dr. Caligari* and the plays of Max Reinhardt, Ernst Toller, and Georg Kaiser. "The aim of the expressionist," wrote Frederick Hoffman, "was to project in outer symbols a state of mind, an inner crisis, a psychological condition."

A 1923 play embodying this principle of abstractions in motion was *The Adding Machine* by Elmer Rice, whose purpose was to represent the results of "Fordized" industry, in this case to a member of the white-collar group, and the reign of Babbittry, all in the flavor of Mencken.

The main character is Mr. Zero, who works in a department store, where his life consists of adding figures, with an assistant who has the glamorous name of Daisy Diane Dorothea Devore. The entire first scene consists of a harangue delivered by Mrs. Zero to her husband, which is a flood of clichés garnered from movies and the tabloids. Their friends are ciphers, too—Mr. and Mrs. One, Mr. and Mrs. Two, etc. Their social conversation is a regurgitation of the obvious and commonplace.

On the twenty-fifth anniversary of his starting to add figures, Mr. Zero thinks that his boss will at last recognize his contribution by shifting him to a new locus, and his boss appears on the scene to do exactly that. He announces that he is shifting him to the open air by replacing him with a mechanical adding machine. Thereupon Mr. Zero kills his boss, is executed, and we next see him in the Elysian Fields, where he is so bored doing nothing that he would rather be alive. So he is put to work for another twenty-five years adding figures.

The officer in charge tells him that he is sending him back to earth to reenact his slave existence and to wind up operating a superb super adding machine to be installed in a coal mine where the output of each miner will be recorded without any effort except the light pressure of the great toe of the right foot. This, says the officer, is the final triumph of the evolutionary process—through millions of years "step by step, down through the ages—a gain here, a gain there—the mollusk, the fish, the reptile, the mammal, man. And all so that you might sit in the gallery of a coal mine and operate the super-hyper-adding machine with the great toe of your right foot.

"Back you go to your sunless groove—the raw material of slums and wars—the ready prey of the first jingo or demagogue or political adventurer who takes the trouble to play upon your ignorance and credulity and provincialism. You poor, spineless, brainless boob. . . ."

By the beginning of the decade, popular interpretations of Freud were available, and his beliefs were already influential. Liberation from repression was the springboard to acceptance of the life of freer sexual morals. Awareness of the important role of the unconscious evoked a response in literature in works in which the mind turned into itself. William Faulkner devel-

177

oped a special style to explore the deep recesses of depravity and obscenity among the fine families of the South.

The psychological wellsprings of human motivation were a focus for the greatest playwright of the era, Eugene O'Neill, who was chronically preoccupied with dark and devious human impulses, the twisted and macabre, and often the despair brought about by frustration. Born in 1888, the son of an actor, he spent his early years around the stage, attended Princeton for a year, went to sea, and did odd jobs. After a period of introspection during a spell of bad health in 1912, he embarked on a course of deep study, in which he read and reread the classics and studied English at Harvard. He then gravitated to Greenwich Village and to Provincetown, Massachusetts, where he became associated with a pioneering theater group, the Provincetown Players, and started to write plays. In 1920 he was a success on Broadway with *Beyond the Horizon* and *The Emperor Jones.*

He was a bold experimenter, and his works were varied from his early play *Before Breakfast,* with one character, through *Strange Interlude,* produced in 1928, which lasted from 5:30 P.M. to 11 P.M. (with a break for dinner) and whose characters not only talked to one another but often spoke in asides to the audience. It was widely said that O'Neill came as close to the humor, irony, tragedy, and human understanding of the Greeks as any modern playwright did, and in fact, he was deeply influenced by Aeschylus. He himself acknowledged his debt to the modern playwright and Expressionist August Strindberg, who, as he said, was "the greatest interpreter in our theatre of the characteristic spiritual conflicts which constitute the drama."

O'Neill took a whack at Babbittry, reiterating the main theme by Expressionist devices. In *Marco Millions* he satirized the American businessman disguised as Marco Polo who is palpably out of place in the land of Far Eastern dignity and culture. His *The Great God Brown,* which preceded it in 1926, offered a more complicated approach. In this play the experimenter has the characters wear masks and take them off, indicating multiplicity of character in a single human being and also the difference between appearance and reality.

Brown is a businessman, therefore a "Great God" in our society. According to O'Neill's own description, "Brown is the visionless demi-god of our new materialistic myth—a Success, building his life of exterior things, inwardly empty and resourceless." His boyhood friend is an imaginative but feckless artist, Dion Anthony (Dion suggested by Dionysus), who has married Margaret, the woman Brown loves. Brown always envied the creative power of Dion—even when as a child he crept up on the four-year-old Dion who was drawing a picture in the sand and struck him on the head.

Brown hires Dion as an artist in his architectural firm and cashes in by using Dion's ideas as his own. (The heinous charge by the intellectual leveled at the businessman—that he exploits the artist for profit—is here given a literal translation.) Brown is tortured by his love for Margaret and also, as Dion says, "by that germ which wriggles like a question mark of insecurity in his blood, because it's part of the creative life Brown has stolen from me." Despite his Nietzschean pride, Dion is crushed by the crude man of business and, dying, wills him his mask. Assuming the mask, Brown pretends to be Dion and thus enjoys Margaret's love. But the devil of mocking doubt enters him, and in the end he is forced to wear, as well as Dion's mask, the mask of his success, William A. Brown, before the world, and thus perishes.

This excursion into social criticism was no doubt an exhilarating exercise for O'Neill, but it was rough going, even for the literati. It was certainly incomprehensible to the masses. It is a good example of the huge gulf of noncommunication that existed between the artist and the milling mob.

The disaffected intellectuals, with their gnawing discontent with the arid world of Coolidge, parallel the political Progressives of the Norris and La Follette type, who were also a thorn in the side of the majority will. But the rebels—intellectuals and Progressives—could not define what was wrong or agree on what to do about it.

Chapter VII

CULTURE—FOR THE MASSES

After visiting the United States at the end of the decade, the editor of the English journal *Punch* wrote, "The whole energy of the cinema industry appears directed toward the filming of human interest stories without the faintest infusion of instruction or idealism to the many-headed mob. In short, to provide 'dope.'"

By 1920 there were 14,000 movie theaters throughout the country, a number which would increase by only a couple of thousand in the next ten years. A large segment of the population had found a new home away from home. The average weekly attendance was estimated at 50,000,000, and 700 feature films a year were being turned out, almost all in Hollywood.

The growth of the cinema had been fabulously fast. In April, 1894, an invention of Thomas A. Edison was put to commercial use on Broadway when the public could see peep shows, rows of kinetoscopes with flashing images, one-minute shows of James J. Corbett boxing or of Annie Oakley shooting. By 1907 there were 7,000 dingy nickelodeons, catering mostly to the lower-income classes. The hunger for this new medium proved insatiable, a romantic device to bring entertainment to the common man, and theaters supplanted the nickelodeons, sprouting everywhere, not only in the city but in the remote hamlet. "This is not a business," gasped one overnight success, "it's a dissipation."

A Hollywood producer was publicly quoted in 1921, "The

picture industry is not different than the underwear industry. It is all the law of supply and demand." It was a get-rich-quick business, and its moguls, as listed by Raymond Moley in his book *The Hays Office*, came from such unlikely professions as fur merchant (Adolph Zukor and Marcus Loew), jewelry merchant (Lewis J. Selznick), manager of a little clothing store in Wisconsin (Carl Laemmle), cloth sponger (William Fox), retail druggist (Joseph M. Schenck), and glove salesman (Sam Goldwyn).

The moviemakers found early that what sold best on the screen was the vicarious experience of illicit passion, and movie titles such as *A Shocking Night, Hot Romance,* and *Virgin Paradise* abounded. An advertisement for one picture read, "Brilliant men, beautiful jazz babies, champagne baths, midnight revels, petting parties in the purple dawn, all ending in one terrific climax that makes you gasp."

The garish lives and loves of the new movie colony became notorious. In 1921, after the unsolved murder of director William Desmond Taylor, his liaisons with two stars considered innocent young babes, Mabel Normand and Mary Miles Minter, came to light. When the actress Virginia Rappe died after a drinking and sex party in a San Francisco hotel, the famous comedian Roscoe "Fatty" Arbuckle was put on trial for homicide. He was acquitted after his third trial, but his career was ended because of the storm of public protest. In the United States Senate the industry was thus denounced: "At Hollywood is a colony of these people where debauchery, riotous living, drunkenness, ribaldry, dissipation, free love seem to be conspicuous. Many of these stars it is reported were formerly bartenders, butcher boys, sopers, swampers, variety actors and actresses who may have earned $10 or $20 a week. Some of them are now paid salaries something like $5,000 a month or more, and they do not know what to do with their wealth, extracted from poor people in large part by 25 or 50 cents admissions, except to spend it in riotous living and dissipation."

The industry, intimidated by mounting protests, induced Will H. Hays, Postmaster General of the United States, and former Republican national chairman, to become czar of the industry, much as Judge Kenesaw Mountain Landis became czar of baseball after the Black Sox scandal. Said Hays on taking his new office, "We must have toward that sacred thing, the mind of a child, toward that clean and virgin thing, that unmarked slate—we must have toward that a sense of responsibility, the same care about the impressions made upon it that the best teacher or the best clergyman, the most inspired teacher of youth would have."

Hays' first big job was to head off censorship of the industry, and he organized a propaganda campaign in Massachusetts, where a referendum on the issue was held in November, 1922. The measure was handily defeated, and state censorship continued only in Pennsylvania, New York, Ohio, Kansas, Maryland, and Virginia. Congressman William D. Upshaw, the temperance crusader, introduced a bill for federal censorship in 1926 which received considerable support, but the proposal died after President Coolidge spoke out against it.

The industry would have welcomed some outright accolade of approval from Coolidge, but that was not forthcoming. He had only a desultory interest in the movies, though on a rare occasion he would consent to view a special showing in the White House of one of the "epics" of American history, complete with orchestra supplied by the company. Nonetheless, in 1926 the trade paper *Film Classic* reported, "President Coolidge is the first national Executive to depend on motion pictures as his sole recreation. It is true that the President does not burst into riotous applause, but then he never does. However, it is to be noted that he almost lets his cigar go out in the intensity of his interest."

Hays managed to insert clauses in contracts with movie stars permitting the studios to cancel the contract for even an accusation of immorality. Under what was termed the formula the studios voluntarily agreed to clear with the Hays Office any book or play before purchasing it for the screen. In 1924 no fewer than sixty-seven vehicles which had proved popular in other media were rejected by the Hays Office. Later a Production Code was adopted with specific do's and don'ts.

The Hays regime was highly effective in maintaining purity on the screen during the twenties; the walls came crumbling down only in the Depression, when the companies frantically tried to pull in the customers. Lewdness or the suggestion of lewdness was not present in the movie house, which a whole family could attend without embarrassment. Somerset Maugham's *Rain* and Sidney Howard's *They Knew What They Wanted* could not be made. I recall seeing as a youngster Tolstoy's *Resurrection*. The seduction by the aristocratic officer Rod La Rocque of the servant girl Dolores Del Rio was portrayed by his walking across the grounds of the dacha toward the light of her room. The cause and effect of her ruin, which is the subject of the story, left me completely baffled.

Sex ticklers might be sneaked in. Every Cecil B. De Mille picture could be counted on to have a sequence showing the heroine bathing. Wild parties or revelry might be shown, but it was usually pointed out in a subtitle that this was a sign of moral decadence that must be shunned at all costs.

Hays proclaimed, "Motion pictures contain a potency of life as active as the soul whose progeny they are. Motion pictures have carried the silent call of humanity, ambition, virtue, patriotism, love of country and of honor to audiences speaking fifty different languages. They have clothed the empty existence of far-off hamlets with joy, they have lifted limitless laboring folk until they have walked the peaks of romance and adventure."

One of the outstanding features of the silents of the twenties is their downright silliness and hokum, their divorce from real-life situations. There is a great deal more plausibility in a comedy like Chaplin's *The Gold Rush* than there is in most serious dramas. Any obstacles of space or time were vaulted over with carefree abandon. Facts were treated as a nuisance. David Wark Griffith's *Orphans of the Storm* converted the French Revolution into a Western.

As far as film technique was concerned, it all stopped with Griffith even before the twenties began. Richard Griffith and Arthur Mayer stated in their excellent history of the movies: "Between 1909 and 1916, David Wark Griffith created the art of screen narrative almost singlehanded. After 'Intolerance' there was almost no significant addition to film syntax until the advent of sound and of the wide screen, both mechanical rather than artistic innovations." Griffith was born in Kentucky, the son of Colonel Jacob Wark Griffith, a hero of the Confederacy.

Proud of his family tradition, the son became a writer and playwright and drifted into films as an actor in order to eat regularly. He was so ashamed of this disreputable occupation that he took the name of Lawrence Griffith and wrote his wife, "You know we can't go on forever and not tell our friends and relatives how we are earning our living."

Griffith revolutionized film making when he became a director. Instead of the standard "one scene–one shot" fixed-camera method of shooting film, he varied camera positions to the "long shot–mid shot–close shot" combination. He also invented the fade-out, explored the use of light and shadow, and was a pioneer in filming the fluid narrative feature. It had been the belief that twenty minutes, or two reels, was the most that an audience could take without eyestrain or boredom. Griffith changed all this with the four-reel spectacle *Judith of Bethulia* in 1913. He experimented in color by dying film prints and even used a corps of girls to add extra colors, frame by frame. For even more striking color effects he instructed projectionists in the theaters when to throw red or blue beams onto the screen.

In 1915 came the first showing of his monumental *Birth of a Nation,* a project dear to his Southern heart since it concerned the story of the Confederacy during and after the Civil War, based largely on Thomas Dixon's novel *The Clansman.* It was a nationwide sensation and continued to be so for years. It cost $100,000 to produce and by 1939 had grossed at least $39,000,000. The film was rehearsed for six weeks and shot in nine by one camera and one cameraman. There was no prepared script. Its star, Lillian Gish, recalled, "He carried the ideas in his head—or I should say in his heart."

President Wilson viewed it in the White House and said with awe, "It is like writing history with lightning." On the other hand, with regard to its treatment of historical fact, President Eliot of Harvard said, "It presents an extraordinary misrepresentation of the birth of this nation."

Negro groups protested strongly against the image Griffith gave of the Negro during Reconstruction. Stung by this criticism, Griffith next undertook *Intolerance,* which has been described as "the only film fugue ever made." It interwove four stories from four different eras—Belshazzar's Babylon, sixteenth-century France, modern slum life, and the time of the Crucifixion—bound into a whole by intermittent shots of Lillian Gish rocking a cradle. The sets were the most opulent ever seen, and its lack of financial success was equally spectacular.

Griffith's decline had begun. By 1925 the father of the modern cinema was working on scripts prepared by others. By the thirties he was no longer receiving any screen credits for what he did. Finally, he sank into indigent alcoholism and lived, a recluse, in a room in a shabby hotel near Hollywood, where he died in 1948.

All M-G-M films opened with a roaring lion and the words *ars gratia artis* (art for the sake of art), a nonsensical slogan belied by the movies pandering to the lowest denominator of taste. Hollywood's concept of "culture" was corn, such as the eye-filling, opulent spectacles which were the run-of-De Mille productions. There were a few isolated pictures of artistic merit such as King Vidor's vivid reenactment of the grimness of the Great War, and its camaraderie and fleeting romances in *The Big Parade,* and his *The Crowd,* in which he dissected the regimentation of city life. The motion pictures gave no true representation of America. Most of them took place in New York City, to show scenes of wealth and power. An analysis of forty pictures in which American homes were shown in some detail revealed that 69 percent of them accented the life of the rich and only 4 percent that of the poor. In a rare excursion into social realism, Erich von Stroheim filmed *McTeague* by Frank Norris. He cut it from fifty reels to an irreducible twenty-four, but M-G-M issued it in ten under the title of *Greed,* making the plot practically unintelligible.

The Western had great customer appeal both here and abroad. Two stars dominated the Western, William S. Hart from 1914 until 1924 (he earned $2,200,000 in two of those years) and, after Hart left the scene, Tom Mix. Both men were the genuine article and had worked in the West, which was more than could be said for other screen cowboys. Hart had been born in New York in 1870, but his parents soon moved first to Minnesota and then to Wisconsin. Hart could speak Sioux by the time he was six; in his teens he had extensive experience as a ranch hand. He became an actor somewhere along the line playing many Shakespearean roles, but when he got into films, he specialized in portraying cowboys. He tried to give his films the flavor of the real thing and bridled at all the absurdities in the first American film epic, *The Covered Wagon*. He said that showing oxen swimming across a river with their yokes on was an "error that would make a Western man refuse to speak to his own brother." Yet there was a lot of hokum even in his films.

After taking part in the Spanish-American War, Tom Mix wandered into the Oklahoma Territory, became sheriff of a Kansas county before he was twenty-five, and spent three years as a Texas Ranger. A movie company came to the Oklahoma Territory in 1910, and Mix, who had been hired to advise on locations and hire extras, found himself an actor. His white hat and suit and his horse, Tony, were familiar to millions of movie-goers. He was to make 400 feature films and $4,000,000. As time went on, the Western became more and more stylized. The cowboy was no longer a man who worked with cows, but a rootless person of no fixed occupation who acted as an itinerant Robin Hood.

The great creative surge in the cinema took place in Germany. A series of remarkable psychological films were produced in the postwar years. The monumental *The Cabinet of Dr. Caligari,* released in 1919, told of the weird Dr. Caligari who carried around fairs a coffinlike box containing the somnambulist Cesare (played by the later famous Conrad Veidt), who escaped at night to commit horrible murders. The plot, which conveyed the wavering of the soul between tyranny and chaos, turned out to be a madman's dream, and Dr. Caligari was none other than the supervisor of a mental asylum. In this and later German films there were all kinds of innovations—a highly mobile camera, externalization of dreams, use of distorting mirrors as an act of defiance to conventional thought, heavy symbolism.

The Last Laugh of 1924 introduced the great German actor Emil Jannings to American audiences. The Brooklyn-born Jannings was capable of acting with the most delicate nuances and usually played elderly men, although he was only in his late thirties. *The Last Laugh* had no captions and needed none. Jannings portrayed an elderly porter at the door of a Berlin Grand

Hotel who wears a gorgeous, bespangled uniform which gives him a sense of dignity and causes him to be treated with awe and reverence in the slum quarter in which he lives. When the hotel strips him of his uniform and demotes him to lavatory attendant, his feeling of self-worth vanishes, his neighbors heap ridicule on him, and his relatives turn him into the street. The story seems to end on a note of tragic doom, but in a fairy-tale close that is a satiric thrust at Hollywood, the old man emerges wallowing in wealth. An American millionaire has bequeathed his fortune to the man present at his death, and the man just happens to be the lavatory attendant.

Despite all the admiration they won, *Dr. Caligari* and other pioneering German films had no real influence on the American cinema, and a large factor in the decline in the artistic quality of the German film in the mid-twenties was their "Americanization" to compete in the export market. Immediately after the war, in view of anti-German sentiment here, German films were labeled "Made in Scandinavia," but their superiority became so widely acknowledged that there was a wholesale raiding of German talent by Hollywood. Jannings, Veidt, Pola Negri, director Ernst Lubitsch, and many others were induced to come to California.

The one cinema form to which America made a great esthetic contribution during the twenties was the comedy. Its first master was Mack Sennett, who applied the techniques he had learned working for D. W. Griffith, and the results were lunatic fantasies of endless movement, filled with scamps, scoundrels, fakers, and Keystone Kops who reduced authority to absurdity. They all were splashed with pies and struck by autos and endured other indignities without bodily harm and in the cause of good fun. Sennett's cameras were cranked slowly in sequences such as the inevitable chase, which made them whiz when they were seen by audiences. He worked without a planned script, improvising as he went along. His mode of comedy was called slapstick, after an implement used by stage comedians which consisted of two pieces of wood, slapped together when an object, such as a human posterior, was hit.

His finest star was Charlie Chaplin, who arrived in the United States from England in 1913. In the London music halls Chap-

187

lin had learned the invaluable secret of timing, and from his observation of a character on the London streets he fashioned a little tramp with derby, oversized shoes, and a funny walk. In time he left Sennett to develop his own style. Sennett wanted his gags to be finished in 20 feet of film, and Chaplin wanted 100 feet just to get started. Finding the two-reel comedy inadequate, he went into feature films.

Of him Sennett said in later years, "Oh, well, he's just the greatest artist that ever lived." Highbrow critics joined in the praise. Concerning his gift for pantomime, James Agee said, "He could probably pantomime Bryce's 'American Commonwealth' without even blowing a syllable and make it paralyzingly funny in the bargain." Gilbert Seldes wrote:

> It is a miracle that there should arise in our time a figure wholly in the tradition of the great clowns, a tradition requiring creative energy, freshness, inventiveness, change, for neither the time nor the country in which Charlie works is exceptionally favorable to such a phenomenon. He has created that trajectory across the screen which is absolutely his own line of movement. No matter what the actual facts are, the curve he plots is always the same. It is one who seems to enter from a corner of the screen, becomes entangled or involved in a force greater than himself as he advances upward and to the center, there he spins like a marionette in a whirlpool, is flung from side to side, always in a parabola which seems centripetal until the madness of the action hurls him to refuge or compels him to flight at the opposite end of the screen. He wanders in, a stranger or impostor, an anarchist, and passes again, buffeted but unchanged.

Buster Keaton was the second of the great film comedians of the era. He had acquired his name Buster from the magician Harry Houdini, who laughed at his many pratfalls when he was a child with his parents in vaudeville. Keaton's face was a blank, gazing at the world in frozen bewilderment—"a smile was as deafeningly out of key as a yell"—and atop his head perched a hat as thin as a phonograph record. "One can never forget him," wrote Agee, "standing erect as the prow of his little boat is being launched. The boat goes grandly down the skids and just as grandly straight to the bottom. Keaton never budges. The last of him you see, the water lifts the hat off the stoic head and it floats away."

The biggest financial success was Harold Lloyd, a comedian whose artistic talent did not match that of Chaplin or Keaton but whose assumed character, clean and sympathetic, struck a chord with Americans. By 1920 Lloyd was making $1,200,000 a year. He was trained by Sennett before shifting to Hal Roach, whose *Our Gang* comedies were then the rage. Lloyd experimented first with a character named Willie Work, next with Lonesome Luke for whom he borrowed heavily from Chaplin, and hit el dorado with "the glass character" who wore his glasses whether to bed or in a football game. This last creation was an ineffectual momma's boy whose virtue, à la McGuffey's Reader or Horatio Alger, triumphed over superhuman odds in unexpected ways. Lloyd himself explained, "My character symbolizes something important. I symbolize the little struggling man working at a menial type of job. He might be a soda jerk, a ribbon salesman or somebody trying to get a job. In any event he was always struggling against the bigger man in a difficult situation."

Lloyd's film of 1923, *Safety Last,* in which he played a human fly on a skyscraper, illustrates a type of humor which has become extinct, the multiplication of gags, one topping the other, all built on and growing out of a single situation. The higher he climbs, the more horrifying his ordeal becomes—he gets fouled up in a tennis net, the pigeons treat him like a statue, a mouse runs up his leg, and he hangs on by an eyelash. He is driven to the end of a flagpole by a furious dog, the pole breaks, and he falls, just managing to grab the minute hand of a huge clock which circles around carrying him along; the clock face falls out and slants perilously with trembling springs above the street; he manages to get off the face of the clock, but then his feet get caught in the springs, etc.

The golden age of comedy disappeared with the talkies as verbal gags supplanted the wonderful art of pantomime and mimicry.

Like the automobile, the movie palaces of the twenties emphasized nonutilitarian glitter. The first of the kind was the

Central Park, built in Chicago in 1917 by the Balaban brothers. They lined the interior with crimson velvet and with marble, adorned the walls with paintings, and filled the lobbies with uniformed and bowing ushers. In a swirl of color and splendor they experimented with prologues, singers, dancers in diaphanous robes, and so forth. The theater was sensationally successful, and by 1928 the Balabans had eleven others that were similar.

Every city of any size now had a movie palace. The moving picture theater acquired mystic and quasi-religious virtues. In New York City the 54th Street Theater was called the Sanctuary of the Cinema; the Capitol, the Theater with a Soul. Of the Paramount Theater in New York, an English visitor said, "This is what the American peasant conceives a European castle looks like—and doesn't." The one with the most lavish and useless opulence was the Roxy, the Cathedral of the Motion Picture. It cost $10,000,000 and had three organs and more than 6,000 seats. Its marble lobby, which was as big as a good-size railroad station, contained a huge chandelier and was filled with statuary and paintings. On the floor was a flaming red rug, which cost $100,000 and weighed two tons.

At the opening of the Roxy in March, 1927, a draped prophet atop a pedestal declaimed, "Ye portals bright, unite us all to worship at beauty's shrine." Immediately thereafter a blaze of light staggered everybody in the front seats of the orchestra, and deafening music welled up. The *Independent* wrote:

> The Cathedral has been planned by a minor master in what by press agents is described as the "plateresque" (why not the "plasteresque") mode but which appears to be a Neo-Hebraic-Ultraistic style with suggestions of the supposed golden glories of King Solomon's temple, coy hints at the Moorish and reversions to the Italian Renaissance. After all, P. T. Barnum is not dead.

What dividends of pleasure such movie palaces gave have been described by Lloyd Lewis:

> In the dim auditorium which seems to float in a world of dreams, an American woman may spend her afternoons alone. Romantic music gives her a pleasant sensation of tingling . . . on this music as on a mildly erotic bridge she can let her fancies slip through the darkened atmosphere to the screen where they drift

in rhapsodic amours with the handsome stars. . . . All of this splendor has been planned for her delight and with a luxuriance that she imagined was enjoyed only in Cleopatra's court, oriental harems or Parisian and Viennese society. She strolls voluptuously through lobbies and foyers that open into one another like chambers in a maze, her feet sink in soft rugs, she is surrounded by heavy Renaissance tables, oil paintings, and statues of nudes. When she goes home that evening she will perhaps clean spinach and peel onions but for a few hours attendants bow to her, doormen tip their hats and a maid curtsies to her in the ladies' washroom. She bathes in elegance and dignity; she satisfies her yearning for a cultural atmosphere. Even the hush that hangs over the lobbies means refinement to her . . . in the de luxe house every man is a king and every woman a queen.

It became apparent as the decade rolled on that movie attendance was declining because of the competition from the radio. As it became harder to fill theaters, the new movie palaces with their heavy overhead felt the pinch most. Novelty attractions were added. In New York's Paramount Theater, there was Paul Whiteman and his band at $10,000 a week, Sousa and his band, and Gertrude Ederle swimming in a tank. Obviously some decisive new fillip was necessary to fill empty seats.

It is surprising that the talkies did not come much earlier. Hollywood, though well aware that the necessary technology was available, hung back. The movie companies had millions tied up in stars who might not make the grade in talkies, as well as other millions invested in equipment for which the cost of conversion would be staggering. Then, too, 40 percent and more of revenues came from sales abroad, and what would happen if movies were spoken in English?

In April, 1923, Lee De Forest showed the first sound movies in the Rivoli Theater in New York. They were shorts of vaudeville acts. In early 1924 he shot a six-minute sound film of Al Smith to be used in his campaign for the Democratic nomination. Later he made a film of Coolidge speaking on economy. Because of lack of equipment in theaters, it could not be widely shown. De Forest organized a company, Phonofilms, and tried to sell stock to the public. Coolidge, when informed that the film he made in 1924 was being used in demonstrations, cracked

191

down on De Forest. In May, 1925, De Forest wrote to Presidential secretary Clark that he was amazed by the President's displeasure and that he was donating the Coolidge film to the Smithsonian Institution.

De Forest abandoned his project, but meanwhile, two other systems had been perfected. One, which became known as Vitaphone, was that developed by Bell Telephone through its Western Electric laboratories and consisted of a disc revolving on a turntable geared to a projecting apparatus. The other and more practical method was that of the Case Laboratories System in which sound was photoelectrically reproduced on the edge of a strip of film; Fox Movies and Case joined in the Fox-Case Company. On June 25, 1927, the Roxy Theater started showing Lindbergh's takeoff as recorded by Fox Newsreels. The audience was thrilled to hear the roar of the motor, shouts of "goodbye," and cries when the plane soared.

Warner Brothers, which was teetering on the edge of insolvency, decided to take the plunge with Vitaphone. The first Vitaphone products from Warner Brothers were shorts of operatic arias and comedy skits. The first sound film was *Don Juan* with John Barrymore and Mary Astor. There was no audible talking, only a musical score and a few sound effects such as the click of dueling swords. At the time people thought the chief utility of the new technique would be to permit small-town theaters to have the kind of musical accompaniment that had formerly been available only through large orchestras in big-city theaters.

In October, 1927, Warner Brothers forged ahead with *The Jazz Singer,* starring Al Jolson. Although only 500 theaters in the entire country were then wired for sound, it set the box-office record for the year. The sound sequences consisted only of Jolson singing "Kol Nidre" and "Mammy."

Tenderloin, the first film with spoken dialogue, was a piece of claptrap, but it scored a big box-office success. For history, let it be recorded that the first exchange of words in sound occurred when Dolores Costello, a pure dancing girl, is awakened from her sleep by the villain, Conrad Nagel, who demands that she give him some stolen money. His hand is at her throat while she proclaims her innocence.

HE: All right. You're not bad to look at, and my night shall not be wasted.

SHE: Not that, not that. Surely you have a sister.

The rustling of a newspaper, unless dampened, was a deafening noise, and the patter of raindrops sounded like thunder. A major problem was that sibilants were turned into lisps. Thus in *Tenderloin* Miss Costello was heard to say, "Why do you perthitht in perthecuting me? I am innothent."

There was great skepticism that talkies would supplant the silents. Recently actress Mary Astor, looking back forty years, stated:

> We the artists—the superior, solid conservatives, the steady-working actors, directors, writers—we would come out of the projection room exchanging satisfied quips about how the noise would simply drive audiences from the theaters. Seriously, it was nothing but a poor imitation of theater itself. We were in an entirely different medium, a very successful medium. It was a way of telling a story—images created the emotion—a direct appeal. There were many reasons why "talkies" were completely impractical. Everything would have to be straight cuts, no fade-ins or fadeouts, no dissolves. And the fluid motion of the camera would be lost. It would be static, dull. How would you go outdoors? How would you ever get such scenes as Borzage's taxi army in "Seventh Heaven"? Or Renee Adoree running after the column of doughboys in "The Big Parade"? Even in more intimate scenes you could never speak while moving around.
>
> Then they began to make awful things called "part-talkies." Everything was normal until the final big scene. And then Bam! Yakity-Yak! Audiences loved it and we the artists shuddered. Or was it shivered?

As late as October, 1928, an article by noted director Monte Bell appeared in the *North American Review* saying, "Sound is simply an accessory. I do not look and hope for continuous dialogue in pictures but simply for added dramatic effectiveness—the sough of winds, the ceaseless murmur of waves, the barking of dogs, the crashing of thunder. I do not believe the public is going to throw over Clara Bow, Mary Pickford, Buddy Rogers, John Gilbert and Charles Farrell." In four years they all would be gone.

Since the most rudimentary sound equipment cost half a million dollars, most of the first talkies were merely the filming on sound stages of such Broadway plays as *The Letter, Interference* or *The Trial of Mary Dugan*. Without the music to which theater patrons were accustomed they sounded hollow, and they dragged badly because the need for pantomime in the silents had set the pace of filming slower than real life.

Critics lamented the poor quality of the films, and a good many agreed with Charlie Chaplin that "movies need dialogue as much as Beethoven symphonies need lyrics." There was a film, *Lilac Time*, a tearjerker about the war, which was made as a silent and in the revolution released with a sound music track. The producers felt that if the audiences wanted another fillip, they would give them one. At the most poignant times in the story, lilac perfume was wafted through the theater. Many critics had the same comment: that at least this film smelled better than most they had to review.

The transition had come swiftly. In the very month that Coolidge left office it became clear that sound was here to stay. In March, 1929, a large studio, Fox, announced that henceforth it would make only "all-talkies," although even then only 2,500 of the 16,000 movie theaters in the country were wired for sound.

In reviewing the decline of culture in an article for *Harper's* in 1927, Aldous Huxley said on the subject of recreation for the masses:

There is another way in which machinery adversely affects culture. It removes man's incentive to amuse himself. In the past when people needed recreation, they were compelled to a great extent to provide it for themselves. If you needed music, you had to sing or play an instrument. If you wanted a pictorial record of some person or scene you had to draw or paint. If you lived in a village or out of the way town and wanted drama, you had to act, yourself. Today you need none of these things. Recreation is provided ready-made by enormous joint-stock companies. The play-instinct, which found active expression in the past, is now passive.

During the Coolidge Era the radio became the chief source of mechanized entertainment. Radio as a home accessory came into being accidentally. Wireless was familiar as a means of ship-to-shore communication. Radio telephony was hastened by the invention by Lee De Forest of the audion, or vacuum tube valve. Successful experiments in this field were conducted in 1906. Ten years later pilots of airplanes flying over Manhattan were carrying on conversations with operators in buildings under them, and radio amateurs were talking with one another.

All amateur licenses were suspended during the war, but the government permitted Dr. Frank Conrad of Westinghouse in Pittsburgh to continue experiments in the defense interest. In a laboratory atop his garage, as part of his tests, he started sending out transmissions twice a week on Wednesday and Saturday nights, playing records, giving ball scores, and inserting news items. An ingenious schoolboy could make a receiving set, the crystal set, and soon Conrad had an audience.

One morning in early October, 1920, Harry P. Davis, vice-president of Westinghouse, came across an ad by a department store in a Pittsburgh paper selling "A special line of radio receiving sets suitable for listening to Dr. Conrad's concerts." An idea clicked in his mind. "If a retail store saw enough in radio to set up a department to sell goods on the strength of this twice-a-week entertainment, suppose the entertainment were provided daily, broadcast on greater power, and a variety of features were added?" Then Westinghouse could manufacture and sell equipment in quantities for a mass audience.

Davis called Conrad in and said he was discontinuing his pygmy operation in favor of a regular station. An application was made to Washington which granted a license to station 8ZZ. On election night in 1920, this station, with a transmitter of 100 watts housed in a rough box atop a high building, broadcast the returns announcing the election of Harding and Coolidge. The broadcast was heard as far away as New Orleans and Manchester, New Hampshire. Soon this station was rebaptized KDKA.

By 1922 there were twenty-two radio stations on the air. A milestone came the same year, when the station belonging to American Telephone and Telegraph in New York, WEAF, broadcast the first commercial, for the Queensboro Realty Company. Henceforth, thanks to the beneficence of capitalism, free entertainment on an expensive scale could be beamed into the

American home. Newspapers found that they had a new competitor for advertising revenues, and they refused to give radio anything but the skimpiest coverage until Roy Howard of the Scripps-Howard chain broke the boycott. Telephone wires were used to bring programs into the studios, obviating the need for performers to be there physically. The broadcasting chains were launched in 1926, when the National Broadcasting Company was formed by the Radio Corporation of America; by 1929 it had fifty stations. In 1927 the rival Columbia Broadcasting System was formed.

Originally the wave band allocations for radio stations were regulated voluntarily with Secretary of Commerce Herbert Hoover acting as arbiter. The industry generally abided by Hoover's decisions though he received this letter from a chronic wave jumper whom he tried to keep in bounds: "Please order your minions of Satan to leave my station alone. You cannot expect the Almighty to abide by your wave-length nonsense. When I offer my prayers to Him, I must fit into His wave-length reception." Its sender was the controversial Aimee Semple McPherson, an evangelist who propounded her Four-Square Gospel from the Angelus Temple in Los Angeles.

When a station in Chicago broke away and maintained its independence in court against Hoover's weak statutory authority, Congress in 1927 passed the legislation establishing the five-man Federal Radio Commission to allot ninety-eight wavelengths to 732 stations; this was possible because most stations could be heard only within a small radius.

The listener of today, with his mechanically durable and reliable radio which he takes for granted, does not realize the inconvenience that his counterpart had to endure in the twenties. A typical set in 1926 was a Freshman Masterpiece costing about $150, a huge piece with dials galore. Although a great advance from the earlier crystal set with headphones, it had a horn loudspeaker. An outside aerial 100 feet long had to be strung. The radio required two sets of batteries—the A battery was a storage battery which had to be recharged every two weeks, and the B battery was a set of dry cell batteries which had to be replaced every three weeks or so. By 1927 radio sets could get their power from the ordinary electric socket in the home. Even after the user put up with much trouble and expense, for a good part of the time his radio had to be shut off because of the chronic problem of static from moisture in the air. The growth of the radio was phenomenal, but by the end of the decade there were only 10,000,000 in use compared with 180,000,000 today, including automobile radios. Only 30 percent of homes had radios compared to 40 percent with phonographs, 60 percent with telephones, and 67 percent with automobiles.

Radio in those days was a sprawling infant, uncoordinated, directionless, and malformed. In 1929, although there were fifty stations in the Chicago area, a survey revealed that 50 percent of the potential audience listened to only three stations, leaving an average of 12,000 listeners to the other forty-seven. On the small stations the programs were often plain garbage. Medical quacks who were denied space in newspapers and magazines peddled their wares on them; thus KFKD in Milford, Kansas, was used by "Doc" John R. Brinkley to sell his "rejuvenation" operation, and KTNT of Muscatee, Iowa, promoted the Tangley Institute with its surefire cure for varicose veins.

Aural advertising was new. It was believed that if a name were repeated often enough, it would induce the listener to buy Tweedledum brand instead of Tweedledee. As Stuart Chase put it:

A little music, a good stiff sales talk, a little more music. The motto was: if the magazines can do it, why can't we? They could and they did. The eager fans stupefied with the sensation of getting anything, even a hiccough out of the air, were ready to listen greedily to whatever might come along. The output of soap and sealing wax appeals was enormous but it is to be doubted that it sold much merchandise. Father was too busy twisting grapevine aerials and playing with static eliminators to pay much attention to what was actually being said.

After protests rose from the audiences about the advertising to which they were constantly subjected, the big stations swung to another approach, an effort to win goodwill for the product by a churchly dignity which mentioned the sponsor only at discreet intervals. At any rate, by the end of the decade, the big stations, despite their hustling sales departments, had only the foggiest notion about where they were going. "No advertiser

197

can get a real appraisal of what his radio expenditure is worth. He will be shown maps, charts, letters, and figures. But no sound technique for evaluating the radio benefit has yet been evolved," wrote Chase.

There was one certainty, and that was that the programs were of poor caliber. In order to cultivate the mass market, the precious few or the elite had to be ignored. There was very little classical music. There were no "good music" stations, as there are today. There was far less news on the air. There was less variety. One heard an endless cacophony of jazz, the blare of trumpets, the twang of banjos, and the crooning of saxophones. A survey of 387 hours of broadcasting from the larger stations in New York City showed 56 hours given to talk, 42 to classical or semiclassical music, and 289 to jazz, but the talk and serious music were crammed into the early hours of daytime when few were listening. There was a raft of musical troupes, such as the Happiness Boys, the A&P Gypsies, the Humming Birds, and orchestras without number, among which that of Rudy Vallee was outstanding in its appeal.

Just as in the case of the movies, the magic electronic box could create public personalities, and the popularity of Rudy Vallee paralleled that of Valentino. At an early age Hubert Prior Vallee ducked his duties in his father's drugstore in Westbrook, Maine, to play the saxophone in theaters. He worked his way through college, first at the University of Maine and then at Yale, from which he was graduated in 1927, by playing at night; after college, he formed his own band which was an instant success on the air. Thousands of letters from young women deluged the stations; when a New York department store announced that he would appear at the early hour of ten in the morning to sing some of the songs on his records, the crowds of ladies of all ages who appeared gave the place the air of a football afternoon at the Yale Bowl. Martha Gellhorn wrote of "God's Gift to Us Girls" in the *New Republic:* "It would seem that American women want a beau. Their husbands are busy earning the money that sends the ladies to the movies and buys their radios. The poor men cannot be expected to come home from work, hurry through a shower, gussy up in white linens and start singing in a languid, cajoling way 'I Kiss Your Hand, Madame.' Rudy fits the bill. And that is that."

Another personality who was a household word was Graham McNamee, the top sports announcer for the National Broadcasting Company. In 1923, McNamee was a man of thirty-three who was broke and jobless and whose only salable experience was that he was a baritone who had done concert work. While wandering along lower Broadway in the spring of 1923, he passed the American Telephone Building and decided to drop in and try for a job doing some singing on fledgling radio. An executive to whom he talked said, "Well, we need young men like you. It's a new racket, and so we'll give you a trial for $30 a week." In 1924 he vividly reported the wild Democratic National Convention and was shifted to sports work.

His main asset was his vibrant voice which made events exciting to listeners, but many pointed out that he knew very little about his subject and was guilty of egregious errors in his reporting—or nonreporting. This is an excerpt which conveys the flavor of McNamee:

> It's raining. No, by gosh, it's snowing. I don't know. Phil Carlin says it's doing both. Wow! Four Georgia men tackled Flanagan at once, and—and—and—ha, ha, ha, when they hit the ground they slid twenty feet on their faces. They'd have to be introduced to their mothers the way they look now. I don't know whether it's raining or snowing, but somebody's turned something on, and well—I'm jealous of you folks who are sitting in front of the fireplace. No, I'm not either. I'd rather be here even—they've lined up again. Flanagan is back for a forward—no—no—a punt—no. . . .

The air waves were flooded with the musical innovation called jazz. About the origins of jazz and its anatomy as a form of musical expression there is a good deal of doubt, and this doubt extends to the origin of the word itself. Some years before Lafcadio Hearn had found that the word "jas" in the Creole patois of New Orleans meant to speed up. It may have been connected with the French word *jacer* meaning to prattle, or it may have had African roots. The word was used for copulation, but this was probably a derivative application. At any rate, jazz was the new music, strident but full of the spirit of youth, free in expression, joyous, humorful, and zestful.

199

It evolved from ragtime of the early century, and the Negro influence seems to have been a commanding one. What was first recognizable as jazz cropped up in the Negro minstrel shows as opposed to the blackface ones. In an analysis Don Knowlton wrote:

Rhythm is the backbone of jazz. While I hesitate to go as far as some and ascribe a Freudian motivation and a phallic symbolism to jazz, nevertheless the fact remains that the beat of the tom-tom which drives savages into orgiastic ecstasies and the beat of the drum which sets the pace for the dance orchestras are identical. Jazz serves primitive rhythm on a civilized platter.

Syncopation, the shifting of the usual musical accent, was a hallmark of jazz. For example, the tone could begin on an unaccented beat and continue through the accented beat. Syncopation might have become a feature of symphonic music itself if it had not been directed into the world of dissonances by the influence of Richard Strauss and Arnold Schoenberg. There was some kinship between the two, and dissonance in jazz was called the blues. Despite its origins, artistic merit in jazz was recognized by musical authorities such as Leopold Stokowski, who said, "It is an expression of the times, of the breathless, energetic, superactive times in which we are living."

What was more offensive to the ear than the music were the lyrics of the songs, "mere sensuous sentimentality expressed in baby talk jingles." These lyrics were in part a carry-over from ragtime where the words had drifted into slush and kisses; since skilled writers shunned jazz, they were written by the musicians themselves or by vaudeville actors or cranks.

On February 12, 1924, at Aeolian Hall, a sanctuary of classical music in New York City, the King of Jazz, Paul Whiteman, gave a concert before a distinguished audience. The sensation was a work commissioned by Whiteman and composed by a twenty-five-year-old musician, George Gershwin, *Rhapsody in Blue,* orchestrated by Ferde Grofé. The veteran conductor Walter Damrosch said, "Various composers have been walking around jazz like a cat around a plate of hot soup, waiting for it to cool off so they might lift it to the level of music respectability. George Gershwin seems to have accomplished that miracle." The next year, under a commission from Whiteman, Gershwin in a month's time composed a jazz piano concerto and scored it himself for 100 members of a symphony orchestra.

George Gershwin, born Jacob Gershvin, an authentic musical genius of this century who died at the early age of thirty-eight, was largely self-taught. Until he was thirteen, he had no musical training whatsoever; at that age his family in Brooklyn acquired a piano, and his older brother, Ira, started taking lessons at fifty cents an hour. George became fascinated with the piano and sat playing and playing. His parents realized that George was the one with the talent; Ira stopped taking lessons, and George began them. Breathlessly he ran through all that was offered and after $10 worth of lessons had nothing more to learn from his teacher. Although he took further lessons from others, he became a wizard piano player mostly by learning aurally.

At the age of seventeen he took a job as a song plugger at $15 a week for the music firm of Remick, where he played ditties for the trade for ten hours a day. Two years later he quit to earn $35 a week as a pianist for rehearsals of a new show by Jerome Kern. He became acquainted with the actress Vivienne Segal, who sang two of his songs one night at the Century Theater, and Al Jolson interpolated his "Swanee" into the musical comedy Sinbad. The firm of Harms & Co., which controlled 90 percent of show music, signed him up for a handsome figure. His first big success was La, La, Lucille in 1919. With his brother, Ira, as lyricist he then wrote the music for a succession of musical shows—Funny Face, Rosalie, and Lady, Be Good—before his smash success in symphonic jazz with Rhapsody in Blue.

Although they were called jazz, Gershwin's works for symphony orchestra were actually an individual creation, the synthesis in his own style of the classical music of nineteenth-century Romanticism and the new jazz idiom. Paul Whiteman had been brought up on classical music and had been a violist in his youth in the Denver Symphony Orchestra and then the San Francisco People's Symphony Orchestra. His success, when he turn to jazz, was fantastic—in 1925 he earned $680,000 and his recording of "Three O'Clock in the Morning" sold 3,400,000 copies. He brought stature to the dance band expanding it from the usual seven- or eight-piece ensemble to include larger brass and reed sections.

Writing on the occasion of his death in the New York *Times* in December, 1967, John S. Wilson said that Whiteman was a misunderstood pioneer. "When the public became more aware of jazz—the 'real thing' as it was often called in the nineteen-thirties to distinguish it from the dance music that had been called jazz in the twenties—followers of Benny Goodman and Count Basie, of Louis Armstrong and Duke Ellington and later of Charlie Parker and Dizzy Gillespie were apt to look on Mr. Whiteman as an impostor." By the swing era of the thirties, the semisymphonic style in which Whiteman had been dressing his music for a decade had become dated. One of Whiteman's most important contributions was his development of personalities who later became prominent in their own right. The list includes Bing Crosby and the Dorsey brothers.

Newspapers expanded in size during the decade, and more magazines, particularly those appealing to lower tastes, were on the market. As a recreation, reading was very cheap, compared to today. In 1929 at the height of the boom, the New York *Times* and other morning papers in New York cost 2 cents and the mammoth Sunday papers only 5 cents. Printing costs were low, even in view of the fact that the consumer price index was a little more than half of what it now is. This is evident from the price of a hard-cover book which then ranged from $2 to $2.50. Reliance on advertising revenue, however, was the main reason for the cheapness of mass-media publications.

The *Saturday Evening Post*, a far cry from the emaciated magazine of today, cost 5 cents. A single copy of the *Post* in December, 1929, weighed 1 pound 14 ounces and ran to 272 pages, containing 295 square feet of paper. The advertising revenue ran up to $1,500,000 an issue at the rate of $12,500 a page. Almost 3,000,000 copies a week were printed. The advertisers ran the gamut of American industry. As Lowell Schmaltz, "The Man Who Knew Coolidge," said, "Yes, sir, a fellow that wants to understand the United States, all he has to do is to study The Saturday Evening Post and he'll see why we're the most advanced nation in the world and the most civilized."

Advertising was in its heyday. J. Thorne Smith wrote in

Civilization in the United States, "Do I understand you to say that you do not believe in advertising? Indeed! Soon you will be telling me that you do not believe in God." We were now, said Smith, in a "world where every prospect pleases and only the reluctant spender is vile." By 1928 it was estimated that $1,782,000,000 a year was being spent for advertising, which meant that $1 was being expended to educate consumers in what they might or might not want to buy for every 70 cents spent for all levels of education, from primary to university.

Claude Hopkins, the president of Lord and Thomas, in his 1923 book *Scientific Advertising* began, "The time has come when advertising in some hands has reached the status of a science." H. L. Mencken labeled advertising as "the most gorgeous development of imposture as a fine art that Christendom has ever seen. I speak of fine art in the literal sense—it enlists such talents as under a less pious civilization would be devoted to the confection of cathedrals and even perhaps masses."

Goods were sold not for quality and usefulness but "to titivate the essential monkey in us." Photographs were skillfully contrived to make the consumer want the product in order to appear young, exclusive, socially or sexually desirable and, most important of all, to keep up with the Joneses. Advertising copywriters who played on prestigious urges were a new priesthood to what William James had aptly called "the bitch-goddess, Success." J. Thorne Smith wrote:

> With an accurate stroke, but with a perverted intent advertising coddles and toys with all that is base and gross in our physical and spiritual composition. The comforts and happiness it holds out to the reader are forever contrasted with the misery and misfortunes of another. Thus, if I ride in a certain make of motor I have the satisfaction of knowing that everyone who rides in a motor of another make is of a lower caste than myself and will certainly eat dirt for the rest of his life. Again, if I wear a certain brand of underwear, I have the satisfaction of knowing that my fellow-men not so fortunately clad are undoubtedly fouled swine. This is one of the most successful weapons used in advertising. It is a pleasure drawn from the same source that feeds so many people's sense of satisfaction when they attend a funeral or call on a sick friend.

When all is said and done, commented Stuart Chase, this much can be said in behalf of advertising, that it gives "a certain illusion, a certain sense of escape in the machine age. It creates a dream world: smiling faces, shining teeth, schoolgirl complexions, cornless feet, perfect fitting union suits, distinguished collars, wrinkleless pants, odorless breaths, regularized bowels, punctureless tires, perfect busts, shimmering shanks, self-washing dishes, backs behind which the moon was meant to rise."

Joseph Pulitzer, when he was actively running the New York *World*, once dictated to an editor working for him his concept of what a newspaper should contain to score with the public. "What is new, what is original, distinctive, dramatic, romantic, thrilling, unique, curious, quaint, humorous, odd, apt to be talked about without shocking good taste. . . ."

Notably lacking in this summary is any mention of what is socially important or what the public ought to know. This credo for success was applied with a vengeance by the press of the twenties which swelled with news of sex, violence, conflict, mystery, suspense, and the foibles of personalities.

The change in emphasis is shown in a survey comparing the content of 100 leading journals between 1893 and 1923:

> Editorials—minus 77 percent
> Letters to the editor—minus 80 percent
> General and political news—plus 1 percent
> Business news—plus 4 percent
> Foreign news—plus 9 percent
> Sports news—plus 47 percent
> Crime news—plus 58 percent
> Illustrations—plus 84 percent

The year 1923 was only the beginning of the Coolidge Era. After that, the papers became sated with news of sports and crime. A survey of papers in 1929 showed that the space devoted to sports ranged from 15 percent to 40 percent of total news coverage. Then, too, in the twenties there was a new type of newspaper, the tabloid, which frankly and unapologetically peddled thrills. The leading one was the New York *Daily News*, which soon had a circulation of 1,000,000, several times the circulation of the old standard papers. When in 1923 Thomas A. Edison deplored this trend, the *News* retorted editorially, "Newspapers print the news. That's why they're called newspapers. That part of the news happens to be scandalous is the fault of the people who make it, not the fault of the papers."

A leading educator, President Charles W. Eliot of Harvard University, died at the same time as Valentino, and some pointed out that for every line about Eliot in the papers, there were columns about the death and obsequies of the screen lover. The most respected American newspaper, the New York *Times,* devoted no fewer than fifteen pages to Lindbergh when he returned to New York and printed 22,000 words on two days of the Snyder-Gray murder trial in 1927.

Newspapers had become capitalistic enterprises, and there was little room for craftsmen and conscientious old-style editors, such as William Allen White and Josephus Daniels. In his obituary in 1925 of the publisher Frank A. Munsey, White wrote that he had contributed to journalism "the talent of a meat-packer and the manners of an undertaker. He and his kind have about succeeded in transforming a once-honorable profession into an 8 per cent security."

The leading columnist of the day was Arthur Brisbane, who wrote about 500,000 words a year, including his syndicated column "Today." He was the close associate and personal friend of William Randolph Hearst, and his views reflected those of the Hearst papers. He was an ardent exponent of capitalism and an equally ardent militarist.

When Brisbane became a personal friend of Hearst at the beginning of the century and they were both bachelors, he was filled with high ideals. Having imbibed Socialistic principles from his father, he was indignant about the exploitation of the masses. However, his economic views underwent a transformation when he accumulated wealth. He and Hearst made large sums of money in real estate ventures through the Hearst-Brisbane Properties, which built the Ziegfeld Theater and the Warwick Hotel in New York City in the twenties. In later life, as W. A. Swanberg wrote, "Money was so much on his mind that on meeting people for the first time, he would often say, 'I'm delighted to meet you, sir. Did you know that Hearst paid me

$260,000 last year?' He liked to make estimates of the millions he had made for Hearst."

A leading publisher in the twenties was the health addict Bernarr MacFadden, who for years had been putting out the highly successful magazine *Physical Culture*, in which he promoted his faddist ideas, such as living on five cents a day on a diet of watercress, crumbled oats, kidney beans, and dried peas, all washed down with water; standing on one's head not only to promote blood circulation but also to combat baldness; and sleeping on hard boards instead of mattresses (which his wife's biography revealed he never did). Living with Bernarr was a hair-raising experience as she described it—when she was five and a half months pregnant with her first child, he made her dive from a pier sixty feet into the English Channel to publicize his theory that pregnant women should not be coddled, and when the baby was three days old she was horrified to find him dipping it in ice-cold water. He himself was a great physical specimen, and at the age of eighty-three he jumped by parachute for the first time from an airplane.

MacFadden was a crackpot in his health ideas. However, like Henry Ford, he was aware of the free publicity that could be had by appearing to be a crank. Thus, when he walked barefoot twenty-three miles from his home in Nyack to Manhattan's Flatiron Building, it was for the benefit of photographers. He and Ford became personal friends, and they found a lot in common to talk about.

During the twenties, MacFadden launched an expansion program which brought him from 50,000,000 to 70,000,000 readers for his various publications. His *True Story* magazine, which gave a monthly prize of $1,500 for the best piece of fiction, was fabulously successful and soon outstripped the *Saturday Evening Post* in circulation. Although the stories had to be accompanied by affidavits that they were true, they were in fact written mostly by professional writers. He absorbed the magazine *Liberty,* making his protégé Fulton Oursler editor; the chief staff writer on foreign affairs was George Sylvester Viereck, who had been a German propagandist before our entrance into the war and who filled *Liberty* with pro-German views—former Crown Prince Wilhelm of Germany was the author of the first series of articles. There followed a forest of MacFadden magazines of the *True Story* caliber, such as *True Romances, True Ghost Stories, True Lovers, True Detective, Movie Weekly.*

MacFadden set New York on its ear when he started a daily newspaper, the flaming *Evening Graphic,* which was so smutty that it was dubbed the Daily Pornographic. It failed because MacFadden made the difficult mistake of pitching it too low. He tried to use it as a vehicle for his political ambitions, hoping that it would promote him to a new post in the Cabinet as Secretary of Health. The *Graphic* left its mark through the new personalities it brought to journalism—there was a young man hired to write about sports by the name of Ed Sullivan and a vaudeville hoofer who was hired to write a column about Broadway by the name of Walter Winchell.

Although it was fashionable to sneer at MacFadden, the other mass media magazines were not much better. The *Saturday Evening Post* was described by one critic as "artistically trite, intellectually puerile, socially conventional. The heroes of its stories are little more than modernized versions of Horatio Alger's paragons of Social Darwinistic virtues."

The greatest public appetite was for news about crime, particularly about murder. One big murder case followed another in the headlines. In December, 1927, an extremely vicious killing took place in Los Angeles. A nineteen-year-old discharged bank messenger, William E. Hickman, kidnapped twelve-year-old Marion Parker, the daughter of a bank officer against whom he had a grudge. After collecting a small ransom, he returned her dead, mutilated body. The identity of the kidnapper was established by fine detective work, and Hickman was arrested a few days later in Echo, Oregon. When he was apprehended, his first words, according to police, were, "Will I get as much publicity as Leopold and Loeb did?" referring to the sensational case of 1924, when nineteen-year-old Nathan Leopold, Jr., and eighteen-year-old Richard Loeb, sons of wealthy Chicago families, confessed to the thrill slaying of fourteen-year-old Bobby Franks.

Charles Merz, in an article in *Harper's* entitled "Wanted—Bigger and Better Murders," wrote:

207

Time was when the country had to wait for its great national murders until they actually occurred. Today if a really first-class murder does not come along after a decent interval of time, some second-class murder is taken by the hand, led to the center of the stage and advertised so successfully with all the modern art of ballyhoo that claiming to be a first-class murder it actually becomes one.

During the Hall-Mills murder trial in Somerville, New Jersey, in 1926, 5,000,000 words were transmitted over the wires in the first eleven days, making it the biggest story since the invention of printing. At the end of twenty-four days, 12,000,000 words had gone over the wires; this number, it was calculated, were enough to make a shelf of novels twenty-two feet long. The *Evening Graphic* gave a prize for the best letter on the solution of the crime, and the New York *Journal* polled its readers on whether the defendants were innocent or guilty. Those on trial were Mrs. Frances Stevens Hall and her two brothers, Henry and Willie Stevens, charged with the murder, four years before, of Mrs. Hall's husband, the Reverend Edward W. Hall and his mistress, choir singer Mrs. Eleanor R. Mills. They were acquitted, despite the testimony from a bed in the courtroom of the "pig woman," Jane Gibson, who claimed that she saw Mrs. Hall and Willie Stevens at the murder scene.

In the Snyder-Gray trial there were four rows of tables for the correspondents who had come from all over the nation, each row with ten tables and with three correspondents to a table. Among those who covered the proceedings were the novelist Mary Roberts Rinehart, the revivalist Billy Sunday, the moviemaker David Wark Griffith, the historian Will Durant, the adviser to the lovelorn Dorothy Dix, the churchman Reverend John Roach Straton, and the former wife of Rudolph Valentino, Natacha Rambova. The Reverend Aimee Semple McPherson, writing about it in absentia for the *Evening Graphic,* called on God to teach young men to say as a lesson from the case, "I want a wife like Mother—not a Red Hot Cutie."

What was the great fascination that the Snyder-Gray murder trial had for the public? Undoubtedly it was that this apotheosis of bourgeois murder was one that could happen in any household. Alexander Woollcott wrote that the case "held the country spellbound not because Mrs. Snyder was extraordinary but because she wasn't. Indeed she was so like the woman across the street that many an American husband was soon haunted by an unconfessed realization that she also bore an embarrassing resemblance to the woman across the breakfast table." Likewise, Damon Runyon wrote that "the thought of it probably makes many a peaceful, home-loving Long Islander of the Albert Snyder type shiver in his pajamas as he prepares for bed."

The trial started on April 26, 1927, in the Queens County Courthouse in New York City in a courtroom which was the largest in the nation. For the first time microphones were set up on tables and amplifiers on the walls to enable those present to hear all, but the apparatus did not work too well. Damon Runyon thus described the defendants for the New York *American:*

A chilly-looking blonde with frosty eyes and one of those marble you-bet-you-will chins and an inert scare-drunk fellow that you couldn't miss among a hundred men as a dead set-up for a blonde or the shell game or maybe a gold brick. . . .

She is not bad-looking. I have seen much worse. She is 33 and looks just about that, though you cannot tell much about blondes. She has a good figure, slim and trim with narrow shoulders. Her eyes are blue-green and as chilly-looking as an ice-cream cone. If all that Judd Gray says of her actions of the night of the murder is true, her veins carry ice water.

Gray was neatly dressed in a dark suit with a white starched collar and a subdued tie. He has always been on the dressy side, it is said. He wears big horn-rimmed spectacles and his eyes have a startled expression. You couldn't find a meeker, milder looking fellow in seven states, this man who is charged with one of the most horrible crimes in history.

Runyon commented on the fact that the trial was being covered by some philosophers.

I have been requested by my Broadway constituency to ascertain what if anything philosophy suggests when a hotsy-totsy blonde with whom a guy is enamoured tells him to do thus and so. But then a philosopher perhaps never gets entangled with blondes—or he wouldn't be a philosopher.

It was called the Dumbbell Murder. Early on a morning in March, 1927, the police were called to the home of Albert Snyder, art editor of the magazine *Motor Boating*, in Queens Village. In his second-floor bedroom they found Snyder dead, having been bashed over the head, chloroformed, and strangled with picture wire. The floors were strewn with pots and pans, the contents of bureau drawers, and an Italian newspaper torn into shreds. Mrs. Ruth Brown Snyder, the mother of their nine-year-old daughter, who had been sleeping in an adjoining room, claimed that she had been bound and gagged by burglars. There were no bruises on her body, no marks on her wrists, but there were specks of blood on her person. She was arrested immediately, and the next day her lover, Henry Judd Gray, a married traveling salesman of corsets, was taken into custody in Syracuse. His alibi, which he thought was airtight, was quickly smashed.

They confessed that together they had planned and committed the murder. His story went back to Eve—that she had enticed him into joining the plot. Lest one should think that she was a coldhearted murderess, this mark of gentility should be noted. When her confession was being read back to her, she was quoted as having said, "We discussed various ways of killing him." Upon hearing her words, she exclaimed, "I don't like that, it sounds so cruel." The deputy district attorney said, "Well, that's what you did, isn't it?" She replied, "Yes, but I would rather change that to 'getting rid of him.' "

Then she repudiated her confession and claimed that she had been coerced into the murder by Gray. "I know now that he is a coward, a low, cringing, sneaking jackal, the murderer of my husband, who is now trying to hide behind my skirts and who is trying to drag me down into the stinking pit that he himself willingly wallowed in. The women in his life! And he reads the Bible! What a fantastic lie!"

She tried to get a separate trial but in vain. His attorneys wanted a joint trial since they counted on the fact that no jury in Queens County had ever sent a woman to the electric chair.

An agent for the Prudential Insurance Company testified at the trial that Snyder had been tricked into signing a double-indemnity life insurance policy. He had been sold an endowment policy for $1,000, and he had been then asked to sign a blank policy as if it were a routine matter. It was a policy for $50,000 with double indemnity for violent death, which somehow came out to $96,000. Mrs. Snyder and the agent filled in the blanks afterward. She herself sent the checks for all the premiums, she instructed the company to address all the mail about the policy to her, and she told the mailman to deliver all the insurance-company mail to her personally.

Gray told substantially the same story in his police confession and on the stand. He had met Ruth for the first time in 1915, when he was escorting the girl he later married, and then met her again in 1925, when they became lovers. Their first tryst was on a hot night in the Bien Jolie Corset Company office on Fifth Avenue, and then they transferred their lovemaking sessions to the Waldorf-Astoria Hotel. She told him that she had tried to kill her husband seven times. "I think you're terrible," he chided her. She had twice opened up the gas in his bedroom, but he had both times risen and shut it off. She had once closed the garage door while the auto motor was running. She had twice put bichloride of mercury in his whiskey, but he had not drunk it because it tasted bitter. She had twice doped his medicine, but both times he had become sick and thrown it up.

She hounded Gray about helping her kill her husband. "With some veiled threats and intensive love-making she reached the point where she got me in such a whirl that I didn't know where I was at."

He bought an iron sash weight, which he delivered to her beforehand. On the night of the murder he arrived from Syracuse and went to her home, carrying with him chloroform, cotton waste, and an Italian newspaper he had picked up on the train. She let him in and secreted him in a room. She went to a bridge party with her husband where she persuaded him to swallow her drinks, as well as his own. They returned late and undressed for bed. When he was asleep twenty minutes, she went to the room where Gray was waiting, and they kissed. It was 3 A.M.

"She took me by the hand. She opened the door. I followed her." There was only an arc light in the corner of the room. He put on suede gloves and hit the sleeping Snyder with the sash weight wrapped in white paper. "He was apparently full of

211

fight. He got me by the necktie and a struggle ensued in which I was getting the worse, because I was being choked." In panic, Gray cried out, "Mommie, Mommie, for God's sake, help me." She took the sash weight and whacked her husband unconscious with it. They stuck the cotton waste up his nostrils and mouth; they tied his hands and feet; they buried his head and mouth in the pillow saturated with chloroform. Then she tied the picture wire around her husband's neck, and Gray pulled on it. They went downstairs and had a drink. She put his shirt and her nightgown stained with blood in the furnace and she gave him a fresh blue shirt belonging to her late husband. Then they set about to make it look like burglary.

On the witness stand Mrs. Snyder told a different story. She had fought to save her husband's life. She found Gray kneeling over Mr. Snyder, hitting him with the sash weight. She tried to drag him off, but Gray—pistol in hand—threatened to kill her if she interfered. "I was mortally afraid of him. I saw what a terrible man he was. I couldn't see any other way out than to do what he asked me to do."

Under cross-examination she admitted that she knew that Gray had come to kill her husband, but she nonetheless had let him in and had hidden him. She also admitted that she had joined in the arrangements of the faked burglary.

In a play for sympathy, her lawyers put her nine-year-old daughter on the stand. In a tearful plea to the jury, her lawyer said, "Oh, the Sunday-school hymns taught to the little daughter! And the pretty lamp shades made by Ruth's own hands and the jars upon jars of preserves in the cellar!"

They both were sentenced to die in the electric chair. The verdict was unanimously upheld by the Court of Appeals. She was a Lutheran but turned Catholic after the trial, some said because Governor Alfred E. Smith was a devout Catholic and she believed that he would not permit a Catholic woman to die in the chair. Governor Smith listened stonily to the plea for clemency and then issued a statement that he had searched his conscience in vain for any extenuating circumstances.

She maintained the premiums on the policy on her husband's life to the very end. At her death a suit by her against the insurance company for the $96,000 which it refused to pay was still pending. She and Gray were executed at Sing Sing Prison at eleven o'clock on the night of January 12, 1928. She sobbed as she was strapped in the chair, "Father, forgive them for they know not what they do." The New York *Daily News* filled its entire first page with a photograph of Mrs. Snyder in the electric chair. It was a remarkable feat of photography snapped by a camera attached to the ankle of a reporter.

Chapter VIII

THE RULE OF MELLON

When Coolidge assumed the Presidency, he inherited Harding's Secretary of the Treasury, whose thinking on the paramountcy of business in American life was so close to Coolidge's that each became the activator of the other's mind, and it is hard to say in retrospect who was master and who was servant. Together they carried out policies based on the philosophy that what was good for American business was good for America.

In early 1921, when President-elect Harding was assembling his Cabinet in typical hit-or-miss fashion, Senator Philander Knox of Pennsylvania suggested that Andrew W. Mellon of Pittsburgh would make a fine Secretary of the Treasury. "Who is he?" asked Harding, and Knox, who was on Mellon's payroll as a legal counsel, replied, "He is a very wealthy man, but more than that, he is one of the greatest constructive economists of this century."

Harding was interested and, on checking, found that Mellon was indeed rich, the third richest man in the nation. Having been excellently shielded by his associates and the Pittsburgh press, Mellon was largely unknown. Even in the New York *Times* his name had been in print only in some lists of corporate directorships. Harding asked advice from his closest political associate, Harry M. Daugherty, who said, "I certainly do know of him." He had heard of Mellon as the fattest of the fat cats in support of the Republican Party in Pennsylvania. "If

214

there's one thing he knows, it's money. He will make for you the greatest Secretary of the Treasury since Alexander Hamilton."

Harding was skeptical that he could be confirmed without some fireworks in the Senate and was gratified that his name glided through quite easily. He had worked in obscurity, had no public record of any kind, and since he had lived in Pittsburgh, the label of Wall Street could not be fastened to his name. Mellon was to remain Secretary of the Treasury for eleven years, under Presidents Harding, Coolidge, and Hoover, and he was to become the dominant symbol of the marriage of high finance and government. Senator George W. Norris summed it up this way, "Three Presidents served under him."

Today the Mellon fortune is several billion dollars and ranks with the Rockefeller fortune as the greatest in America. It was launched by Thomas Mellon, born in 1813 to a family of Scotch-Irish Presbyterians from northern Ireland. He was graduated in law from the University of Western Pennsylvania, now the University of Pittsburgh, and early in his law practice, when he was thirty, had accumulated $12,000 from investments in the booming real estate of that area. In 1869, after a ten-year term as judge of the common pleas in Allegheny County, he founded the bank T. Mellon and Sons on Smithfield Street in Pittsburgh. When he turned the bank over to his sons, Andrew William and Richard, in 1882, his holdings were worth close to $100,000.

Andrew gave the date of his birth as 1855, which would have made him sixty-six at the time he became Treasury head, but he was probably older; earlier editions of *Who's Who in America* had listed his birth as 1852 and then 1854. He attended the University of Western Pennsylvania until a few months before graduation and then entered the bank. The son vastly increased his father's fortune and in that process played a considerable role in the building of industrial America.

His principle was to bet on a man with an idea. In a conference at the bank in 1889 Arthur Vining Davis, a young promoter, exhibited to him a light shiny metal in biscuit shape produced under a patent by Charles Martin Hall. Mellon, greatly impressed, advanced funds in return for stock. This was the beginning of the Aluminum Company of America. In

215

1895, Mellon lent money, in return for a stock interest, for the production of a silicon carbide made by fusing sand, coal, and coke under intense heat in an electric furnace. This was the beginning of the Carborundum Company. He developed oil properties around Pittsburgh which he had to sell out to the all-powerful Rockefeller, but in the new century he bought heavily into wells in the fabulous Spindletop area of Texas. This was the genesis of the Gulf Oil Company. Other ownership interests developed by Mellon were in the Standard Steel Car Company and the Koppers Company. He expanded the steel industry around Pittsburgh in conjunction with his friend Henry Clay Frick and made the Union Trust Company in Pittsburgh one of the most powerful banks in America.

His great passion had been the pursuit of wealth. When he was over forty-five and seemed a confirmed bachelor, he met on a ship bound to Europe twenty-year-old Nora McMullen and conducted an ardent courtship. In the divorce case in 1910 she filed a statement which read in part, "Nights that I spent in my baby boy's bedroom, my husband locked in his study nursed his dollars, millions of dollars, maddening dollars, nursed larger and bigger at the cost of priceless sleep, irretrievable health and happiness. Always new plans, bigger plans for new dollars that robbed him and his family of the time he could have devoted far more profitably to a mere 'Thank God, we are living.' " The girl from Hertfordshire, England, had a dream of improving the lives of the steelworkers, but he dismissed it, saying, "They are foreign, Huns and Slavs and such as that, and you can't do anything with them." She added, "The whole community spirit was as cold and hard as the steel it made and chilled the heart to the core." Now, with his children grown up, perhaps surfeited with money-making, Mellon was ready for a new challenge, in government service.

His reputation as a Merlin of finance was enhanced by his appearance. He was elegantly slender, painfully shy, "remote like the portrait of one's ancestor," and his face bore a look of faraway sadness. Even more than Coolidge he made silence a virtue. It was said that when they got together, they conversed in "unpregnant pauses." When he read a statement before a Congressional committee, he spoke so softly that his words could

216

hardly be heard. He was a worshiper of beauty, and in his Massa-chusetts Avenue apartment he was surrounded by paintings of the masters supplied by Joseph Duveen. The art works he collected made possible one of the nation's great cultural assets, his gift of the National Gallery of Art in Washington.

This was a face and dignity that inspired trust, one who seemed a selfless, public spirit, not an ogre of capitalistic greed. Yet there is no doubt that his philosophy of government was one-sided, and there still remain questions about whether he promoted his personal fortune while head of the Treasury.

Senator James Couzens of Michigan, the former Ford partner, was Mellon's great antagonist. The feud started in December, 1923, when Couzens wrote a letter to Mellon, a quite friendly letter he later insisted, in which he asked for "proof" for the Secretary's claim that high surtaxes on big incomes hurt productive enterprise by driving money into tax-exempt channels that would otherwise flow into investment in industry. The reply by Mellon was "resentful," and Couzens construed it as saying that such matters should be left to persons who understood them.

Couzens accused Mellon of trying to impose his views on the nation, while Mellon claimed that Couzens' big fortune was all invested in tax-exempt securities. In return, the Senator asked the Secretary, "So long as you have entered into the record of my securities, will you please tell me what your securities are, how much you own of them and how much you will benefit by the reduction of surtaxes as proposed by you?" Moreover, he said that Mellon money was invested in the Overholt distillery. Was money used for making industrial alcohol that undoubtedly ended up in bootleg whiskey preferable to money raised by tax-exempt bonds issued by states and municipalities for public improvements?

The battle was on, and in February, 1924, Couzens introduced a resolution for an investigation of the Bureau of Internal Revenue which the Senate approved. Couzens' obvious purpose was to embarrass Mellon; he hired an investigator, Francis J. Heney, recommended by anti-Mellon Governor Gifford Pinchot of Pennsylvania, and paid him out of his own pocket. Coolidge made a strong protest to the Senate about

217

what he construed as a personal vendetta. The press generally applauded, though the Democratic New York *World* said, "The utter disproportion of his rebuke to Congress and the gentility toward the Denby and Daugherty resignations [in the Teapot Dome scandal] is too startling. Mr. Coolidge is furiously angry at Senator Couzens because he has had to bottle up his anger at Senators Walsh and Wheeler." Administration pressure was effective in delaying the hearings. Senator James Watson, chairman of the committee investigating Internal Revenue, said, "I am no muckraker. I would rather pull a man out of the mud than push him into it." Couzens suddenly became ill and was taken to Johns Hopkins for an operation.

The investigation did not begin until November 20, and the probe got scant attention in the press, although the testimony was to spread over 4,500 pages in eight volumes.

The Bureau of Internal Revenue filed a suit for a $10,000,000 tax deficiency against Couzens based on his sale of his Ford stock, a suit which Couzens won years later in the Board of Tax Appeals. Couzens claimed that it was a revenge action, pure and simple, by Mellon, and that Mellon tyrannically acquired immunity from printed criticism since it was an easy matter for him to levy a million-dollar tax assessment on any offending newspaper.

Through the years, Couzens maintained his offensive against Mellon, publishing figures on tax refunds that had been granted by the Treasury to large corporations, many of them to Mellon corporations, such as the refund of $3,996,000 to Gulf Refining and $15,589,000 to the Aluminum Company of America. Couzens claimed that Mellon's personal beliefs had become the guiding principles of the Treasury and that 25,000 lawyers, accountants, economists, and tax experts, many of them former bureau employees, were engaged by business in recasting and resubmitting tax returns in order to recoup money already paid to Uncle Sam.

The widest channel for refunds was through tax amortization. If a company built facilities that were useful only for war, then it could avail itself of the quick write-off that would reduce its taxes. It was strange, said Mellon critics, that companies which claimed that facilities were useful only for war production spent a lot of money after the Armistice to complete them. It was also strange that companies such as the Aluminum Company of America should be allowed to use as a test year for peacetime production the depression year of 1921; in 1923 production of aluminum was twice that of 1921.

There were other allowances that resulted in tax refunds. One was the depletion allowance for oil, then called the discovery depletion. The bureau also allowed refunds on the ground that executives should have been more highly paid or allowed companies to inflate their assets, since they were allowed a deduction of 8 percent of invested capital. Couzens claimed that the amount of tax refunds to business in Mellon's regime was more than $2 billion. The exact figure appears to be $1.271 billion, which is high enough for those times. Nowhere was Mellon more vulnerable than in the question of how far his own companies profited by favoritism. Couzens dug up a notation by a bureau employee on a file of the Standard Steel Car Company, "This is a Mellon company." It was claimed in Mellon's behalf that this was made by a young eager beaver who was anxious to ingratiate himself with the boss.

It would have been virtually impossible for Mellon to divorce his actions as an officer of government from an impact on his own wealth, and in fact, he took no real steps to effect such a divorce. When he was reappointed by Hoover, he testified before the Senate Judiciary Committee: "Before I took office in 1921, I resigned every office I then held in any corporation and resigned all my directorships. I sold every share of stock I held in any national bank, trust company or other banking institution. I then owned and I now own a substantial amount of stock in the Gulf Oil Corporation, the Aluminum Company of America, Standard Steel Car Company and other business corporations but in every case my holding is very much less than a majority of the voting stock of such corporations. My active connection with them was severed in 1921 as completely as if I had died at that time."

All of which begs the question. He did remain a stockholder of giant corporations, and his holdings, though less than a majority, may have been the *controlling* interest.

The cornerstone of his program was the reduction of taxes

on the rich. In addition to his claim, challenged by Couzens, that a reduction of surtaxes would benefit the economy and ultimately profit the government by inspiring business, he wanted estate taxes reduced, because, as he explained in a letter to Coolidge in 1924, when they are coupled with inheritance taxes imposed by states, "the need to raise cash results in forced sales and a general lowering of values upon which the credit structure of the country is based."

He was not interested in the reduction of taxes on small incomes. Once he testified against the removal of taxes on incomes under $5,000, saying, "Nothing brings home to a man the feeling that he personally has an interest that government revenues are not squandered but intelligently expended as the fact that he contributes a direct tax however small to his government." The Omaha *World-Herald* found the logic faulty. Since only about 2,500,000 people paid any federal income taxes, it followed under the Mellon logic that "the other one hundred and ten million must be classified as without a country."

There was an outcry against the Mellon program from labor and farm groups. Senator Robert M. La Follette, Sr., said, "Brazenly and impudently, Secretary Mellon has laid down the rule that wealth will not and cannot be made to bear its full share of taxation. He favors a system that will let wealth escape." Mellon said in reply, "I have never viewed taxation as a means of rewarding one class of taxpayer or punishing another." None of the three Presidents in whose administrations he served gave him fuller support than did Coolidge who announced that he would back the Mellon program to the hilt.

Mellon was immediately successful in securing in 1921 the abolition of the excess profits tax which had been enacted as a war measure, but he had difficulty in getting a balky Congress to agree with his program of cutting taxes on the rich. Congress would consent only to reducing the surtax on the highest incomes from 65 percent to 50 percent. In 1924 he was confident that his program would go through. However the opposition was stronger than expected. The surtax rate was reduced to 40 percent, but the estate tax rate was increased to 40 percent from 25 percent, and a gift tax was added, as was a provision for making income tax payments public, a step which greatly displeased

Mellon. The figures for 1923, released in 1924, showed John D. Rockefeller, Jr., with the highest tax of $7,435,000, then Henry Ford with $2,457,000, Edsel Ford with $1,984,000, and Mellon himself with $1,173,000. A commentary on relative rewards in our society was that the most successful writer, Mary Roberts Rinehart, paid $42,000 in taxes.

In the Presidential campaign of 1924 Coolidge left no doubt that he would interpret a victory as a mandate for the Mellon program. His overwhelming triumph was regarded as a vote of confidence by the nation in Mellon, as well as in Coolidge. Senator Watson announced, "The country believes Mr. Mellon is the greatest financial genius in many years. The people believe in him." Coolidge decided that the tax program should be postponed from the short session starting in December, 1924, to the long session of the newly elected Congress starting in December, 1925.

Meanwhile, a great publicity and propaganda campaign in behalf of the Mellon program flooded all the channels of communication. It emanated from the Chamber of Commerce in Washington, from every local Chamber of Commerce, from every trade association, from the American Taxpayers' League, from city and rural banks. It was so effective that a *Literary Digest* poll showed that the people believed that the prosperity of all was advanced by cutting the taxes on the rich. When Congress was assembled in December, 1925, support for Mellon was as freely given by the Democrats as by the Republicans. Mellon actually had to prevent Congress from enacting deeper cuts than he proposed.

In the Senate only two Democrats voted against the new tax law. On February 26, 1926, with Mellon standing proudly beside him, Coolidge signed the bill, the greatest achievement of his administration. The top surtax rate was cut to 20 percent. An income of $1,000,000 dollars, which was taxed $663,000 in 1920, was now taxed under $200,000. The estate tax was reduced to 20 percent, and the gift tax was repealed, thus indirectly lowering the estate tax. The publicizing of tax returns was also repealed.

Income taxes were low or nonexistent for most of the population. The rate of normal tax on the first $7,500 of income was

1.5 percent, with an exemption of $1,500 for a single person and $3,500 for a married person. A married man with a $7,500 income probably paid no more than $60.

The encomiums lavished on Mellon grew more fulsome than ever. The *Saturday Evening Post* said, "Admitting the genius of Hamilton and the value of his constructive work on the rudimentary governmental financial system," no Secretary "was so completely the master of finance as Mellon, nor was there any who had problems one-tenth the size and complexity of his problems"; Mellon was the greatest, *including* Alexander Hamilton. Mellon publicly depreciated these plaudits. At a dinner of Columbia alumni in honor of Alexander Hamilton he said, "I think that each successive Secretary of the Treasury at some time during the incumbency of his office enjoys the distinction of being the 'greatest Secretary of the Treasury since Alexander Hamilton'; however he goes out of office and his glory has departed." Mellon showed uncanny prevision; in the future his career could be summed up as *sic transit gloria*.

Mellon's financial wizardry was vastly exaggerated. Tax reduction and debt reduction were possible not because Mellon was a genius but because war taxes were continued for some time after the war, while military expenditures were drastically reduced. The surplus increased as prosperity brought in greater revenues, particularly from corporations. In the 1926 Revenue Act, which slashed surtaxes on individual incomes, the corporation income tax was actually raised from 12 percent to 13½ percent, though by the Mellon logic, which he applied to personal incomes, this would cut the amount of money flowing directly into industrial production.

Between 1923 and 1929, the years of the Coolidge administration, the public debt was reduced from $22.3 billion to $16.9 billion. The figures are puny in today's terms, but then we are talking of a bygone age. (For purposes of comparison, the interest charge alone on the public debt today amounts to $14 billion yearly, more than four times the cost of the entire federal government in Coolidge's day.) In 1923 expenditures were $3.294 billion, and in 1929 they were $3.298 billion. During an expanding economy Coolidge successfully kept government expenditures down. Thus, in 1927, Interior Secretary Hubert

Work wrote the President that between June 20, 1923, and April 30, 1927, the number of employees of the Interior Department was reduced from 14,247 to 11,365. More than lip service was given to economy in the Age of Coolidge. (In the same letter Work advised Coolidge that the average salary in his department was $2,000.)

Mellon was the Rock of Gibraltar in the administration and an important reason for the general confidence in Coolidge. Mellon was unfailingly bullish on business prospects, always implying that the rosy future flowed from the wisdom of his fiscal policies. In the 1928 Presidential campaign, Mellon spoke in these words: "In no other nation and at no other time in the history of the world have so many people enjoyed such a high degree of prosperity. . . . Productive business by being freed of oppressive rates has taken out of a strait-jacket and permitted to expand in an orderly manner unhampered by artificial restraints."

Although he was in his mid-seventies, Mellon was appointed Treasury Secretary under Hoover, but his path now became progressively more rocky. Hoover did not repose the same confidence in him as did Coolidge, relying increasingly on the Undersecretary, Ogden L. Mills. Then came the Crash, and the man who had hitherto been considered sacrosanct was now assailed as the symbol of the diabolism of the Republican business regime. Senator Joseph T. Robinson of Arkansas, Democratic minority leader, in a Senate speech said, "Whatever causes contributed to the trouble, it must be admitted that the present Secretary of the Treasury, the greatest since Alexander Hamilton, we are told, nor any other leader or agent of the Administration, took adequate steps to prevent the collapse, which they should have known must follow the orgy of speculation stimulated by their utterances."

Criticism increased. Democratic Congressman Wright Patman brought impeachment proceedings, based on Mellon's huge stockholdings and the actions he had taken to favor his own companies. Mellon said he would continue in office despite the attacks. "As Benjamin Franklin said, 'I am deficient in the Christian virtue of resignation.' " However, soon thereafter he departed for the honorific post of ambassador to the Court of

St. James's. The New Deal further marred his image. It was claimed that he had hired the brightest men in Internal Revenue to serve as his personal tax counsel and devise tax-avoidance schemes such as organizing dummy corporations. He was sued for $3,000,000 in back taxes. His case was presented to a grand jury which refused to indict him, and after some furor it ended in his exoneration. But "the greatest Secretary of the Treasury since Alexander Hamilton" had become a sorry jest, the relic of a shattered era.

A lasting contribution made by Mellon was the construction of magnificent federal buildings in Washington and over the country. By a paradox, Mellon proposed this as an economy measure.

During the Coolidge administration a $250,000,000 program for constructing federal office buildings was launched. This resulted in the imposing row of buildings in Washington in what is known as the Federal Triangle, between Pennsylvania and Constitution avenues. The first to be erected, the new Commerce offices, was completed about the time of Hoover's inauguration. The government in Washington and elsewhere had previously lodged its bureaus mainly in privately owned buildings. The genesis of the new program was in a letter that Mellon sent to Coolidge on June 2, 1925. In the long run, Mellon wrote him, it would be much cheaper for the government to have its own buildings. When the government rents commercial space, there enter local and state taxes that the federal government does not have to pay on its own property, interest on the investment in excess of what the government has to pay on its borrowings, and a profit to the owner, and also because of the characteristics of dealing with the government, "the owner generally wishes to add something for nuisance value." Coolidge used these arguments of Mellon (except for the one about nuisance value) in recommending the new building program to Congress, which approved it.

If Mellon's influence was strong in national policy, he dominated Pennsylvania politics. The Progressive Governor Gifford Pinchot was not his man, but the two United States Senators,

David Reed and George Wharton Pepper, did what Mellon told them to do. In May, 1926, Pepper, distinguished-looking and unctuous, ran for another term in the Republican primary, tantamount to election in then rock-ribbed Pennsylvania. His opponents were Pinchot and William S. Vare, a ward heeler who had become Republican boss of Philadelphia. Pepper ran largely by parading his friendship with Coolidge, obviously hoping that Coolidge's great popularity would rub off on him. Vare ran as a wet.

In a surprise result, Vare won with something to spare. The dry vote had been split between Pepper and Pinchot, but the main factor was the huge majority which Vare rolled up in Philadelphia, where the vote total for Pepper and Pinchot was zero in many so-called zero precincts. Senator James Reed of Missouri headed a Congressional investigation of the primary after charges of voting fraud and whispers about how much the campaign had cost. Reed found that Pepper, who had been financed by Mellon, had spent $1,086,000, more than the Democratic National Committee had spent in the Presidential campaign of 1924, and that in Pittsburgh the Pepper forces had hired one out of every four voters as poll watchers, paying men $10 and women $5 for their services. Vare had spent $605,000— an amount which, if laid end to end in dollar bills, would almost reach from Philadelphia to Washington.

Vare won easily, as was expected, against his Democratic opponent in the November elections. However, when he presented himself to take his seat in the Senate in December, 1927, he was barred pending further study of the amount spent to win the nomination, although the sum was far less than Pepper's. At the same time, the Senate in a striking exhibition of chastity in politics, the likes of which it has not displayed since, also prohibited Frank H. Smith from taking his seat as Senator from Illinois, both because of excessive campaign expenditures and because as chairman of the Illinois Commerce Commission he had received $158,000 for his campaign from Samuel Insull, the Chicago utilities king. Insull, a generous contributor to both Republican and Democratic candidates, was compared to Jay Gould, who once said, "In a Democratic district, I am for the

Democratic candidate, in a Republican district, I am for the Republican candidate—but always I am for Jay Gould."

A close friend of Mellon from Pennsylvania enters the picture. Joseph Grundy was the pet abomination of the liberals in Congress. The multimillionaire sixty-seven-year-old president of the Pennsylvania Manufacturers' Association was the dean of high-tariff lobbyists and had been the Moses of the movement ever since the Dingley Tariff of 1897. Said the New York *Times,* "He is a bachelor and taking the place of wife and children is the doctrine of protection of American industry." At a committee hearing Grundy once exhibited a stock of goods needing protection, which Senator Norris called "Grundy's Main Street Piggly-Wiggly Store." Norris said in disgust, "I think we ought to give Grundy and his crew a few sawed-off shotguns like the Chicago bootleggers. If they killed each other off it would not be bad for the consumers."

In the hearings of 1929, leading up to the passage of the Hawley-Smoot Tariff, Grundy was hyperactive. Before the Caraway Committee investigating lobbying activities, Grundy was, to quote the *Christian Science Monitor,* "most startling and fantastic" in his frankness. He had raised $700,000 to elect Coolidge in 1924 and $547,000 to elect Hoover in 1928, and those contributing expected results for their money. Small "backwoods commonwealths" of the West should hold their peace since they "have no chips in the game."

GRUNDY: It was a great mistake each state was given two senators.

CARAWAY: When it comes to the interests of Pennsylvania, the people of Idaho ought not to say anything?

GRUNDY: They ought to talk darned small.

WALSH [of Montana]: How would you silence Borah and myself?

GRUNDY: Your own intelligence would suggest silence in such matters.

The Senate had hardly recovered when it got a real jolt. Vare had just been excluded for good from the Senate. Now Governor John S. Fisher of Pennsylvania, a Mellon man who had succeeded Governor Pinchot, made an astounding choice to fill the vacancy, none other than Mr. Grundy.

A few Progressives howled. Senator Norris said that the appointment was "a stench in the nostrils of all honest men" and that Fisher "has disgraced the office he holds." Senator Gerald Nye said that Grundy had got the seat at "an auction sale." There was adverse newspaper comment, the Raleigh *News and Observer* saying, "Pennsylvania has sent some very bad actors to the Senate. But it has never before sunk so low as to elevate the chief lobbyist who has no higher moral perceptions than to avow that he spent months in Washington to see that contributors 'got their money back' and then some."

However, it is a revealing commentary on the regnant spirit of the times that Grundy was seated with so little public commotion, and even with some commendation. In a rebuke to traitors such as Senator Norris, the Indianapolis *Star* said, "His reputation will be enhanced by comparison with the Progressive stalwarts from those 'backward' states whose political amnesia has caused them to forget that they were elected on a Republican ticket." The New Haven *Journal-Courier* said, "Grundy's philosophy possesses the merit of being brazenly sincere."

In the Depression years ahead, "Grundyism" was to become an epithet on the same level as "Hooverism."

Speaking to the American Society of Newspaper Editors in January, 1924, President Coolidge said, "After all, the chief business of the American people is business. They are profoundly concerned with producing, buying, selling, investing and prospering in the world. I am strongly of the opinion that the great majority of the people will always find these are moving impulses of our life." Speaking to the New York Chamber of Commerce in 1925, he said that American business "rests squarely on the law of service . . . reliance on truth and faith and justice . . . in its largest sense it is one of the great contributing forces to the moral and spiritual advancement of the human race."

Business was the *summum bonum* in our society. Glen Buck wrote in *This American Ascendancy* that "I am convinced that almost the finest achievement of mankind is the very tangible thing which we call *American Business*."

The press had done an about-face, abandoning its muckraking stand of the early century for a fond adoration of business and leading businessmen. Suddenly, John D. Rockefeller, who had been vilified for years, was revered as a second St. Francis of Assisi. In *Nation's Business*, Merle Thorpe wrote, "I'll stake my reputation on the belief that half of our richest men do not know what they are worth—nor do they care. Their zeal is directed toward achievement." (Rockefeller had a balance sheet of his wealth presented to him at the end of every day of his business life.)

Business "served" America. Said Mencken, "The Cult of Service is half a sop to conscience, half a bait to catch conies." Slick public relations experts contrived highfalutin soft soap to clothe the simple profit motive. As John T. Flynn conceived it, the chairman of a trade group which had got together to make a pact to maintain uniform prices would thus address it:

> Brothers, it must be clear to every monkey-wrench manufacturer present that the great vocation of making monkey-wrenches for this free people summons us to higher efforts of service. We want profit but there are things more sacred than profit. First comes our God, then our Flag. Then our monkey-wrenches. We must first make America monkey-wrench conscious. Then we must give her a monkey-wrench that represents the highest ideals of patriotism.

Although it is well known that many successful businessmen have often been unable to do more than write their names, business now received academic accolades. George F. Baker, the banker, gave $6,000,000 for a school of business at Harvard, and in granting the first degrees of Master of Business Administration to graduates, president Abbott Lawrence Lowell said, "By virtue of the authority delegated to me, I testify that you are well trained to enter upon one of the oldest of the arts and the latest of the professions." A profession!

In the *North American Review* for November, 1928, an article by Max McConn, the dean of Lehigh University, defended Greek letter fraternities as a "new instrument for learning." He said that most college students do not, and should not, seek old-fashioned learning. What undergraduates "admire and wish to emulate are those qualities of character and mind which make for practical 'success' in the world of business and organization, such moral qualities as the fighting spirit, the will-to-win, initiative and such intellectual capacities as are involved in meeting and dealing with other people." In the "mimic world" of college activities, of which fraternity life is a prominent part, "they have an almost perfect school for the 'go-getter.'"

Coolidge applied the word "spiritual" to American business. Thus, in a speech to the American Advertising Council, he put forth the idea that "advertising ministers to the spiritual side of trade." Before he became President, at a dinner of Amherst alumni, Coolidge said that "the man who builds a factory builds a temple, the man who works there, worships there."

An intimate connection between religion and business was often in evidence. The dean of the Divinity School of the University of Chicago said, "Business is the maker of morals. What else but business can make morality?" The most popular nonfiction book in 1925 and 1926 was *The Man Nobody Knows* by Bruce Barton, which sold Christianity by showing how much it resembled American business. Christ was pictured as a virile go-getting he-man of business, the first great advertiser, a premier group organizer, master executive, a champion publicity grabber. "He picked up twelve men from the bottom ranks of business and forged them into an organization that conquered the world. . . . Nowhere is there such a startling example of executive success."

The Metropolitan Casualty Insurance Company of New York issued to all its agents a handsomely illustrated booklet written for it by the Reverend Dr. S. Parkes Cadman, president of the Federal Council of Churches of Christ of America and a prominent radio personality. It read in part, "Moses was one of the greatest salesmen and real estate promoters that ever lived." On occasions when the Israelites became discouraged, "metaphorically they gave Moses the Ha! Ha! and not infrequently gathered behind the main tent and set up various gods and Golden Calves, all of which was nothing but studied efforts to avoid their responsibilities and cancel their contracts."

The New York *Sunday World* ran a success story about Fred F. French, a nationally known real estate operator, whom it quoted as saying, "The best example of a sales talk is the life of

Jesus Christ. He was the best salesman of his time. He said, 'Knock and it shall be opened to you.' What he meant was 'Keep knocking until the door is opened and if it isn't opened pretty soon, kick down the door!' That's my philosophy too."

Churches were bestowed the highest praise when they were said to be run on sound business principles. A donation to a church was, moreover, the soundest business investment one could make toward personal salvation. The Swedish Immanuel Congregational Church of New York gave those who contributed $100 or more to its building fund an "engraved certificate of investment in the preferred capital stock of the Kingdom of God," and a church billboard in New York read, "Come to Christian worship and increase your business efficiency."

In John Dos Passos' *U.S.A.*, the office of the stockbroker exuded a religious atmosphere to Margo Dowling. "It always affected Margo a little like a church, the whispers, the deferential manners, the boys quick and attentive at the long black-broad marked with columns of symbols."

There was nothing particularly spiritual about the way the buccaneers in the world of finance frantically chased the dollar in that era.

On the New York Stock Exchange the wild boom was assisted by manipulators such as William Crapo Durant of General Motors fame. There was Arthur W. Cutten, described by Dana L. Thomas in *The Plungers and the Peacocks* as "a mild man with rimless glasses who looked like a high school teacher of biology and who had taken millions out of the Chicago grain pits." There was Jesse L. Livermore, the former boy wonder, King of the Bears, who as the twenties opened was fortyish but looked twenty years younger and who betrayed his inner tension only by "polishing off expensive cigars at a furious pace. He wore luxuriously tailored suits, liked his women and kept several of them in villas around the world. He drove a Rolls-Royce painted a gleaming yellow, wenched and fished and drank heavily aboard his yacht during the intense nervous spasms away from work that he called vacations." There was Michael J. "Mike" Meehan, "a short, tubby, explosive Irishman with rimless glasses and fluffy red hair," who met all the leading men of finance as manager of McBride's theater ticket agency in New York, a career he abandoned to become a broker on the Curb Exchange and to open a highly successful brokerage service aboard ocean liners.

As Thomas said, Durant and his associates played on the great bull market "like an artist on a pipe organ, pulling out the stops here, pushing them in there, providing a caressing legato and a booming crescendo there. They had a whole society under the touch of their fingers. Not just a few speculators but a whole nation responded to their tunes."

The manipulators rode up the prices of stocks in spectacular runs, pulling in the general public, squeezing out the shorts, and then unloading when the price was right. Joyrides occurred in stocks such as International Nickel, American Smelters, and Baldwin Locomotive. A stock of the twenties which seemed to have been atom-fueled was Radio Corporation of America, the super glamor stock, which rose from $7 a share in 1924 to more than $500 (taking splits into account) in 1929, without ever paying a dividend. A pool headed by Meehan pushed the stock up by buying and selling to one another—this churning activity was clearly evident since the floating supply was only 400,000 shares, the rest being corporately held, and yet the turnover often amounted to 500,000 shares a day. Since the stock seemed grossly overpriced, many traders sold the stock short, and when Meehan cornered the floating supply, the shorts had to pay through the nose to cover. This helps explain how shares jumped sixty points in four days of trading in March, 1928, during which Meehan's pool extracted $5,000,000 from the public.

The stock rigging was exposed in a Congressional investigation in the early days of the New Deal, between April and June, 1933, with Ferdinand Pecora as counsel, and the resulting outcry facilitated the enactment of the Securities and Exchange Act of 1934, which established the Securities and Exchange Commission. The investigation uncovered stories such as that of the Kolster Radio Company, whose drop in earnings in 1928 worried its directors about the price prospects of its stock. They hired a man named George Breen and gave him options to buy the stock at a low price. His job and his personal incentive were to persuade the public to buy Kolster. A publicity expert got $40,000, and financial newswriters, even those on the most reputable papers, were induced to publish favorable reports on Kolster's prospects. The stock was churned; the public became interested. The price rose from $74 to $95, and then the insiders sold out. In December, 1929, the price had fallen to $6 a share, and the next year the company was in receivership. Breen admitted a personal profit of $1,351,152.50. Even more spectacular was the market operation in the stock of the Anaconda Copper Company, which was run up in price from $60 to $135.

Richard Whitney, president of the New York Stock Exchange (who later was sent to Sing Sing for larceny of a customer's account), defended as "an absolutely usual and customary method of merchandising and distributing securities" the practice by underwriting groups of "pegging" the price, purchasing stock while a sale was going on to the public without letting the public know about it and then "pulling the plug" when the securities had been unloaded. The subsequent drops were often disastrous to investors.

Most illuminating was the testimony about the National City Company, an affiliate of the National City Bank of New York. In a sizzling sales operation, it specialized in stock of the National City Bank. Prospects culled from automobile registrations, tax lists, and the like were forwarded to the sales staff in seventy districts over the country. Salesmen were stimulated by contests and prodded by bulletins, such as one entitled "Loaves from Crumbs," which advised them how to persuade clients with small balances in their accounts to buy National City Bank stock by adding cash. "If you will continue this practice, it will not be long before each client and you will be agreeably surprised by the shares of the National City Bank that he will have accumulated."

Stockholders were not "agreeably" surprised when the price of the stock fell from $575 to $25 a share. Edgar D. Brown of Pottsville, Pennsylvania, told how he had accumulated $100,000, which he entrusted to the National City Company for investment. Somehow he was switched from gilt-edged bonds to stock purchases, and his account started to churn at a furious pace. When National City Bank stock fell to $525 in September, 1929, he wanted to sell out, but terrific pressure was put on him by the sales staff to hold. However, when the price fell to $320 two months later, the company sold his stock without notice or ceremony to protect a loan it had made to him to buy more stock, leaving him penniless. As he wrote them, "I am now 40 years of age—tubercular—almost totally deaf—my wife and family are depending on me solely and alone, and because of my abiding faith in the advice of your company I am today a pauper."

The officers of National City did not suffer. The bank lent $2,400,000 to its officers to protect their holdings in the Crash, without interest and usually without any security. By 1933 only 5 percent had been repaid. This largess did not extend to employees of lower rank who were forced to meet installment payments on stock now selling at a fraction of the buying price. The salary of Charles E. Mitchell, head of National City Bank, was actually raised during the Depression year of 1931 from $100,000 to $200,000. He had an income in 1929 of $4,000,000 but paid no tax, claiming a loss on sale of securities to "personal" or "family" corporations. Criminal prosecution for tax evasion failed of conviction, but $700,000 was recovered from him in a civil suit by the government.

In April, 1932, the nation was shocked by the news that the great electric power king of the twenties, Samuel Insull, was forced out of his companies by bankers representing creditors. His empire was bankrupt: the Insull Utilities Investment Fund had total liabilities of $253,984,000 and assets of $27,473,000; the Middle West Utilities Company had no assets to cover preferred and common stock carried at a book value of $220,924,-000; the Corporation Securities Company had total liabilities of $142,374,000 and assets of $13,146,000.

How could this have possibly happened? Financial expert N. R. Danielian, writing in "From Insull to Injury," said:

> The Insull holding company structure was a skyscraper of many floors. The income-producing properties rested in the cellar; the floors above were occupied by various gradations to the top. It has now been revealed that not only were the top floors vacant but all others occupied by fictitious legal personalities. When creditors forced their way into Insull's labyrinthine corporate structure,

233

they found literally nothing more than empty desks and stacks of account books.

This had been hidden from view for years by feats of financial impressionism, said Danielian:

Like a Moslem minaret during Bairam, the turret was lighted up with colorful lanterns and occasionally a fanatical high priest of finance proclaimed from the top the glories of Allah and the virtues of the prophet Insull.

Now 600,000 stockholders and 500,000 bondholders awoke to find that their investment in a growing industry, the backbone of the country, one which could not fail, had been wiped out. For many their life savings were gone, and they were destitute.

The seventy-three-year-old Insull fled to Canada and from there to Paris while the papers here were filled with news about investigations. During the 1932 Presidential campaign, candidate Franklin D. Roosevelt castigated Insull by name as a malefactor of the old regime. "The Ishmael or Insull whose hand is against every man." In October the absent Insull was indicted by a Cook County, Illinois, grand jury. He fled to Italy and then took a plane to Salonica, Greece. He was indicted by the federal government for using the mails to defraud and for violation of the bankruptcy laws. Greece had had no extradition treaty with the United States, but an extradition treaty was agreed upon. However, the Greek courts refused to give up Insull under the treaty for offenses which were not offenses under Greek law. Throughout the year 1933 all efforts to get Insull out were unavailing.

The State Department under orders from President Roosevelt made things as uncomfortable as possible for Greece, going so far as to prevent private groups from sending funds there. While the nation still refused extradition, it did order Insull out of the country by January 1, 1934, whereupon he chartered a Greek vessel to cruise the eastern Mediterranean while he pondered where he could find haven and whether he might not make an excellent Rumanian minister of electric power. Congress rushed through a law permitting Insull to be seized by any United States officer in a country in which we had extraterritorial rights. His ship put in at a Turkish port for provisions; he was arrested by Turkish officials, given a kangaroo trial, and turned over to a State Department officer, who put him on board the S.S. *Exilona* bound for New York. Withered and wan, the former magnate arrived in May, 1934, to be greeted by a horde of newsmen and the glare of flashlight bulbs. He was whisked by car to Chicago and lodged in the Cook County jail like a common criminal.

In October he was put on trial in federal court on a charge of using the mails to defraud. By this time a considerable amount of sympathy had been generated for him as the "scapegoat for the sins of the era." He was acquitted, and charges against him failed in two other trials. In truth, recklessness in the world of finance had been commonplace; Insull had been only a mammoth operator. There were no adequate regulatory statutes on the books, and the charges brought against him were peripheral to the substance of the offense. He lived until 1938, when he died suddenly in a Paris subway station. How much he had salvaged of his own fortune is a matter of question, but it was not much.

Insull was born in 1859 in London, one of eight children of a couple fanatically devoted to the temperance cause. The boy was educated in a private school in Oxford, where his father had a job as secretary to the British counterpart of the Anti-Saloon League. At the age of fifteen he started his career as an office boy in a firm of auctioneers and there learned shorthand. When he was nineteen and chief shorthand clerk of the firm, he was fired and got another job by answering an advertisement in the London *Times* for a secretary to an American banker resident in London. This was an amazing break for Insull since the banker happened to be the European representative for Thomas A. Edison, who had just invented the electric light. Insull favorably impressed Edison's chief engineer, who came to London to supervise the installation of the first European telephone exchange, and this led to his appointment as Edison's secretary and man Friday.

Insull arrived in America in 1881 at the age of twenty-one, a year before the first electric plant, the Pearl Street Station, was opened in New York City. Initially, Edison, then in his mid-thirties, complained of Insull's Cockney accent, but in time the inventor came to lean heavily on him. Insull took care of his mail, systematized his office, held his power of attorney, bought his clothes, and was his personal confidant.

Edison had been backed by a syndicate of bankers, including J. P. Morgan, and Insull gained his apprenticeship in finance from Edison's successful efforts to remain independent of his sponsors. When he was put in charge of the Thomas A. Edison Construction Company, which sold and built electric stations all over the country, Insull learned the first rule of finance: "Never pay cash when you can give a note."

After the initial surge that followed the Pearl Street Station there was a slump in electrical systems until 1885, when electric streetcar lines were opened in New Orleans and Minneapolis. By 1889 there were 154 such lines in operation, and electrification of buildings, principally office buildings, was making strides. Insull absorbed from Edison the principle of selling as cheaply as possible to attain the greatest market and to reap the profit on big volume. Edison proclaimed, "We will make electric light so cheap that only the rich will be able to afford candles." The price of electric bulbs was cut from $1 in 1888 to 44 cents in 1890 and then to 40 cents in 1897, and all the time the total dollar profit increased.

On July 1, 1892, Insull arrived in Chicago to take over the Chicago Edison Company with the help of a loan of $250,000 from Marshall Field. The city which was preparing for its world's fair the next year, the Columbian Exposition, had 1,000,000 inhabitants but fewer than 5,000 users of electric lights. Insull, adopting the lessons he had learned from Edison, set out to build his company with an aggressive sales policy of cut rates. For advertisement he gave bargain rates to the new Great Northern Hotel. In his first forty-two months in Chicago he increased sales volume from an annual 2,800,000, to 13,300,000 kilowatts. By 1907, when he combined Chicago Edison and Commonwealth Electric, the company was forty-two times larger than when he started. His was a daring spirit of innovation—he built the first huge generating plant in the nation with steam-electric turbines. He said, "In my business the best asset is a first-class junk pile."

In 1912 Insull started down the path of ruin by forming his

own holding company, the Middle West Utilities Company. The financial hocus-pocus began when Insull received $5,000,000 preferred stock and $7,000,000 common stock for assets that were hardly worth the amount of the preferred stock. The holding company was a device that made money almost effortlessly. It could milk the captive operating companies by charging them exorbitant amounts for financing and construction services.

The Insull empire rolled like an avalanche. From 1912 to 1927 the number of people living in electrically lighted homes rose from 16 percent to 63 percent of the population. The growth in the twenties was phenomenal; consumption more than doubled, from 43.3 billion kilowatt-hours to 96 billion between 1920 and 1929. The Insull interests included Commonwealth Edison, Peoples Gas, Public Service of Northern Illinois, and Middle West Utilities. Among them, they provided electricity and gas in 500 communities in thirty-two states. Insull had succeeded Charles T. Yerkes as a transportation magnate, owning elevated railways in Chicago and electric railways between Chicago and the suburbs. In all, the Insull interests were worth $3 billion.

His was a name to be conjured with. Forrest McDonald wrote in his authoritative biography:

> In the hero-worshipping postwar decade, Insull became the Babe Ruth, the Jack Dempsey, the Red Grange of the business world. The people—butchers, bakers, candlestick makers who invested their all in his stocks—fairly idolized him, and even titans viewed him with awe. He measured up to America's image of itself: a rich, powerful, self-made giant, ruthless in smashing enemies, generous and soft-hearted in dealing with the weak. His doings, large and small, became a great spectator sport, and they were reported and followed accordingly.

He became a friend of Presidents from McKinley on and pronounced all of them colossal bores with the exception of Theodore Roosevelt. He was paterfamilias to the thousands of his employees. His door was always open to them, but he would fire a man on the spot for failing to recognize and greet him. He was a patron of the arts in Chicago, and his name became synonymous with the Chicago Civic Opera. The directress, Mary Garden, resigned in a huff, accusing him of vulgarization

237

when he insisted on dropping her favorite French operas for German and Italian works because there were more Germans and Italians than French around Chicago. He built a new home for the opera on the ground floor of a forty-two-story office building, and when it was unveiled, it had an astonishing feature—there were no boxes where the grand ladies of Chicago's society could bask in the public eye.

As time rolled on, Insull became the prisoner, as well as the master, of the forces he had set in motion. As McDonald said, "Even as his grip on the reins of great and growing power had tightened, their grip on him had become inescapable. . . . His hands and the reins had become one; whatever happened, he could no more let go than they could slip loose."

Throughout the nation the utility holding company became the vogue, and one holding company was built on top of another. Since they operated in more than one state, they were free from the control of the state public utility commissions. The Insull Utilities Investments Fund (IUI) shot up from $12 a share in the beginning of 1929 to $150 by the summer, and Insull's personal fortune rose to about $150,000,000.

Insull had learned the uses of propaganda as head of the Illinois State Defense Council during the war, and he profited by this experience when he set up the Committee on Public Utilities Information. By the mid-twenties hating utilities was as rare as hating the flag and motherhood. He also had found that the best way to win friends for a cause was to get them to invest something in it, so he set about convincing the public, particularly his consumers, to buy stock in his companies, each of which had a security sales department. At the end of the war Middle West had 6,000 security holders, and ten years later it had forty times that many.

A Chicago investment house had a radio hour of semiclassical music which was interrupted for a talk by the Old Family Counsellor, who urged his listeners for their personal security to buy the safest possible growth stocks and bonds, which were, of course, Insull's. It was later revealed that the soothing voice belonged to a University of Chicago professor who was paid $50 a broadcast to read the script that was prepared for him.

Even hardheaded bankers thought Insull was a rosy investment. Insull's bookkeeper James McEnroe said, "The bankers would call us up the way the grocer used to call my momma, and try to push their money at us. 'We have some nice lettuce today, Mrs. McEnroe—we have some nice, fresh green money today, Mr. Insull. Isn't there something you could use—maybe $10,000,000?' "

The securities sold to the public in the holding company structure represented phony values. The investments, shuffled back and forth among the subholding companies at constantly rising values, were acquired by the superholding company at a grossly exaggerated price. Sometimes the parent company would buy properties and sell them to a subholding company, which, in turn, would sell preferred and common stock to the public. The preferred would be the equivalent of the cost of the properties and the common would be retained by the parent company, representing nothing but being carried on the books at a fictitious value. There were other malpractices—dividends were declared when there were no earnings; expenses such as those of organization were listed in the accounts as assets; capital was used to finance speculative undertakings, such as the refloating of bankrupt textile mills and real estate promotional schemes.

Insull did not fail because of the Depression, wrote Danielian. "Insull only failed in hiding any longer the lack of success in his financing activities." In 1930 and the early part of 1931 the utilities business of Insull enterprises actually boomed. He was in the forefront of rescue operations and gathered more than $50,000,000 to pay policemen and schoolteachers when Chicago hung on the lip of bankruptcy. He embarked on a large plant expansion program for his utilities. His Achilles' heel was that to raise money, with the stock market gone to pot, he had to resort to debt financing from banks, and he put up his stock as collateral. When the prices of the stock fell catastrophically and he could put up no more collateral, the game was up.

Chapter IX

THE SUPREME ILLUSION— THE NEW ERA

> No Congress of the United States, ever assembled, on surveying the state of the Union has met with a more pleasing prospect than that which appears at the present time. . . . The great wealth created by our enterprise and industry and saved by our economy has had the widest distribution among our own people and has gone out in a steady stream to serve the charity and the business of the world. The requirements of existence have gone beyond the standard of necessity into the region of luxury. Enlarging production is consumed abroad.
>
> The country can regard the present with satisfaction and anticipate the future with optimism.

Thus spake the prophet Calvin Coolidge, mantled in the public mind with omniscience and infallibility, in his final State of the Union message to the Congress on December 4, 1928. This date was one month after Herbert Hoover had been elected as his successor in the "prosperity election" of 1928. It was also only ten months before the great stock market crash of October, 1929, which would bring his era to a decisive close and usher in the blackest depression in American history.

Actually the economic situation at the time was not as rosy as Coolidge pronounced it. The country had recovered from a mild recession in 1927, but the indexes showed that the rate of expansion was slowing down. Moreover, there was an increasing number of sick sectors of the economy. A few weeks after the Coolidge address, Professor Wesley C. Mitchell, the foremost student of business cycles, concluded a massive study with these words: "Even on the face of affairs, all is not well. Americans have seen more fortunate times. . . . The conditions of agriculture, the volume of unemployment, the textile trades, coal mining, the leather industry, present grave problems not only to the people immediately concerned, but also their fellow-citizens. How rapidly these conditions will mend, we do not know. Some may grow worse." Yet at this time, with danger signals apparent, the greatest bullishness prevailed. The stock market soared to stratospheric heights, and business pundits joined in Bernard Baruch's prediction that we were on the verge of a "great forward movement." Secretary of Commerce Herbert Hoover said that the time was near when the poor-house would be only a remembrance of the past. Talk was rampant of perpetual and never-ending prosperity. What were the bases for this vision?

Industrial production had soared through the decade, and national income had increased from $59.4 billion in 1921 to $87.2 billion in 1929, all with remarkably little inflation. The wholesale price index had never fluctuated more than 10 percent. Unemployment for most of the decade was small. Workers had more to spend. As calculated by the University of Chicago economics professor Paul Douglas, the annual earnings of wage earners in terms of constant purchasing power was 8 percent above the 1914 level in 1921, 19 percent above in 1923, and 32 percent above in 1929.

In the shimmering vision, wages would keep on rising, and consumer demand, which would increase as living standards rose, would be enhanced by new technological developments for making life easier and more enjoyable. The radio and airplane were only tokens of what lay ahead. In a *Nation's Business* article, "This Amazing Decade," Merle Thorpe wrote: "The period just ended has leaped forward by arithmetical progression: 2, 4, 6, 8, 10. The high gear of our industrial machine will bring changes in the next decade by geometrical progression: 2, 4, 8, 16, 32. It is glorious to contemplate."

The class war concept which had poisoned relations between capital and labor abroad did not exist here. As George Soule explained:

> It was true that large profits were being amassed but they belonged not to the few but to the many because of the ever-widening participation in the ownership of American industry. Not only small businessmen and professional people but also the workers with their high wages were becoming partners in ownership and therefore a better kind of collectivism was being established without disturbing the freedom and efficiency of business.

Capitalism, the great creator, worked while Socialism did not, a fact which was abundantly proved by the backwardness of industry and the failure of the experiment in the Soviet Union.

Could there be any more convincing symbol of the future than the Kellogg-Briand Multilateral Treaty for the Renunciation of War, signed by sixty nations in 1928 and ratified by the United States Senate in January, 1929, the last major action of the Coolidge administration? During the entire life of man, he had been engaged in mutual slaughter and cannibalization, but now this all would come to an end. Reason would supplant madness, and the swords would be turned into plowshares.

Coolidge was hostile to expenditures on our armed forces because he couldn't see whom in the world we were going to fight and because such expenditures contravened his cherished economy program. The propaganda by the military to get more money from Congress was a nuisance. On one occasion he exploded at a press conference, "I don't know why it is, when other appropriations go through without any effort to alarm the country—the Post Office has an appropriation of over $750,000,000, I think, and it isn't considered necessary to resort to inflammatory statements to secure the passage of that bill— that it is supposed that the passage of the appropriation bills for the Army and Navy won't go through unless somebody asserts that the country is about to be engaged in war." There was a gust of laughter from the newsmen, and Coolidge resumed, "Well, I say that in all seriousness . . . you know the very alarming criticism that the press would make if anybody suggested

242

to men in the Army and Navy that they ought not to say things of that kind. It would be asserted on all sides that they were muzzled and that someone was trying to cut down their privilege of free speech and so on. I find in my own case that my privileges of free speech are a good deal curtailed because I am President."

In 1927 the appropriation for the Army, which numbered 119,000 men, was $300,000,000. Said Coolidge, "I suppose as long as we continue to spend $300,000,000 a year that the General Staff will be able to provide the nation with a fair degree of defense." An apocryphal query often attributed to Coolidge is: "If the military must have aircraft, why can't they buy a plane and take turns using it?" In September, 1924, the President declared to his press conference that the government was spending all of $32,174,000 for military aviation, "the largest amount that is expended by any government, with the possible exception of France."

The real budgetary problem was the Navy, which then had 75,000 men and maintained a very expensive fleet. Coolidge delayed construction of all but two of the eight 10,000-ton cruisers that had been authorized by Congress in 1925, each of which cost $16,500,000. However, work on two aircraft carriers, the *Saratoga* and *Lexington,* went on. When Coolidge became President, America had only one carrier, the converted battle cruiser *Langley,* which had a speed of fourteen knots.

The Navy people felt that part of the problem was that Coolidge was not Navy-minded. Perhaps it would help if he reviewed the fleet. Coolidge wanted to, but he had a weak stomach and was afraid of being seasick. His naval aide, Wilson Brown, persuaded him that if the *Mayflower* floated down the Potomac and anchored well inside the Virginia capes, there was very little chance of motion, and the fleet could parade by on its way to anchorage farther up Hampton Roads.

However, it did not work out according to plan. Weather conditions seemed favorable, but during the night a heavy ground swell began piling in through the capes, and when the *Mayflower* anchored, it had a roll. The President became seasick and stayed in his bunk all morning, protected from the newsmen who were being entertained elsewhere on the ship.

243

"When the flagship came into sight," recalled Brown, "a queasy Coolidge rose from his misery and his bunk and came to the bridge with binoculars and yachting cap. During a full half hour he posed for the photographers, looking sternly through the long signal glass pointing to each ship as she came abeam, returning salutes endlessly while trying to stand at attention and steady himself against the roll with his unengaged hand."

After the battleships had passed, Coolidge sank weakly into a sofa behind the afterdeck. Newsmen had been kept away, but a photographer slipped in when the commanding admiral came aboard, and he snapped a photograph of a grim-lipped, disconsolate President. Brown concluded his tale: "This rather comic picture was given greater publicity than any other. Calvin Coolidge never uttered one word of reproach to any of us for causing his embarrassment, but neither did he give any support to a naval building program."

In time Coolidge did alter his views. The event which brought about this change was the failure of the Geneva Disarmament Conference which opened in June, 1927, with the United States, Britain, and Japan as participants and France and Italy as observers. Hopes were high. The purpose was to put a limit on cruisers and destroyers as the Washington Conference of 1921 had put a limit on battleships and aircraft carriers. But it was soon evident that the United States and Britain had a fundamental difference of outlook.

The American negotiator, Hugh Gibson, wrote to Secretary of State Kellogg that his British counterparts were Navy men rather than diplomats. "The British delegation is so imbued with strictly technical admiralty doctrine that they cannot give weight to broader considerations." Kellogg wrote to Coolidge, "Either the British Navy has gone mad or Great Britain has felt compelled to continue shipbuilding to furnish employment." On July 25 Coolidge replied, "I must confess that it is very disappointing to have the British opinion revealed to us. In my opinion they are very short-sighted and cannot hope to secure any advantage by building a navy larger than ours. Of course, there is no other navy against which they need to build."

Japan was not seen as a threat by Coolidge or others, even though there were reports that she was building battleships and aircraft carriers in violation of the Washington Treaty and was fortifying the Caroline and Marshall islands in the Pacific. In the Geneva negotiations the Japanese representative said frankly that no treaty could be ratified in Japan that did not provide for parity with the United States and Britain.

A most interesting sidelight to the Geneva Conference erupted into the front pages in September, 1929, two years later. William B. Shearer, who was a big man with a big, booming voice, a self-proclaimed "American, Christian, Protestant and patriot," was well known as an exponent of a big Navy. He had brought suit, futilely, to prevent the scrapping of our battleships under the Washington Treaty and had been most visible in Geneva in 1927 during the Disarmament Conference, where he lived sumptuously and entertained lavishly. He had agitated against any agreement to limit navies, he had issued press releases in his cause, he had given technical data to both sides, and he had generally exacerbated relationships between American and British delegates. When asked who was financing him, he had said he was working for a Pittsburgh doorknob manufacturer, "because ships have doorknobs." Some English and European papers had hailed him as "the man who broke up the Conference."

Now, in the fall of 1929, Shearer brought suit against the Bethlehem Shipbuilding Company for $275,653 for services rendered to the satisfaction of his employers. The services, he claimed, were the wrecking of the Geneva Conference. Senator Borah indignantly called for a Congressional investigation, and hearings were held by a subcommittee of the Naval Affairs Committee. Charles M. Schwab, chairman of Bethlehem, said he did not know Shearer, but maybe "my boy, Grace," did. Eugene G. Grace, president, also denied knowledge of him. Finally, a vice-president, Samuel Wakeman, admitted he had hired Shearer, in a "damn fool decision. I was just jazzed off my feet by Shearer." It developed that Shearer had actually been hired not only by Bethlehem but also by the New York Shipbuilding Corporation and the Newport News Shipbuilding and Dry Dock Company and that he had been paid almost $50,000 previously by the companies.

Contrition was displayed, and explanations were voiced: "I

went along with the others," "I realize now it was a foolish thing to do," etc. They claimed that they had not even bothered to read Shearer's reports. Schwab avowed that he would gladly scrap his armor-plating and shipbuilding plants if it would bring peace on earth and he was really against such "interference" by Shearer.

Having fought the war to end wars, the civilized world in the twenties was engaged in the search for some formula for ending wars. In those times a contest was considered the way to find the right answer to anything, and the philanthropist Edward Bok offered a prize of $100,000 for the best plan. This created a good deal of commotion. There were 22,165 entrants, including Franklin D. Roosevelt and William Jennings Bryan. Solutions ran a wide spectrum. Some suggestions urged birth control and the division of wealth, and one elaborate idea was a system of music based on the theory that harmonious sound is a socially unifying agent. A committee of seven headed by Elihu Root awarded first prize to Charles H. Levermore, secretary of the New York Peace Society, for a plan entitled "Progressive Co-operation with the Organized World, Sustained by the Moral Force of Public Opinion," which basically called for our entrance into the League of Nations with reservations. Half the prize was to be given immediately, the other half to be given when the plan was put into effect or when there was "sufficient popular response." Mr. Levermore collected only $50,000.

As far back as 1919 a Chicago lawyer, Salmon O. Levinson, had started promoting the idea that war should be outlawed as an illegal method for achieving national ends—which would be contrary to the existing concept in international law, which recognized its legality. Levinson enlisted many people in his cause, including John Dewey and the Reverend John Haynes Holmes. The same idea was also pressed by Professor James T. Shotwell of Columbia, an adviser to Wilson in drafting the Versailles Treaty and now director of the Division of Economics and History of the Carnegie Foundation for International Peace. President Nicholas Murray Butler of Columbia in his frequent journeys to European chancelleries did valuable missionary work.

Some of the plan's greatest enthusiasts were, ironically, those who were actively opposed to every existing institution for the prevention of war. Thus, Senator Philander Knox backed it as an alternative to the League of Nations, as did that most energetic opponent of the League, the chairman of the Senate Foreign Relations Committee, Senator Borah.

On April 6, 1927, the tenth anniversary of our entry into World War I, the French Foreign Minister, Aristide Briand, made a proposal to the United States (purportedly written by Professor Shotwell) for the banning of war as an instrument of national policy between the two nations. This treaty would not provide for mutual assistance but would merely pledge the United States to stay neutral if France were involved in war with, say, Germany. France, stripped of the Russian alliance it had enjoyed before the war, was feverishly engaged in international diplomacy, and Briand felt that such a pact with the United States would enhance French prestige in Europe.

Secretary of State Frank B. Kellogg, a nervous man—Nervous Nellie he was called by former Senatorial colleagues—was described by associates as obstinate in the pursuit of a course of vacillation. He was swamped with telegrams and petitions backing the Briand plan, a great deal of support having been whipped up by public personalities interested in the cause, such as President Butler, Professor Shotwell, Jane Addams, Mrs. Carrie Chapman Catt, and Raymond Robins. An emotional factor was Lindbergh's flight in May of that year which had produced a great surge of rhetoric about the undying friendship between the United States and France.

Kellogg was unenthusiastic about the Briand proposal, well aware of France's ulterior motives in using it to play power politics in Europe. He also resented being pushed around by a "lot of damned fools," his characterization of the amateur diplomats. He took the matter up with Coolidge, who found this the first business after returning from his summer vacation. Coolidge raised the question of whether the constitutional provision giving Congress the power to declare war did not prevent any such international treaty, but Senator Borah argued that the peace pact would obviate the necessity for a declaration of war

247

hereafter. In a tentative mood both Coolidge and Kellogg decided to pursue the matter.

On December 22, Kellogg appeared before the Senate Foreign Relations Committee and discussed his answer to the Briand proposal. He had a mania for arbitration treaties, and he proposed to reply to Briand that in an arbitration treaty with France the preamble would call for "condemnation of war as an instrument of national policy." Borah asked, "Is that all that is to be done with the Briand proposal?" The white-haired Kellogg, flustered and uncertain, said, "I believe the preamble will be satisfactory to M. Briand." Borah growled, "I can't feel that that is all that ought to be done with it. I feel that it ought to be treated as a separate, independent proposition. Moreover, it ought to be extended to all nations because an outlawry of war pact with France alone implies a willingness to fight others." Other Senators joined Borah. Borah told Kellogg, "This committee would like you to make a proposal to accept the bilateral treaty if it could be extended to a multilateral one."

Kellogg conferred with Coolidge, who instructed him to move ahead along that path. On December 28 the Secretary finally replied to Briand, suggesting a multilateral pact, in which other nations would join the United States and France. There was intense disappointment in the French Foreign Office. Such a treaty would dilute gravely the glory of a pact with the United States. President Raymond Poincaré objected to any idea that might outlaw war with Germany. Further opposition was expressed on the ground that France's obligations to the League and to other nations in its network of alliances might stand in the way. Borah, in a letter to the New York *Times*, said that he could not see how outlawing war could be inconsistent with the League if the League was indeed an instrument of peace, and if France favored a bilateral pact, a multilateral pact could effect no basic change in France's relationships to other nations.

Briand countered that a multilateral pact would be the most sweeping declaration of faith in words since the Sermon on the Mount. He tried various gambits to derail Kellogg from his project. He suggested that Kellogg and he sign a pact first and that then an international conference be held. Kellogg replied that they would get entangled with all sorts of suggestions and would get nowhere. Briand proposed a conference of legal experts, and Kellogg replied that "legal representatives of all the countries would not agree on the Ten Commandments without an amendment."

Briand had no choice but to fall in line when other European nations agreed to sign. In a letter of April 23 to the great powers, Kellogg wrote that the treaty excluded questions involving self-defense, the Covenant of the League, the Locarno treaties, and those treaties in the French alliances. Nonetheless, letters from various powers stated to Kellogg additional individual reservations. Britain exempted from the pact "certain regions of the world," which Sir Austen Chamberlain, British Foreign Minister, explained to the British public meant colonial wars.

Within the administration and the State Department itself there was a good deal of skepticism. Assistant Secretary of State William Castle confided to his diary, "Actually it is futile, it appeals enormously to the pacifists and the Earnest Christians." However, Kellogg was becoming more and more excited about it and wrote to his wife in May, "If I can only get my Treaty through, it will be the greatest accomplishment of my administration or any administration lately." It was now his personal conception.

The pact initiated by Briand and Kellogg, in which the signatories agreed to renounce war forever "as an instrument of national policy," would be signed by fourteen nations in the Clock Room of the Quai d'Orsay Palace in Paris on August 27. Kellogg agreed to be there. Coolidge was to make a speech before the American Legion at Wausau, Wisconsin, on August 15, in which he would discuss the pact. He asked Kellogg to review an advance text. An unsigned message to secretary Sanders from a White House staff member of August 3 reads, "Kellogg is so nervous and wrought up at the prospects of his trip that it was very difficult to get him to read the speech carefully. I made a second visit this morning with the result that he made the enclosed suggestions." In his Wausau address Coolidge asserted, "Had an agreement of this kind been in existence in 1914, there is every reason to suppose that it would have delivered the world from all the misery inflicted by the Great War," a doubtful statement indeed, since all the nations, including Germany, believed they were fighting in national self-defense.

The British government chose this juncture to present to Kellogg an outline for a new attempt to reach a naval accord in place of the failure that had occurred in Geneva the year before. When Coolidge, who was vacationing in South Dakota's Black Hills, heard about it, he sent a wire to Kellogg to ignore the proposal and followed the wire up with a sharp letter. "What I desire to have done at present is nothing at all. I would not have you even ask the British Government for any explanation of the proposals which they have made. Let the entire matter stand in abeyance."

Coolidge was apparently suspicious that the European nations would use the peace treaty to approach Kellogg on other matters, such as disarmament and the war debts, and find him softened. Before his departure, Kellogg wrote apologetically to Coolidge:

> I regret exceedingly that any inquiry was made of the British Government . . . I am also very sorry that I agreed to go to Paris to sign the Treaty . . . it was suggested to us that it would be a great compliment to France if I would agree to sign the Treaty there with the other ministers. I have not the slightest idea that anybody expects to discuss with me any other question at all. . . . All the talk in the press about discussing debts with me is the same talk which always appears when Mr. Mellon goes abroad.

In the impressive signing ceremony, M. Briand made a speech that was far from accurate, stating among other things, "I never contemplated for one moment that the suggested engagement should only exist between France and the United States." The occasion was drowned in all the appropriate clichés: "Noble conception" (from Coolidge), "milestone in the history of civilization," "new spirit," "turning swords into plowshares," "Parliament of Man," "testimony to the ties of brotherhood," "deepest aspirations of the human conscience," "dawn of the new day," "one of the greatest events since the birth of Christ."

There was a good deal of skepticism, if not cynicism, expressed on these shores. Senator James Reed said that it was "an international kiss" and nothing more. The New York *Herald Tribune* said, "In order to renounce war a substitute for war must be developed. The renunciation should come last, not first." The Hearst press and the Chicago *Tribune* said that they had no objection to the Kellogg Pact if it did not interfere with our new program for building more heavy cruisers and other armaments. Elmer Davis wrote in the New York *Times:* "If only he [Kellogg] will add a clause that sorrow and suffering on and after January 1 shall be forever prohibited, I am with him." He compared the treaty to the forlorn sign found at Gettysburg after the battle was over: "Shooting prohibited on these premises under penalty of the law."

On August 25 Kellogg sent a message from Paris to the State Department to be relayed to Coolidge: "I plan to leave Wednesday noon on the cruiser Detroit for Dublin returning in time to catch the Leviathan on September 4th at Cherbourg. Admiral Burrage is anxious for me to return on the cruiser landing at Washington. McDermott [State Department press officer] who is in touch with the press is of the opinion that if I should return on a cruiser to the U.S. it would bring a reaction in the press against the treaty and the sincerity of the signatory powers and under the circumstances it might be best for me to follow my original plan and return on the Leviathan."

Coolidge on reading this must have lost all patience with "Nervous Nellie." The same day he wired the State Department: "Tell Secretary Kellogg to use his own judgment about coming home." Kellogg played it safe and decided to sail on the *Leviathan* instead of on a warship.

The hollowness of the treaty was evident in the Senate debate on its ratification in January, 1929. Senator Borah was put on the defensive. In answer to a query he said that the United States could have gone to war against Spain in 1898 even if the Kellogg Pact had been in effect since our battleship *Maine* had been blown up. In answer to another query he said that we could have sent an expedition to Mexico under General Pershing in 1916. "We would have a perfect right to send an expedition anywhere to protect the lives and property of our citizens." Senator Hiram Johnson said that the treaty "like the characters of a Henry James novel has been analyzed by its proponents into disintegration. The explanations and interpretations have made its nothingness complete." Senator Carter Glass said, "I am unwilling to have anybody in Virginia suppose that I am simple enough to imagine that this Treaty is worth a postage stamp in bringing about peace, but it would be psychologically bad to defeat it." The treaty was ratified by a vote of 85 to 1, the sole adverse vote being that of Wisconsin's Senator John J. Blaine.

In July, 1929, in an elaborate ceremony President Hoover declared that the Peace Pact was in effect. Soon thereafter fighting erupted in Manchuria between Japan and Russia, and then in 1931 came the Sino-Japanese hostilities. The one concrete contribution of the Kellogg Peace Pact was the invention of the fiction of the "undeclared war." The Kellogg Pact is in effect today, never having been abrogated by the signatories. After the Second World War the prosecution in the Nuremberg trials rested its case in part on the violation of the treaty by Germany when it went to war against Poland. It has not been mentioned since in international diplomacy.

Secretary of State Kellogg was awarded the Nobel Peace Prize. It might better have gone to Senator Borah, who had prodded Kellogg and the administration into adopting a multilateral pact stand.

Strangely enough, the two chief architects of our foreign policy of the time, Coolidge and Borah, had never been abroad. It was said that Borah had never visited Europe since he had been told by a fortune-teller that he would die by drowning. The two men were close friends; Coolidge courted Borah with frequent invitations to dinner and *Mayflower* cruises. Borah's feelings for Coolidge in turn were warm. The differences could hardly have been greater between the two—the one a New Englander, conservative, trim, self-effacing, silent in public, who had made his way by doing the conventional and expected; the other a Westerner, radical, shaggy, filling the public eye, always voluble, who had made his way by doing the unconventional and unexpected.

Yet the rapport between them was such that Coolidge wanted him for his running mate in 1924. The Senator had not been consulted by a President since he entered the Senate in 1907. Now Androcles had drawn the thorn, and it was no wonder that the lion purred. He supported Coolidge warmly in the 1924 campaign; he was for Coolidge in 1928 before Coolidge withdrew; in the 1928 convention he showered Coolidge with praise.

In her 1961 biography *Borah,* Marian C. McKenna referred to Borah as a "destructive statesman" and one having a "passion for wreckage." All Borah ever had to offer was opposition and criticism. He distrusted all machinery of government and once wrote to Walter Lippmann his approval of a quotation of the historian Buckle that "the most valuable additions made to legislation have been enactments destructive of preceding legislation."

Although a liberal, he was against the Child Labor Amendment. He said that it would be treason not to develop a program to help the farmer, but all he had to put forth was a devastating criticism of the McNary-Haugen bill. He defended the rights of the individual but was an ardent supporter of Prohibition. He was opposed to our getting too close to European nations and even opposed the World Court, but he was all for recognition of Soviet Russia. Of his leadership in promoting the Kellogg Pact, Walter Lippmann commented, "How much easier to arouse a large audience by a denunciation of war, than to persuade them to agree on the principles of a code!"

Borah was a super individualist. The symbol of his rugged independence was the lonely rides he took on his horse every day through Rock Creek Park in Washington. He retired for long hours in his study and was so much of a loner that it was hard to get him to spend any length of time in a committee room, much less on the floor of the Senate. Now and then he would deliver a Senate speech which would draw a big audience, but then, having given play to his histrionic talents and basked in the admiration of his colleagues and the press, he would disappear and not be heard from for weeks. He never entertained and rarely attended a social function. Since his state of Idaho was in his pocket, he did not have to do any of the usual politicking. A Democratic opponent of his for the Senate said, "I run for advertisement only."

One principle that Borah surely stood for was *integrity.* In 1923 he was adamant with Coolidge that Harry Daugherty must resign as Attorney General to redeem the honor of the administration. When Congress in the closing days of the 1925 session raised Congressional salaries from $7,500 to $10,000, Borah alone among members of Congress refused to accept the raise for the remainder of his term, saying that he had been elected to a $7,500 office. When the facts came to light in 1928 that oilman Harry F. Sinclair had donated $200,000 to the GOP, a gift carefully concealed, Borah said that the honor of the party must be redeemed. When Republican chairman William M. Butler refused Borah's demand that the money be returned on the ground that it had already been spent, Borah organized a campaign to raise the sum by contributions from rank-and-file Republicans, a move which fizzled.

There were many who were skeptical about Borah's pretensions. The Baltimore *Sun* once said editorially, "Borah cries, he beats his breast, and then votes with the boys." On his death in January, 1940, two dispatches in the New York *Times* caused a good deal of conversation in Washington. On January 21, there was this caption: "Think Borah Left Little." The story stated that the Borah estate would be small since his sole income was his $10,000 a year salary as Senator. He was so poor that he could not afford to own a home in Boise and rented an apartment when he visited there during the summer recesses. Then on February 1 came this surprise: BORAH BOX YIELDS $200,000, DISCLOSED IN OPENING VAULT, SURPRISES SENATOR'S WIDOW. There has never been an explanation of where the money came from.

In the twenties, profits of business boomed; incomes and salaries of executives and employees were larger; dividends of shareholders were larger. During the decade savings bank deposits and life insurance policies doubled in amount. The Coolidge-Mellon policy of reducing the income tax surtaxes on the rich had the unlooked-for effect of making more tax-free money available for speculation in stocks.

There was also an abundance of credit. In the spring of 1927, Norman Montagu of the Bank of England, Hjalmar Schacht of the German Reichsbank, and Charles Rist of the Bank of France visited the United States and asked the Federal Reserve Board to reduce interest rates here in order to discourage the outflow of gold and money from Europe for investment in the United States. Such a step would enable England to maintain the pound at its fixed price in dollars and stabilize other foreign currencies. The Federal Reserve Banks cut the rediscount rate to 3½ percent as they established an easy money policy. Between the middle and the end of 1927, Reserve Banks bought $435,000,000 of government securities in the open market. In the last six months of that year loans and investments of member banks rose by $1.764 billion, but only 7 percent of that increase went into business loans. A large amount went into speculative building, and funds were pouring into the stock market. Brokers' loans, for purchasing stocks on margin, rose by 24 percent.

As stocks started to climb, the word swept through the public about an open sesame to riches. The "Coolidge confidence" permeated the marketplace. John J. Raskob, vice-president of General Motors, wrote an article in the *Ladies' Home Journal* entitled "Everybody Ought to Be Rich," and everybody *could* be rich by investing in the market. In time the public came to believe that Wall Street was paved with gold, just as Dick Whittington had believed it of the streets of London. The hallowed standard for stocks had been that they should be priced at ten times the current earnings. Raskob claimed that fifteen times the earnings was the sounder yardstick. The public started to discount the future, and the yardstick went to thirty times the earnings, and then stock prices soared above any measurement as buyers discounted not only the future but the hereafter.

While the public viewed President Coolidge as the repository of wisdom and prudence under whose guidance nothing could go wrong, evidence brought to the surface in later years shows that Coolidge knew very little about economics and regarded the stock market as beyond his jurisdiction. When in a series of articles in the *Atlantic Monthly*, which later became a book, *Main Street and Wall Street*, Professor William Z. Ripley of Harvard wrote on the subject, Coolidge invited him to the White House. Ripley claimed that when corporations sold stock to the public, management by various devices such as the issuance of nonvoting stock retained full power. Thus, an artificial silk concern gave voting rights to only 2,000 out of a total of 600,000 shares. Control of many electric light, gas, and power companies lay in only one-tenth of the capitalization.

In two sessions on February 15, 1926, Coolidge listened to

him, feet on desk, cigar in mouth. The next day Coolidge commented to his press conference, "He didn't think there was anything Federal legislation could do. . . . It isn't interstate commerce and there is difficulty for that reason in reaching it." He further stated, "These concerns are not national but state concerns. They get their authority under the laws and charters that are granted to them by the various states."

As far as actions of the Federal Reserve Board were concerned, Coolidge adopted a hands-off attitude. Mellon was ex officio a member of the board, and it appears that Mellon did keep him informed. In a letter dated July 27, 1927, J. W. McIntosh, Comptroller of the Currency, wrote Coolidge saying that since Mellon was out of town, he would like to pass on information about reductions in rediscount rates made by Midwestern Federal Reserve Banks. "The situation in Europe made it almost imperative that this should be done in order that discount rates in central banks of Europe should not be advanced to a point where it would interfere with the purchase of raw materials and agricultural products from the United States." It is evident that the policy was explained to Coolidge not as an aid to Europe, which would not enlist much sympathy from him, but as an aid to American business which would command his support.

Under any circumstances Coolidge would favor a low interest rate policy because it would further his policy of economy—it would effect some saving by lowering the interest charges on the public debt. It is clear, however, that Coolidge took no part in the decisions of the board. On September 13, 1927, when he was asked at a press conference to comment on the easy money policy, he replied, "I think I have indicated a great many times that it is a board that does function and ought to function entirely in the nature of a judicial position. I have sometimes made some comment on what they have done and the beneficial effect that I thought had accrued from it, but I do not recall that I have ever made any suggestion to the Board as to any action that it ought to take."

At a press conference in January, 1928, he did make a direct statement about a condition in the stock market. It concerned the amount of brokers' loans used to finance margin purchases.

In the early twenties such loans outstanding amounted to about $1.5 billion. But by the end of 1927 they had swelled to almost $3.5 billion, a rise causing a good deal of uneasiness since it signaled a great burst in speculative activity. (At this time, one could buy stocks on as little as 10 percent margin.)

I am not familiar enough with the workings and practice of the Federal Reserve System so that comments that I might make relative to the amount of brokers' loans and so on would be of much value. I do know in a general way that the amount of securities in this country has increased very largely in recent years. The number of different securities that are dealt in on the stock exchange are very much larger than they were previously. The deposits in banks are also larger. And those two things together would necessarily be a reason for doing more business of that kind that is transacted by brokers and would naturally result in a larger sum of money being spent for that purpose. Now, whether the amount at the present time is disproportionate to the resources of the country I am not in a position to judge accurately but so far, as indicated by an inquiry that I have made of the Treasury Department and so on, I haven't had any indications that the amount was large enough to cause particularly unfavorable comment.

The President's statement was thus reported in the New York *Times* of January 8: "President Coolidge does not see any reason for unfavorable comment. The President, it was said at the White House today, believes that the increase represents a natural expansion of business in the securities markets and sees nothing unfavorable about it." Other papers in reporting the statement gave the impression that the President had spoken with firmness about the matter ex cathedra.

The press greeted the President's intervention in this matter as unfortunate. The New York *Times* said, "These are not matters which the Chief Executive should feel himself called upon to discuss." The Newark *News* said it was "ill advised." The Baltimore *Sun* said that it "was received by the conservative-minded with regret." The New York *Journal of Commerce* said that the President "has entered upon a dangerous field from which both prudence and propriety should dictate that he remain absent."

Coolidge's actual words show that he spoke hesitantly and dis-

257

claimed any pretense of authority on the subject. Whether he spoke at Mellon's suggestion to hearten Wall Street, we do not know. That he spoke at all may have been due to his fondness for discoursing to the press. It was unfortunate that Coolidge's White House Spokesman rule forbade any direct quotation. As happened so often, the press turned his wishy-washy position into a virile stance. It was the one and only time he had anything to say about the stock market. Although there were repeated questions in succeeding months from correspondents, as the White House files show, he ignored them all.

H. Parker Wills, of the New York *Journal of Commerce,* a cousin of Coolidge, related that a few days after the President had made his statement about brokers' loans, Coolidge said to him in an after-luncheon talk, "If I were to give my personal opinion about it, I would say that any loan for gambling in stocks was an 'excessive loan.' "

His thinking may have run along these lines: he would not gamble with his own money in Wall Street, but then he could not prevent other people from being foolish. As he could not prevent Americans from drinking poisoned liquor or slaughtering themselves with their cars on the highways, as he could not reform the human animal in other acts of foolishness; he could not undertake a cure for the national delirium of becoming rich without work. That was to him a sin, but the only remedy was to let people learn by sad experience as in the Florida land boom mirage.

Throughout 1925 land values in Florida were bid up in frenzied buying, as the prices of lots in mythical cities, and often in swampland and jungleland, tripled and quadrupled. The spectacular collapse came in 1926, assisted by two ravaging hurricanes, which punctured the dream of Florida's idyllic climate on which the boom was built in large part.

At any rate, the public was much less interested in whether too much money was being used for speculation than it was in whether stock prices would go higher. Two months after Coolidge's pronouncement, in early March, the market started on a rampage, and prices skyrocketed, although business in some sectors was a good deal less favorable than it had been in 1927. Before March, 1928, there had been only eight sessions in which more than 3,000,000 shares had been traded, but in this month alone there were sixteen days in which volume surpassed that figure and four days in which volume exceeded the 4,000,000 mark.

Hitherto the market had been an occupation for the rich and professionals. Now for the first time the man in the street plunged in on a large scale. The value of a seat on the exchange which had reached a peak of $80,000 in 1924 rose to $375,000. B. C. Forbes in his financial column said, "The stock market has palpably lost its head. It has ceased to fulfill a legitimate, orderly function. Instead of a sane market-place it has become a seething Monte Carlo." The *New Republic* said:

> Playing the market has become a national institution for the large class of the prosperous and for many others as well, making, in the intensity of its interest, a fascinating sport in which for a long time it has seemed possible for everybody to win, matching their wits against each other only by the extent of their comparative gains. The stock market is the national gaming table comparable to the lotteries in Latin American countries but more suitable to the American temperament, since it seems to offer a large opportunity for the substitution of shrewdness for mere chance.

In the early part of the Presidential election year of 1928 the Federal Reserve Board became alarmed and tried to apply a brake by raising the rediscount rate. In his press conference of April 24, Coolidge, when asked about the new policy, said, "No information has come to me concerning the increase in rediscount rates except that which I have seen in the press. That is a matter entirely for the Federal Reserve Board, a matter that I wouldn't happen to know anything about."

Throughout the year the speculative fever mounted, crowds filled the brokers' boardrooms, newspapers devoted more and more news to the market and stock prospects, and prices of stocks steadily ascended. Further magic had arrived on Wall Street in the form of the new investment trusts. In the diversification of stocks offered by these trusts there was absolute safety for the investor, they were masterminded by the greatest experts, and the huge funds they commanded would ensure that with their mammoth purchasing power they would shore up the market if there were ever any faltering in its march upward. These trusts were eagerly grabbed up by the gullible public at prices ridiculously higher than the net asset value per share.

From time to time the Federal Reserve twisted the tourniquet of credit, but to no avail since the price of credit, the interest rate, became a progressively less important factor to the speculator who looked forward to large capital gains. Even though the rate for call money rose ever higher, brokers' loans, which were $3.5 billion in January, 1928, when Coolidge discussed them in his press conference, amounted to $5.5 billion by September, only nine months later.

While Coolidge discussed economic prospects with undiluted optimism, the Federal Reserve Board was wrestling desperately with the problem of how it could check the speculative orgy. It could not raise the rediscount rate above 5 percent for fear of interfering with necessary commercial borrowing. On February 2, 1929, it issued a letter to the Federal Reserve Banks asking that they request member banks to refrain from using Reserve Bank funds to finance speculative purchases of stocks—an injunction which was words thrown into the wind. A month later Calvin Coolidge was out of the White House.

It is not easy to find specific grounds for bringing an indictment against Coolidge for the Crash. It is unfair to have expected him to be more clairvoyant than others. The overwhelming number of trained economic analysts was bullish, and the few who had twinges of doubt did not anticipate the catastrophe which was in the offing. Coolidge was a man of his times and for his times. He was typically American, perhaps Babbitt-like, in his optimism when he told Hoover that worry was a futile type of activity. "If you see ten troubles coming down the road, you can be sure that nine will run into the ditch before they reach you, and you will have to battle with only one of them."

How much could there have been in the way of federal action since the regulatory controls of today did not exist then? Even so, let us suppose he had been a Jeremiah crying out public warning. There would have been an answering howl of rage since a President cannot afford to be a prophet of doom. William Allen White in his book *A Puritan in Babylon,* though implicitly indicting Coolidge for the sins of his era, concedes his helplessness:

> But what if the President through some miracle of insight and by some onrush of will had started to stem the flood? His action would have been the order for a minor panic! How quickly the Congress would have left him. . . . And indeed back of Congress, back of the courts, supporting both in their check of the Executive would have been a raging populace roaring at the White House to let the carnival go on. The Coolidge boom was ordained by the American democracy . . . democracy was having its will and going mad in its appointed way.

Whether or not he put words in Coolidge's mouth, Senator James Watson reported a conversation they had about the market three months before Coolidge left office. They were discussing the dangers in the speculative boom:

> Coolidge responded that if he were to give a statement from the White House warning people against a situation of this kind, they naturally would think there was something wrong in the whole financial system and perhaps would begin dumping their securities on the market all at once, which would result in an even greater disaster than if the fever of speculation were permitted to run its course like the smallpox or measles.

Undoubtedly if there had been a public opinion poll at the time, the vast majority would have agreed with the comment of *Nation's Business* in March, 1928, regarding proposals that the Federal Reserve Board adopt radical measures to curb speculation: "Apart from the technical criticism of these proposals, they are objectionable because they would radically interfere with the constitutional right of the citizen to lose his money if he so desires."

Extraordinary Popular Delusions and the Madness of Crowds points out that mistaken popular belief turns into dogma precisely at the time that the premises for the belief become the most shaky. From 1927 to 1929 the general public and the experts agreed that we were entering an era of perpetual prosperity—precisely at the time when it should have been apparent that the props under our national economy were becoming weaker.

It is extraordinary that stocks should have doubled and tripled from 1928 to 1929 when many businesses were complaining of "profitless prosperity." In the relentless drive for expansion they were running up against the law of diminishing returns, as the cost of a unit of expansion was exceeding the dollar per unit sales return.

Retail sales growth was slackening. The boom in residential construction faded after 1927. While private investment spending picked up in 1928 after the recession of 1927, it was mostly in inventory building rather than in capital spending. There were many weak spots. The textile industry in the North had been languishing for some years. The anthracite coal industry had been dealt a death blow by the competition from oil heating, and the bituminous coal industry saw increased suffering as 250,000 men lost their jobs in mine closings between 1923 and 1929.

From time to time some economic observer raised the question of whether the mass purchasing power was sufficient to maintain indefinitely a high level of consumption of consumer goods since the increasing incomes had started from a very low base. The Brookings Institution in a 1928 finding that got little notice reported that six out of ten families had less than the $2,000 needed to supply only the basic necessities of life.

The gains from prosperity were maldistributed. Too much went into business profits and too little into wages. Dividends went from 4.3 percent of the national income in 1920 to 7.2 percent in 1929, an increase which far outstripped wage boosts. Profits which remained undistributed in corporate treasuries rose from $230,000,000 in 1922 to $2.3 billion in 1926. When the call-money rate rose over 8 percent in 1928, a great deal of this corporate money went into Wall Street to finance speculation in stocks, instead of going into increased wages.

At the time discouraging talk was dismissed lightly. In December, 1927, Professor Irving Fisher of Yale University produced figures to show that most of the population was just making expenses and had nothing to set aside for a rainy day. To his scholarly analysis, the Hartford *Courant* replied, "Here are sav-

ings banks fairly bulging with deposits, our highways fully over-
flowing with automobiles, our colleges turning away thousands
of young men and women who never before had money to go to
college, our homes filled with pianos, radios, phonographs, washing machines, vacuum cleaners and goodness knows what not.
Here are all the seeming evidences of prosperity and yet our
prosperity is largely mythical! We would ask for more light on
the subject if we thought that it could possibly benefit us, but
we feel that our ignorance is too deep to be penetrated by the
shining rays of statistical truth." In his column, Will Rogers
wrote, "Give the people four more years of this unparalleled
prosperity and the people will get so tired of having everything
they want that it will be a pleasure to be poor again."

However, most of these worldly goods which filled the home
and the garage were being acquired by installment credit plans.
"You furnish the girl, we'll furnish the home" and "Enjoy while
you pay" were typical of the slogans which were plastered on
billboards and in newspaper advertisements. Previously credit
had gone only for permanent acquisitions like houses, but now
85 percent of furniture and 75 percent of washing machines and
refrigerators were being bought on time.

In a press conference Coolidge defended installment buying
as sound, and his views were given wide circulation. "When a
commodity is bought on installments, it means that there is then
laid out a plan on which it is to be paid. . . . I recognize that it
can be overdone like any kind of credit, but I think it is an advance over the old kind of credit that was given without any
plan of repayment."

The owner of a clothing store wrote to Coolidge asking him
whether the mania for buying things on the installment plan
wasn't getting out of hand. He related a true conversation he
had overheard in a railroad car:

> Have you an automobile yet?
> No, I talked it over with John and he felt we could not afford
> one.
> Mr. Budge who lives in your town has one and they are not as
> well off as you are.
> Yes, I know. Their second installment came due, and they had
> no money to pay it.

What did they do? Lose the car?
No, they got the money and paid the installment.
How did they get the money?
They sold the cook-stove.
How could they get along without a cook-stove?
They didn't. They bought another on the installment plan.

The gravest aspect of the general economic situation was the distress in the farm sector of the economy. While wage earners were better off in purchasing power than they had been before the war, farmers on the whole were worse off, and the farm share of the national income dwindled. Farmers had enjoyed fabulous prosperity during the war years, but after the Armistice, when demand fell off and Europe started to produce its own food, prices dropped catastrophically. In 1921 the price of corn fell to a third of its 1919 high; prices of cotton, wheat, and hogs to half. There was a recovery in the years 1923 to 1926 and then a further relapse. Meanwhile, freight rates rose, and the farmer had to pay more for farm labor to compete with city wages.

There are some interesting features on the ways in which changes in postwar civilian life hurt the farmer. For example, the supplanting of the horse by the automobile destroyed the market he once had for hay and oats, while the need for good roads sharply hiked taxes. People ate less on the average in the postwar world, partly because the electric machine age and shorter hours required less food for energy for work and partly because slim figures became fashionable among women. People ate less meat and more dairy foods, vegetables, and citrus fruits, and so the number of cattle were reduced, while dairy farmers, truck farmers, and citrus growers prospered. Shorter, sleeveless dresses for women and lighter clothes for both sexes reduced the demand for cotton and wool.

The most acute distress came because during the war the farmer bought much additional farmland to grow more crops and needed more agricultural machinery to cultivate it. He was now stuck with heavy debts. The value of agricultural land tumbled from $79 billion in 1920 to $58 billion in 1927. A wave of bank failures in the Midwest farm belt made matters even worse.

The farmer turned to political weapons and started agitating for federal relief through organs such as the American Farm Bureau and the National Grange. A farm bloc took shape in Congress. In the Harding administration specific legislation was passed to help the farmer; this included the setting up of twelve Federal Intermediate Credit Banks and the Capper-Volstead Act, which exempted farm cooperatives from the antitrust laws.

The farmer wanted more in the way of help. The trouble lay in heavy crop surpluses that dropped prices whenever a recovery seemed under way. The farm organizations finally united behind one piece of legislation to deal with the surpluses, the McNary-Haugen bill. In 1924 it applied only to grains and was defeated in the House. In 1926 it won Southern support when it was broadened to include tobacco, cotton, and rice. In February, 1927, the controversial bill passed both houses and sat on Coolidge's desk.

It was an ingenious measure which made separate provisions for the domestic and the foreign market. At home the crop would be sold at the world price, plus a protective tariff figure. Abroad the surplus would be dumped. To reimburse the Federal Farm Board, which would do the dumping, the farmer would have to pay an equalization fee. In an oversimplification, if the domestic market could absorb only 650,000,000 bushels of an 800,000,000-bushel wheat crop, the farmer would sell the 650,000,000 bushels at the world price of $1, plus the tariff of 42 cents, or $1.42. Then the board would dump the other 150,000,000 bushels over the tariff wall at what it could bring, say, 90 cents, and the farmer would pay, say, a fee of 10 cents a bushel, giving him a healthy profit.

Coolidge vetoed the bill in a message which Chief Justice Taft rightly termed in a private letter a "sockdolager." The equalization fee, he said, was unconstitutional; the price-fixing was obnoxious, as well as unconstitutional. The fee would be too difficult to collect, the result would be to encourage our surpluses, not to reduce them, and to dump the crops abroad would help foreign businesses lower competitive costs to the detriment of our nonfarm production.

It was said in defense of Coolidge's position that he was a farmboy and therefore understood and sympathized with the farmers' problem. However, the farms Coolidge knew were the

Vermont farms which yielded only a small living to those who had to scratch for it. The tale is plausible that he once said to the chairman of the Federal Farm Loan Board, "Farmers have never made much money. I don't know that we can do much about it."

Nothing was done in 1927 to override the Coolidge veto. In 1928, on the eve of the Republican National Convention, another McNary-Haugen bill, passed by both houses, came again to Coolidge's desk. Again he vetoed it, in a message which contained stinging phrases such as: "cumbersome," "crudely camouflaged," "autocratic authority," "bureaucracy gone mad," "plague of petty officialdom," "intolerable tyranny," "swarms of inspectors," "impenetrable maze of contracts," "ponderously futile," "folly," "nonsense."

The Des Moines *Register* commented, "Probably never in a hundred and fifty years of Congressional government has the deliberate act of two Congresses been dismissed with such want of appreciation. Mussolini has not said anything about Parliamentary government in Europe that this message does not say by implication of Congressional government with us."

To the chagrin of the farm bloc the veto was upheld, and so the farm problem remained vexing and unsolved when Herbert Hoover took over in March, 1929.

Chapter X

DREAM'S END

As is customary in American politics, discussion about the 1928 Presidential campaign began the year before, in the spring of 1927. The belief was widely expressed that the American people would want another four years of Calvin Coolidge, the patron saint of prosperity and the guardian of tranquillity at home and abroad. It was also generally assumed that Coolidge would want to fill the highest office for another term. He was in the prime of life; in 1928 he would be only fifty-six years of age. His perennial critic Frank Kent wrote in early 1927, "As to Mr. Coolidge's wanting another term, that is too obvious to argue. No President ever liked the White House better than he. No President ever wanted to hold on to it more."

A problem was posed here—Coolidge had served a year and seven months of Harding's elected term before beginning his own term. Would this period mean that if elected in 1928, he would violate American tradition by serving a third term? Arthur Brisbane, who was beating the tom-toms hard for Coolidge, wrote that if the President ran, it would be for a "second elected term" and thus perfectly consonant with the precedent set by Washington. Yet no matter how you sliced it, the result was the same. Coolidge if elected in 1928 would serve a longer time than any previous President of the United States. Venerable Republicans Elihu Root and Chauncey Depew declared that Coolidge's reelection would not break the tradition. On the other hand, president Nicholas Murray Butler of Columbia University said that it would. Coolidge's dyed-in-the-wool foe Senator Norris said that it would be a "long step toward monarchical government."

There was no doubt how the Republican Party organizations felt about it—they were eager for Coolidge to head the ticket because his almost certain victory would sweep in with him state and local candidates. The Washington *Evening Star* took a poll of the Republican National Committee which showed a "virtually unanimous opinion" that another term would not constitute a third term. A procession of party leaders visited Coolidge in the White House to express the hope that he would run in 1928. There was no reaction at all from Coolidge, no change in facial expression, not even a nod or deprecatory smile. "He just looked down his nose at me," reported one state leader after leaving the White House.

In early June, after he had given Lindbergh the big welcome home, Coolidge and a large entourage entrained for the longest summer vacation any President ever took. His destination was the Black Hills of South Dakota, which are in reality mountains 7,500 feet high. His residence at the State Game Lodge would not be far from Mount Rushmore and the town of Deadwood where once Wild Bill Hickok, Buffalo Bill, and Calamity Jane roamed. Every day he would drive to his office at Rapid City, thirty miles away, where he would occupy an empty schoolhouse.

Coolidge had previously vacationed in the East, and his choice for his 1927 vacation was explained by political writers as purposefully connected with the 1928 campaign. Western farmers were disgruntled by his veto in the just-concluded session of Congress of the McNary-Haugen bill, and this sojourn was labeled "The Winning of the West." He would meet with Western political leaders and would confer with representatives of farm groups to work out with them a suitable substitute for the vetoed legislation.

Coolidge fished for photographers and seemed to enjoy entering into the spirit of the unfamiliar environment. He attended a Wild West show and rodeo at Belle Fourche. On his birthday in July he was greeted as "Cal, Our Pal" by a troop of Boy

Scouts and a granddaughter of Buffalo Bill, Cody Allen. When everybody thought that the festivities were over, Coolidge disappeared and made a quick change. When he returned, he was wearing the cowboy regalia that he had been presented with—chaps, a red shirt, blue bandanna around his neck, ten-gallon hat, spurs, and boots. The gesture of appreciation made the party a big success, and the photograph of Coolidge as cowboy was widely printed in the papers around the country.

Amid reports of the President's relaxations there were news stories of the farm bill that the President would unveil to help the farmers, built mostly around a new loan program. All the summer's activities seemed to be standard politicking. Senator La Follette said, "Surrounded by newspaper reporters, photographers and with a corps of publicity men the President is attempting to make the farmer forget his veto of farm-relief legislation by wearing a ten-gallon hat and catching trout with milk-fed worms. The President will have to find better bait than this to catch votes in the West and Northwest." William Allen White in the Emporia *Gazette* expressed his belief that this angling for votes was unnecessary on Coolidge's part:

> They [Americans] would be for Coolidge if he had gone to Florida or Bangor, Maine, for his vacation. Calvin Coolidge represents something definite in the American heart. If a blacksmith with a can-opener would climb Bartholdi's statue, he would find if he cut into the Goddess of Liberty, these words graven to her heart "Let's get the car paid for." Coolidge has poured into himself the incarnation of this sentiment. And that's why you can't beat Calvin Coolidge.

The big surprise was around the corner.

When, at noon on Friday July 29, Coolidge called secretary Sanders into his office and began, "Now," Sanders knew from experience that "Now" meant that Coolidge had something important on his mind. "I am not going to run for President again. I should serve ten years which is too long for any President in this country." Sanders was stunned. "The country will be greatly disappointed, Mr. President," he said. Coolidge then showed him a twelve-word announcement he had written out in longhand. "I do not choose to run for President in nineteen twenty-eight." When asked why he was withdrawing so early, Coolidge replied, "On the second of August I shall have served four years and I think that is an appropriate time for an announcement." The following Tuesday was August 2. At breakfast Coolidge said casually to Mrs. Coolidge, "I have been President four years today," and added nothing. He entered the summer Executive Office at 8:30 A.M., and when Sanders asked him if he intended to go through with the announcement, Coolidge said, "Yes." Sanders then suggested that it be delayed until noon since there was a three-hour differential in time with New York. If the announcement came after the closing of the stock market at three o'clock, that would allow time for the business community and investors to digest the news. Coolidge agreed.

The press filed in at nine o'clock, and he held a routine interview, adding, "If the conference will return at twelve I may have a further statement to make." When the twenty-five newsmen came in at noon, they found Coolidge standing beside his desk with typewritten slips of paper in his hand, which he handed out one by one as they filed past him. There was an audible "Whew!" and they rushed to the telephones outside.

Senator Arthur Capper of Kansas, who was to be Coolidge's luncheon guest, had wandered in and watched the proceedings. They rode back to the lodge together, and Coolidge had no comment on his action other than a crisp sentence that he felt that ten years was too long for any President to serve.

At the lunch they had with Mrs. Coolidge, the President as usual concentrated on food and neglected the social amenities. When he was through, he departed for his usual postprandial nap. Capper, left together with Mrs. Coolidge, said gingerly to her, "That was quite a surprise the President gave us this morning." She asked what it was, and Capper told her. She laughed and said, "Isn't that just like the man. He never gave me the slightest inclination of his intentions. I had no idea."

The news broke like a thunderbolt. The New York *Times* the next day had streamer headlines across its front page and devoted six of the eight columns to the story.

COOLIDGE DOES NOT CHOOSE TO RUN IN 1928
STARTLES PARTY WITH 12-WORD STATEMENT
SOME DOUBTERS, OTHERS SEE FIELD OPEN

From the public reaction one would have supposed that Calvin Coolidge was the indispensable man on whom the welfare of the Republic rested. Prices broke sharply on the New York Stock Exchange in a selling avalanche. Secretary Hoover said, "I regret the suggestion [sic] in the President's statement. However, I still believe as I stated in Chicago two weeks ago that President Coolidge should be renominated and re-elected." A poll taken on the Twentieth Century Limited from New York to Chicago showed that ninety out of ninety-six polled on the train believed that Coolidge should be drafted to run. The New York *Herald Tribune* said that Coolidge had merely expressed a personal preference and that if the call came, "he will respond to it." The chief political writer for the New York *Sun* called it a "masterful move which leaves the President still available as a candidate with the fateful third term issue shifted from his shoulders to the Republican party." The *Wall Street Journal* felt that factors will develop to make the demand "so strong that his personal wishes will have to be submerged for the good of the party," while the Los Angeles *Times* declared that a Presidential nomination "is not to be disposed of purely on the basis of personal wishes." David Lawrence read Coolidge's statement as, "I do not choose to use my office to get delegates and I do not choose to make an active campaign for the Presidential nomination. If my party wishes me to serve, I will gladly do so in the future as I have in the past."

For months the press, without an iota of evidence to support it, kept alive the hope that Coolidge might run after all. There was an endless belaboring of the semantics of "I do not choose . . ." and the phrase became a catchword. (Many Model T Fords bore the sign "I do not choose to run.") The most popular interpretation was that Coolidge had said, "*I* do not choose—" but "*You* can choose—" It was pointed out that Coolidge could have said, "I will not run." Did "I do not choose" mean "I do not want" or "I prefer not to run"? In that case it might be construed merely as an expression of personal wishes which could be overcome by persuasion. If he had put it in the past tense and said, "I have chosen not to run," that would have connoted his completed decision, but "I do not choose" indicated that his mind was only in the process of a

271

choice. Thus, his never-say-die partisans reasoned, and grasped at straws.

On the other hand, Senator Porter H. Dale of Vermont (who had been at the kerosene-light swearing in in 1923) maintained that if a Vermont farmer says, "I do not choose to attend the meeting tonight," a team of horses could not drag him there.

When Coolidge returned to Washington in September and moved into the repaired and renovated White House, the declination was by no means accepted as final. Senator Simeon D. Fess of Ohio, a Republican Party leader, insisted that Coolidge would run again if nominated. The Cincinnati *Times-Star* said that if Coolidge did not elaborate upon the word "choose," then a "lot of political leaders are going to be fit subjects for padded cells." At the end of October the Washington *Evening Star* canvassed members of the Republican National Committee, and of those replying, almost half favored drafting Coolidge. The New York *Herald Tribune,* the most influential Republican organ in the East, ran emotional editorials imploring Coolidge to yield to the national will.

In December the Republican National Committee met in Washington. No one in the party had uttered a peep about seeking the nomination, and Coolidge must have decided that it was time that the party ceased splitting hairs about his statement and started casting about for a candidate. He sent a message to the committee: "My statement stands. No one should be led to suppose that I have modified it. My decision will be respected. After I had been eliminated, the party began and should vigorously continue the serious task of selecting another candidate." This blunt statement jolted the committee out of its daydreams, and in a few weeks Secretary of Commerce Hoover and some others had entered the contest for the Republican nomination. Entreaties to Coolidge continued but waned in time as Coolidge said no more.

Who knew the mind and heart of Calvin Coolidge? There must have been powerful reasons for him to turn away from another Presidential term which would almost certainly have been his, but to this day we do not know why he chose to bow out. With hindsight, his reason must have been his knowledge of his failing health. If Coolidge had been elected to another term, he would have died in office (he died in January, 1933), and for months before then he would have been too weak to discharge his duties fully. During the Presidency he conserved his strength by frequent rests and much sleep, but he complained steadily of indigestion and what appeared to be an asthmatic condition.

People have suggested that Coolidge withdrew because he saw a depression ahead. But it is often these same people who have assailed Coolidge for leading the nation blindly to disaster. In any case, it is ridiculous to suppose that he clairvoyantly, more clairvoyantly than the leading economic seers of the nation, saw the catastrophe ahead. It has also been repeatedly asserted that Coolidge wanted to be drafted for the nomination and was bitterly disappointed that such a draft did not materialize. Everett Sanders was mystified that anyone could have entertained doubts about Coolidge's sincerity. He managed his withdrawal as effectively as it could have been done, said Sanders. If he had said more, he would have been accused of protesting too much.

There is no logic to this thesis, for Coolidge did not have to take the risk of a coy disclaimer. He could have had the nomination on a silver platter by not lifting a finger. Like Roosevelt in 1940, delegations would have been instructed from him, stand-ins would have run in primaries, and he would have been nominated with as few negative votes as Roosevelt. He had to act *to prevent the nomination from being forced on him.* Except for former Governor Frank Lowden of Illinois, who at sixty-nine was considered too old, there were no candidates in sight. Hoover most certainly would not have sought the nomination against Coolidge.

If he had wanted the public to force him to accept, he would have waited a good deal longer before making his announcement. If there were not time to develop another candidate, the pressure from the party would have been too intense. However, in order to avoid that, he withdrew more than ten months before the convention, to give the Republicans plenty of time to find another candidate. When four months passed by and everything remained in a state of suspended animation, his December statement made his feelings obvious.

The person best qualified to judge Coolidge's intentions was Herbert Hoover, who because he had the most to lose, watched the President closely throughout the period before the convention. In his memoirs written two decades later, Hoover said, "I have never been able to explain fully Mr. Coolidge's attitude but I was convinced he was not seeking the nomination either directly or indirectly."

In February, 1928, they discussed the Ohio primaries. Former Senator Frank Willis had entered, and Hoover knew that Coolidge had little regard for his ability. He asked Coolidge if he would enter the Ohio primary, and the President said, "No." He then asked Coolidge if he had any objection to his (Hoover's) entering, and Coolidge snapped, "Why not?" In mid-May he told Coolidge that he had 400 delegates in the bag, but if Coolidge wanted to run, he would have all of them who were legally free to do so vote for Coolidge. Coolidge expressed some skepticism that he had that many delegates and added, "If you have 400 delegates, you'd better keep them." It was Hoover's opinion, reinforced by a conversation with Republican chairman Butler in May, 1929, that what Coolidge really wanted was a deadlocked convention in which he would have the decisive voice in naming the candidate.

"Coolidge prosperity."

These were the magic words which were the talisman for Republican victory in the 1928 elections, the rock on which Republican hopes were built and the rock on which Democratic hopes would be dashed. During the Republican Convention in June every mention of the name Coolidge was greeted with an approving roar. Will Rogers reporting from the convention wrote that his attention wandered briefly from the keynote speaker, and when it returned, he thought that he was speaking of the Saviour but then discovered the subject was Calvin Coolidge.

A Republican advertisement which filled the papers from coast to coast was headed A CHICKEN FOR EVERY POT. It read in part:

> The Republican Party isn't a "poor man's party." Republican prosperity has erased that degrading phrase from our political

274

vocabulary. Republican efficiency has filled the workingman's dinner pail—and his gas tank *besides*—made the telephone, radio and sanitary plumbing *standard* household equipment. And placed a whole nation in the *silk stocking* class. Republican prosperity has *reduced* hours and *increased* earning capacity, silenced *discontent,* put the proverbial "chicken in every pot" and a car in every backyard to boot.

Three years later, Rollin Kirby, an artist with a devastating brush, would have a cartoon in the New York *World* showing a scrawny chicken scratching its way across an empty, dilapidated garage, a golden promise which had turned to dross. But in 1928 America basked in the sunlight, and the ghastly days which lay ahead would have seemed a madman's dream.

On June 18, 1928, a few days after Hoover had been nominated, Secretary Kellogg wrote to Coolidge that Hoover had conferred with him. "I would hate to see Al Smith and Tammany run the country. I do not think that the Republicans have a sure thing in this election. The greatest asset we have is your administration. There cannot be any doubt about that and Hoover's remaining in the Cabinet would show a continuance of policy which I am sure he believes in. In my judgment it will greatly strengthen the campaign."

Hoover solicited, too, the intervention of Mellon, who wrote Coolidge a handwritten note on June 29 before he left for Europe. "I think myself that it would prove helpful to him in his campaign to remain identified with the Administration, and I think that it would tend to keep him in good line and well-advised."

Hoover stayed in the Cabinet until August 21, when Coolidge wrote him that he was reluctantly accepting his resignation which he had long had at hand. He replaced him with William Whiting of Massachusetts. Possibly Coolidge believed that he had arranged the ideal compromise between Hoover's wishes and his own needs since the date was almost equidistant between nomination and election day.

Coolidge's feelings toward Hoover were a mystery, even to Hoover himself. Outwardly they were the best of friends, but Coolidge's inner feelings were never known. There is a ring of authenticity in the tale that Coolidge, once nettled about something, burst out, "Hoover is Secretary of Commerce and the trouble is that he wants to be Undersecretary of everything else." In truth, Washington had never seen anyone grabbing responsibility the way Hoover did, and he was hard to keep in bounds. When he became Secretary of Commerce, he was advised by a former Secretary, Oscar Straus, that the position called for only two hours of work a day: "Putting the fish to bed at night and turning on the lights around the coast." But Hoover made it an around-the-clock job. He turned the Bureau of Foreign and Domestic Commerce into a meaningful aid to business, organized conferences of business for setting standards within industries and eliminating waste, took over the infant civilian aviation industry, and managed the budding radio industry until Congress set up the Federal Radio Commission.

His vast energies could not be contained by one department. As the representative of business in the Cabinet, he claimed that he should have an equal role with the Secretary of Labor in labor disputes. It was he who organized the meetings with Judge Elbert H. Gary and other steel magnates in 1922 which resulted in the elimination of the twelve-hour day. His interest in agricultural problems, which he said were fundamentally problems of business, caused Coolidge to ask him in 1924, upon the death of Secretary Henry C. Wallace, whether he wanted to move over to Agriculture. He usurped conservation projects from the Secretary of the Interior and by prodigious effort obtained agreement from the various states for the Boulder Dam, which was justly renamed the Hoover Dam after completion.

Coolidge leaned on him heavily for advice. With Mellon he was Coolidge's two-man brain trust. As one who knew Europe perhaps better than anyone else in the Cabinet, he seems to have been Coolidge's principal adviser on the war debts—and was strongly of the opinion that the Allies' claim of inability to pay was an arrant fraud, an opinion he continued to hold even during the moratorium he declared as President in 1932. Coolidge appointed him his representative to inspect the damage caused by the great Mississippi River floods of 1927 and to work out a flood control program. The only irritation that Hoover could sense on Coolidge's part came from the threat that Hoover posed to the President's economy program by plans for conservation and irrigation projects and by the ever-increasing size of the Commerce Department.

On one occasion the press believed that Coolidge revealed his displeasure with Hoover's growing role in the administration. On April 15, 1927, Coolidge wound up a lengthy statement to a query on foreign policy with the seemingly gratuitous observation: "While I am on that, I might state again that Mr. Kellogg isn't going to resign. If he does resign, Mr. Hoover will not be appointed Secretary of State." Oblique references to this show of testiness appeared in the press. Four days later Coolidge said in his press conference, "I didn't speak of Mr. Hoover's abilities the other day. . . . His reputation is so well established in the country and indeed abroad for ability and and executive achievement that I doubt very much if I should be able to shake it if I wished to. Certainly I have no desire to do that and shouldn't want to be thought so lacking of appreciation of a man of his abilities as to think that he wasn't well qualified for any position in the Cabinet that he would be willing to accept." However, this statement did not dispel the impression that had formed in the minds of many correspondents.

Hoover paid tribute to Coolidge, not only by wanting to remain in his Cabinet during the campaign, but also by basing the entire campaign on Coolidge's policies and pledging to continue them. His acceptance speech was a dreary affair except for a celebrated passage which was to plague him in later years. "We in America are nearer to the final triumph over poverty than ever before in the history of any land. The poorhouse is vanishing from among us. We have not yet reached the goal, but given a chance to go forward with the policies of the last eight years, we shall soon with the help of God be in sight of the day when poverty shall be banished from this nation. . . ."

Mencken wrote, "[The speech] states the obvious in banal terms and then proceeds to elaborate it without imagination. God made Dr. Hoover virtuous, but He also made him dull." The *New Republic* commented, "He merely took Coolidgeism for granted and paraded it now and then as a perfect creed for Government by the engineer-businessman." The New York *World* said it was "almost indistinguishable from any address

Calvin Coolidge has made on any occasion, be it a dinner of the Chamber of Commerce or the Boy Scouts."

Hoover's espousal of Coolidge philosophy was explicitly stated in his Madison Square Garden speech in New York, the most important speech of his campaign. "When the War closed we were challenged with a peacetime choice between the American system of rugged individualism and a European system of diametrically-opposed doctrine, a doctrine of paternalism and State Socialism." The Republican Party "restored the Government to its position as an umpire instead of player in the economic game. For this reason the American people have gone forward in progress while the rest of the world has halted and in some cases has even gone backward." This was Coolidgeism complete, even to the halo around America and the sneer at Europe and the rest of the world.

The excitement of the campaign was furnished by the Democratic nominee, Governor Alfred E. Smith of New York, who was nominated on the first ballot at the Democratic Convention in Houston after a stirring nomination speech made by Franklin D. Roosevelt, who hailed him, "Victory is his habit—the happy warrior, Alfred E. Smith."

New ground was broken by the nomination of Al Smith. He was the first Catholic nominated for Vice President or President by the Republican or Democratic parties. He was the first candidate from a big city—Theodore Roosevelt, also from New York City, had been in part a Western rancher. Smith had had little more than a grammar school education and was a product of Tammany Hall, a byword for corruption in the nation. He was also a notorious foe of Prohibition. In a telegram to the Democratic Convention after he was nominated, Smith said that while he would enforce the law, "It is well known that I believe that there should be a fundamental change in the present provision for national Prohibition. . . . I feel it is the duty of the chosen leader of the people to point the way."

Most significant for an understanding of the consensus on economic philosophy during the Coolidge years were the positions taken by the Democratic Party and its candidate. Of the Democratic platform the liberal *New Republic* said, "If the denunciatory sections of the platform had been omitted and the customary genuflections to Jefferson and states' rights were cut out, anyone who did not know might easily mistake this for a document the Hoover forces had drafted for the Republicans."

The platform for the first time in Democratic Party history abandoned the position of a tariff for revenue only. Now the party called for a tariff with "equitable distribution of benefits and burdens" and "the maintenance of legitimate business and a high standard of wages for American labor." In a campaign speech at Louisville, Smith took a firm stand explicitly in favor of a protective tariff. On the controversial public waterpower issue, the platform did not mention Muscle Shoals. It did ask for retention of "sovereign title and control" by the government, but this did not exclude leases to private interests. There was no hint of radicalism in the platform, nothing to alarm business or conservatives.

The influence of Coolidgeism was fully revealed by Smith's surprise choice for Democratic national chairman, John J. Raskob, a leading figure in the business world, vice-president of the General Motors Corporation, and chairman of the company's finance committee. Like Smith, he was a leading Catholic layman and a wet without apology, but it was his probusiness philosophy that was the most striking departure from Democratic tradition. He was a member of the Union League Club, open only to Republicans, and it was stated widely and without contradiction from him that he had voted for Coolidge in 1924 and that he was a foe of unionized labor.

Smith was quoted as having made this significant statement in a midnight conference in which he announced his choice to party leaders:

> In 1924 hundreds of thousands of people here in New York who voted for me also voted for that cold fish, Calvin Coolidge. It puzzled me then and I have thought a lot about it since. The only way that I can dope it out is that a whole lot of people who were willing to elect a Democratic governor were afraid for business reasons of a Democratic Administration in Washington.

Many in the Democratic Party were dismayed by the appointment. One of those was the future President Franklin D. Roosevelt, who said it was a "bold stroke to try to end the 99 percent of business, big and little, preference for the Republican party. . . . Frankly I am more and more disgusted and bored with the thought that in this great nation the principal issue may be drawn by what we do or do not put into our stomachs." He would think differently about the paramountcy of the stomach after 1932.

Raskob, on assuming the post, hailed Smith, in words that parroted Coolidge, as a "strong advocate of less government in business and more business in government." He praised the tariff plank of the party and established the Democratic Party offices in the General Motors Building in New York.

The GOP, in the words of one observer, "claimed control over the mechanism of prosperity analogous to the control which the medieval Church claimed over the mechanism of salvation." Smith, the poor boy from the sidewalks of New York, whom some had expected to project a neo-Jacksonian appeal, had elected to challenge the Republican Party on its own grounds by backing from big business. It was a contest he could not win.

But it was the Catholic issue which rocked the country, in the North, as well as in the South, and passions flared everywhere. Protestant denomination organs south of the Mason and Dixon Line dedicated themselves to the crusade against Smith. The Klan had a revival as it issued a Klarion Kall for a Krusade. Photographs of Smith kissing the ring of a papal legate were widely circulated to prove his subservience to the Pope, as was a fake Knights of Columbus oath swearing allegiance to the Pope. The whispering campaign grew into a shout, and Smith himself took cognizance of it in a speech in Oklahoma City in which he attacked intolerance and the Klan. "The cry of Tammany Hall is nothing more or less than a red herring that is pulled across the trail in order to throw us off the scent. I know what's behind it. It's nothing more or less than my religion." Certainly not since the Bryan candidacy in the campaign of 1896 did emotions run so high.

If Smith had violent detractors, he also had wild support not only from the unwashed, but also from a battalion of intellectual liberals, although he was nonintellectual and was clearly a liberal only on the Prohibition issue. Among his partisans were Heywood Broun, Franklin P. Adams, Stuart Chase, Elmer

Davis, Felix Frankfurter, Norman Hapgood, Alexander Wooll-
cott, Arthur Garfield Hays, H. L. Mencken, George Jean
Nathan, Sumner Slichter, Ida Tarbell, Rabbi Stephen S. Wise,
Sidney Howard, John Dewey, and Robert Sherwood.

To a large extent it was a polarization of personalities, with
the mechanical, moonfaced man in the high collar on one side
and the warm person with the brown derby, gold-toothed smile,
gravelly voice, and choice vernacular on the other. To Mencken,
Hoover seemed a crafty self-seeker. "Hoover is a Republican
only by prudent after-thought just as he is an American only
by a prudent after-thought." On the other hand, Smith seemed
"the most refreshing and stimulating phenomenon that America has witnessed since the death of Grover Cleveland. He is for
all his political aptitude the complete antithesis of the normal
American politician. The usual writhing and crawling is simply
not in him. Cocky, vulgar, even low, he is never cheap." More
than that, Smith was loved because the hatred for him was
deemed the worst of backwater yokelism. As Mencken put it:

> The majority of rural Americans with the best blood all
> drained to the cities are probably hopelessly uneducable. Sound
> ideas make no more appeal to them than decent drinks. They
> prefer nonsense to sense as they prefer White Mule to Burgundy.
> Abandoned for years to the tutelage of their pastors they have
> gone so far into the darkness that every light terrifies them and
> runs them amuck . . . in the long run the cities of the United
> States will have to throw off the hegemony of those morons.

The election result was expected, but Hoover's margin in
electoral votes was more lopsided than even the Republicans
had anticipated, 444 to 87. In the North, Smith carried Massachusetts and Rhode Island. He lost his own state of New York
by 100,000. The Republicans carried states in the Solid South
for the first time since Reconstruction—Virginia, North Carolina, Florida, and Texas. The vote had been heavy with
8,000,000 more going to the polls than in 1924, a measure of
the intensity of feeling that the election had generated.

In a large sense the election was an expression of the national
will for Coolidge's philosophy of government. Both candidates
were conservatives; both accepted the primacy of business leadership in our national life; both propounded the doctrine that the

function of government was to promote business health as the best means of fostering national well-being. In neither party was any question raised about the solidity of the prosperity the nation enjoyed, nor was there a word uttered about the speculative boom in Wall Street and the need to restrain it. There was no articulation of feeling among Democrats, if such a feeling existed, that Congress had been laggard in legislating for the benefit of the masses. There was no hint of radicalism in either of the parties and no adumbration of the later New Deal. All this, however, was conveniently forgotten in a later year when Calvin Coolidge became the single symbol for alleged dereliction in bringing about the economic disaster which lay ahead.

Coolidge had taken no part in the 1928 Presidential campaign beyond having lunch with Hoover and being photographed with him. He was restless and irritable in his last few months in the White House. He was in no mood for social functions. He declined an invitation to the Gridiron Club Dinner saying that he did not feel that the Presidential presence was mandatory. The Army and Navy Reception, the big event of the winter season, was disbanded after an hour and a half. He was querulous during a visit by James Derieux of the Crowell Publishing Company and Mrs. Derieux. He complained, "I don't know why people say I am silent, unless it is because I have no table talk. I have made more speeches than any other President." Mrs. Derieux asked him what bothered him most in the White House. Perhaps Coolidge thought that as a woman she was most interested in housekeeping details. He replied, "The White House hams. They would bring a big one to the table. Mrs. Coolidge would always have a slice and I would have one. The butler would take it away and what happened to it afterward I never could find out."

On March 4, 1929, the date of Hoover's inauguration, Mrs. Coolidge lined up some of the White House servants outside the room where her husband was dressing. When he emerged, she said, "Why, Calvin, here are Wilkins and the boys." He did not shake hands but rasped out something which might have been good morning, how are you, or good-bye. Mary Randolph, Mrs. Coolidge's secretary, felt that he was afraid that he might display sentiment, which would be unpardonable for him. He went down to the Blue Room, where Hoover and Vice President-elect Charles Curtis were waiting with some dignitaries and their wives. He shook a few hands and then said curtly, "Time to go." After the inaugural ceremonies, he and Mrs. Coolidge went directly to Union Station, where they boarded the train. The large crowd importuned Coolidge to speak. He said only, "Good-bye, I have had a very enjoyable time in Washington." He would see the city again only once more.

In his *Autobiography*, Coolidge wrote, "We draw our Presidents from the people. It is a wholesome thing for them to return to the people. I came from them. I wish to be one of them again." Cincinnatus in his return to the plow could not have behaved with such simplicity. After an all-night ride on the train, he arrived at Northampton at eight o'clock the next morning to be greeted by a crowd of several thousand. He was accompanied by a corps of twenty newsmen—America would retain its curiosity about Coolidge until his death. Through rain and slush the Coolidges drove to their home, the two-family house on Massasoit Street on which he had continued to pay the $36 a month rent during his Presidency.

The Coolidges had a housekeeper and a man who took care of the lawn and furnace and drove Coolidge to his office in the secondhand limousine that he had bought from the government on leaving. F. W. Plummer, principal of the high school in Northampton, who had lived in the other half of the house since Coolidge was lieutenant governor, always found Coolidge to be extremely reticent. "Mr. Coolidge seems to resent talk," related Mr. Plummer. "I do not mean that he is not always cordial to meet. . . . But if to the essential 'How do you do, Mr. Plummer,' he adds 'Going to be hot,' I feel that I have had a talk with Mr. Coolidge."

Coolidge soon found that it would be impossible to have privacy. He liked to sit on the front porch and enjoy a quiet smoke, as he had done in years past. However, a stream of cars passed, hundreds of cars from every state. His home was a tourist attraction, and guide maps were distributed at gasoline stations to show the location of the house. In the spring of 1930 Coolidge bought an estate in Northampton for $40,000. It was known as The Beeches, and it gave him privacy since its twelve-room house was set in nine acres of lawn and woodland.

His work habits remained the same. He awoke at seven in the morning, was at the office by eight, returned home for lunch and a nap, went back in the afternoon, and closed shop at about five thirty. He worked on his *Autobiography*, having signed a contract while still in the White House for its publication, first as a serial in Hearst's *Cosmopolitan* and then in book form. He would be paid $5 a word. He also wrote three articles on "Peace" for the *Ladies' Home Journal*, and as a new director of the New York Life Insurance Company, he took relish in attending the meetings in New York City on the twelfth of each month. On June 30, 1930, he started a daily article of 200 words for the McClure Newspaper Syndicate with the New York outlet in the *Herald Tribune*. They were homiletic pieces à la Coolidge on thrift, the Boy Scouts, old age pensions, and the like, never political or controversial in tone. Coolidge wrote every word himself, and even in the Depression the public lapped all of them up.

As soon as Hoover assumed the Presidency, he undertook to redeem his campaign pledges by calling Congress into a special session to enact farm legislation and to revise the tariff upward. In June he signed a new Agricultural Marketing Act establishing a Federal Farm Board which would deal with surpluses by buying a portion of the crop and taking it off the market. The new tariff, the highest in history, the Hawley-Smoot Law, was not enacted until a year later.

A fresh forward surge by the stock market followed the inauguration. The speculative frenzy of the public was related thus in a rhyme in the *Saturday Evening Post:*

> O hush thee, my babe, granny's bought more shares,
> Daddy's gone out to play with the bulls and the bears,
> Mother's buying on tips and she simply can't lose,
> And baby shall have some expensive new shoes.

Hoover was worried. He asked the Federal Reserve Board of New York to work out a voluntary plan with the New York banks to withhold credit for stock market purchases, but the plan fell through. Secretary Mellon, who had always been bullish on stocks, gave a veiled warning: "The present situation in the financial markets offers an opportunity for the prudent investors to buy bonds. Bonds are low in price compared to stocks." The call-money rate rose in April from 9 percent to 15 percent and then to the incredible rate of 20 percent, but the market rise could not be stemmed. The Federal Reserve had lost control of the money situation, said financier Paul Warburg.

In August the Federal Reserve Bank of New York took the drastic action of raising the rediscount rate from 5 percent to 6 percent. The market fell for one day, stabilized, and then zoomed higher. The public was not scared away. Brokers' loans which were $5.5 billion in September, 1928, were $8.5 billion a year later.

On September 3, 1929, stocks stood on the peak of Mount Everest. It had been a vertical ascent in the last year and a half. Since March 3, 1928, the price of the Radio Corporation of America (adjusted for a split) had risen from $94.50 to $505, Montgomery Ward from $132 to $466.50, General Electric from $128 to $396, Westinghouse Electric from $91.50 to $313.

In early September the great bull market started to totter. There was a series of declines and a dramatic recovery on September 19. Then the downward move set in for good and gained in force. No specific news started the trend, though blame was put on the discovery of the peculations of a London financial promoter named Clarence C. Hatry which upset the London Exchange and caused a withdrawal of funds from New York stocks. Break after break in prices brought increasing worry and discouragement to Wall Street. On October 15, Professor Irving Fisher of Yale announced that prices stood on "what looks like a permanently high plateau" and after more bad days said on October 18, "I believe the breaks of the last few days have driven stocks down to the hard rocks." It was, however, only the threshold of the catastrophe.

On October 24, Black Thursday, panic erupted as prices fell apart in a frantic day in which 12,984,000 shares were traded. Hitherto 5,000,000 shares had been considered spectacular; now the ticker fell hours behind actual transactions on the floor. At noon leading bankers met in the offices of J. P. Morgan and Company and pledged $30,000,000 to support prices. The Morgan partner Thomas W. Lamont informed the press, "There has been a little [sic] distress selling on the Stock Exchange" owing to a "technical condition of the market rather than to any fundamental cause." Richard Whitney, vice-president of the exchange, representing the bankers, walked on the floor of the exchange placing orders for a dozen stocks at prices above the market—which heartened Wall Street, but only for a short time.

Worse was to come on October 29, Terrifying Tuesday, when almost all stocks joined in a disastrous drop and trading reached the fantastic figure of 16,410,000 shares. Lights burned all through the night in Wall Street. Liquidation had been increased by the setting off of stop-loss orders and by the selling out of one layer below another of margin accounts, whose owners were wiped out. Successive waves of liquidation from foreign accounts had plunged the market through one support level to the next.

President Hoover issued a statement: "The fundamental business of the country, that is the production and distribution of commodities, is on a sound and prosperous basis." Government officials exuded the utmost optimism, as did business leaders. The Federal Reserve Board issued a summary of industrial production for the third quarter which showed business 10 percent above the same quarter of 1928, but it did show declines in steel and auto production and in new building contracts. From Pocantico Hills in New York, John D. Rockefeller, Sr., now ninety years old, made a rare public statement: "Believing that fundamental conditions of the country are sound . . . my son and I have for some days been purchasing sound common stocks." Professor Irving Fisher said that stock prices were "absurdly low"; this seemed to be the signal for a new selling wave.

When the selling subsided in mid-November, the Dow-Jones average measuring the prices of blue-chip industrial stocks was down by 45 percent; in the stocks of lesser quality the carnage was far worse. The market rallied in early 1930 but then turned about as the slide resumed with increased intensity. By 1932 the general level of stock prices in the Dow-Jones industrial average would be only 10 percent of the 1929 highs.

There was no sense of impending doom in the air in November and December, 1929. The consequences of the cataclysm in Wall Street were widely minimized. The *Literary Digest* started its treatment of the event by saying that it would go down in history as the "Prosperity Panic of 1929." The New York *World* called it a "gamblers' and not an investors' panic," and in Britain two of its leading economists, Sir Josiah Stamp and John Maynard Keynes, said that the effect would be a healthy one since it would liquidate unsound speculation. There were news stories, with photographs of beaming countenances, congratulating the canny people who had kept the funds to buy stocks at bargain-counter prices. Samuel Insull announced that stocks were now so safe that he would personally guarantee all stock margin accounts of his employees.

Some repercussions from the Crash were felt immediately. Prices tumbled on all the commodity exchanges. Retrenchment by the upper income group, which was hardest hit, was reflected in lower sales of furs, jewelry and other luxury items, steamship reservations, and even tickets for Broadway shows. Fearing the effect on business confidence, on November 21 President Hoover held a conference with such industrial leaders as Henry Ford, Alfred P. Sloan of General Motors, and Walter Gifford of American Telephone and obtained a pledge from them not to cut wage rates, which was seconded by a larger conference of business representatives two weeks later in the White House. In a New Year's Day message, Secretary Mellon declared, "I see nothing in the situation which warrants pessimism." But already manufacturers were reporting a drying up of orders, and building orders had all but halted. The downward spiral was in full swing. By the summer of 1930, despite all the optimism from Washington, it was undeniable that the nation was in the grip of a severe business slump.

And what of Calvin Coolidge in Northampton, Massachusetts? He did not discuss the economic crisis with the press, and to friends he said that his sources of information were now not much better than their own. His inner feelings, like those of

287

most Americans, including Herbert Hoover, were those of sheer bewilderment. Like others, he tried to see the silver lining, and he pointed out this or that sign of a business turnabout.

But contentment had vanished from Calvin Coolidge, who had been the nation's fat cat symbol, and in remarkable empathy with the mood of his countrymen, his life was turning to gall and wormwood. A friend calling on Coolidge one day found him in a morose mood. "I have been ignored and forgotten," he said. He compared his dingy office surroundings to the magnificence and panoply of the White House. It was a bitter transition from the power and glory of the Presidency to a vacuum. His whole life had been work, and now there was no work to do, especially when he dropped his newspaper column after a year's irksome stint. He filled in his lonely hours as best he could. Hoover appointed him a member of a five-man National Transportation Commission to study the desperate problem of the nation's railroads, which were sinking into a financial mire. Two of the other members were Al Smith and Bernard Baruch. The commission held a few meetings but never really got off the ground.

The Presidential campaign of 1932 rolled in. These were black times of untold personal tragedy, of breadlines and bankruptcies. Hoover's popularity had taken a drastic fall, but Coolidge's remained high. The Republicans realized that Coolidge could be a major asset for Hoover's contest with Franklin D. Roosevelt. Everett Sanders was chosen to be the new chairman of the Republican National Committee, and since he was best known as Coolidge's former secretary, this shed a Coolidge aura on the Republican campaign.

Coolidge was ready to do what he could to help in Hoover's desperate fight for reelection, but his health stood in the way. He wrote Sanders on June 17, 1932, "You know I should be glad to do anything I can to help. My throat, you will remember, always bothers me and it is in such shape that I could not do much of anything in the way of speaking. Just at present I am having some trouble about breathing again." He said he was going up to Plymouth for an indefinite stay and hoped that his health would improve.

Those who saw him in Vermont that summer were disturbed

by his appearance. "He was thinner and his face was paler than usual," said Sanders. Henry L. Stoddard of the New York *Sun* thought that his complexion plainly showed slower heart action and that Coolidge moved around in short, timid steps, indicating that he realized that he had to be careful of himself. Most of the summer was devoted to the preparation of an extensive article to appear in the *Saturday Evening Post* in behalf of Hoover; it would be answered by Al Smith in behalf of Roosevelt. The actor Otis Skinner and his wife lunched with Mr. and Mrs. Coolidge that summer in Woodstock, Vermont. Discussing the forthcoming election, Mrs. Skinner said, "I wish it were you that we were to vote for in November. It would be the end of the depression," to which Coolidge wryly replied, "It would be the beginning of mine."

His article, which appeared on September 12, is interesting for its touches of pure Coolidge. He blamed the Crash on speculation here but more on events abroad. Thus, the Crash was triggered in part by the failure of the Hatry concern in London; by the end of 1930, when the panic should have been almost over, further recession arose from a banking collapse in Germany and Austria and by England's going off the gold standard. He wrote, "It will be observed that all these causes of depression, with the exception of the early speculation, had their origins outside of the United States where they were entirely beyond the control of our government. When men in public office have to meet a crisis which they did not themselves in any way create, the measure of the credit or blame which should attach to such office-holders is not the intensity of the crisis, but the manner in which they may meet it. Perhaps it would be more in accord with the even-handed justice demanded by the facts to stop blaming President Hoover for the condition of depression, the devastating effects of which arose almost entirely outside of his jurisdiction." Coolidge must have been thinking of the blame that might be assigned to himself, too.

With cold Puritan logic he added that Americans themselves were responsible for what had happened to them. "If the advantages and privileges of prosperity were abused by over-speculation, it was something in which the great body of the people were engaged through one method or another to such a degree

289

that they did not heed the warning efforts of the Federal Reserve Board."

Coolidge thought that this article was a complete expression of his views and no further aid would be required of him, but Sanders pressed him to make a speech. He consented to appear in Madison Square Garden on October 11 and was given a great ovation by the capacity crowd. He reviewed the efforts Hoover had made to cope with the economic crisis and praised them. He concluded by stating his belief that the worst was over and that the country was now on the path of recovery.

He looked haggard, and his voice weakened at times. He told Sanders afterward that he had had doubts whether he would be able to finish the speech. A woman came up to him and said, "What a wonderful speech it was, Mr. Coolidge! I stood up all through it." He made his last reported quip, which was a cry from his bone-weary body, when he replied, "So did I."

He was pressed to speak again, this time in Chicago. On October 20 he wired Sanders, "Unable to make speech." He followed this with a letter in which he said that another speech was a physical impossibility, that he had not yet recovered from his New York appearance. Hoover recalled, "After the New York address, he sent word to me that he had found the excitement and effort of that occasion was [sic] more strain than he should rightly put on his heart. I, of course, at once asked that he should not undertake the Chicago speech. It was my first intimation his heart was affected." He consented to speak on the radio on election eve and did so in a well-written appeal of fifteen minutes from his Northampton home.

He seemed more worn after the election. He was visibly depressed by the landslide victory for Roosevelt, which was not only a repudiation of Hooverism but of Coolidgeism. The current of events had clearly outrun the Coolidge philosophy of government. He was depressed, too, according to Mrs. Coolidge, by the appearance of a new book, *The Rise of Saint Calvin,* by Duff Gilfond. The book did not denigrate his character; the word "belittling" would be more appropriate. To Coolidge the book must have appeared as a symbol of a new phase in the assessment of Calvin Coolidge and his lifework, which would be a downgrading in the pages of history.

The air was electric with the spirit of change in the months before the installation of the new regime. Roosevelt's speech of acceptance delivered at the Chicago convention and his campaign speeches indicated that he intended to perform surgery on the old order of things.

Coolidge talked for the last time on national topics with newsman Henry L. Stoddard in New York on December 14. He sensed that great changes were ahead, "socialistic notions of government" which he wouldn't know how to handle even if he were called on to do so. That is why his time in public affairs was past, he said. "We are in a new era to which I do not belong and it would not be possible for me to adjust to it."

On December 27, while thanking Everett Sanders for his gift of a book for Christmas, he wrote a valedictory to all his friends. "Not the least of the reasons why I could not persuade myself to run for office again is the thought of the terrible burden it imposes on my friends. They have to make sacrifices which I can never repay." On New Year's Day his old friend and Amherst classmate Charles A. Andrews visited him at The Beeches, and Coolidge said to him, "I am very comfortable because I am not doing anything of any account, but a real effort to accomplish something goes hard with me. I am too old for my years. I suppose the carrying of responsibility as I have done takes its toll. I'm afraid I'm all burned out."

On January 5, 1933, Coolidge woke early and had breakfast with his wife at eight o'clock. A half hour later he rode down to his office. He went through some matters with his secretary, Harry Ross, and dictated a few letters. At ten o'clock he said to Ross, "I guess we'll go to the house." Ross concluded that he wasn't feeling too well. Only the day before at his home he had said, "I'm getting to be an old man. I have an idea that we might stop going down to the office each day and do our work up here."

He exchanged a few words with his wife, who was leaving to do some shopping. She said she would not need the car. He toyed with a jigsaw puzzle in the library. He said he was thirsty and got a drink in the kitchen. He went down to the cellar and had some small talk with the gardener. About noon he went up to his bedroom to shave. He took off his coat and sank to the

291

floor. Soon thereafter Mrs. Coolidge returned from her shopping and found him there. The previous day had been exactly six months from his sixtieth birthday.

His body was taken to Plymouth for burial in the cemetery where his father and son lay. The headstone bears only the name of Calvin Coolidge, dates of birth and death, and the Presidential seal. His widow survived him by twenty-four years, living to the age of seventy-eight. His son John, now sixty-two years of age, operates a cheese factory in Plymouth, not far from where his father was born.

Ave atque vale. Coolidge passed away almost at the nadir of the Depression, amid widening bank failures, battles by farmers with law officers to prevent farm foreclosure sales and lengthening breadlines. The golden dream of his era had dissolved into bitterness and despair, and America was ready to follow new leaders, who would set a revolutionary course.

The Coolidge Era was a siesta in the life of the nation, a time of some progress and the height of optimism. Somehow the social and economic forces in a vast land and indeed over most of the globe rested for years in equilibrium. Little happened that was politically earthshaking. There comes to mind a passage in the early pages of Edward Gibbon's *Decline and Fall of the Roman Empire.* Discussing the reign of Antoninus Pius in the second century A.D., Gibbon wrote, "Antoninus diffused order and tranquillity in the greatest part of the earth. His reign is marked by the rare advantage of furnishing few materials for history, which is indeed little more than the register of the crimes, follies, and misfortunes of mankind."

From what greater hopes, hopes of everlasting prosperity and everlasting peace, could come greater sorrow? The bulging pages of history in the thirties and forties are due to the "misfortunes of mankind." The world was out of joint. After Coolidge came black depression and a vast reorganization of the concept of government to cope with it, the rise of Hitler in Germany and a second world war. In the subsequent time of so-called peace America has faced staggering problems at home and one foreign crisis after another.

The Coolidge years were by no means golden years for the large segment of the population that had to struggle on substandard incomes or were the victims of racial or religious prejudice. However, it is understandable why America now looks back wistfully on the placid times of Silent Cal as the Golden Twenties.

NOTES

Coolidge, for reasons known only to himself, destroyed his personal papers after his Presidency. One of his White House secretaries, Edward T. Clark, wrote, "This would not involve the loss which you might at first imagine, because, as President, Mr. Coolidge did not follow the practice of other Presidents in trying to explain his administration in letters to his friends . . . the files therefore consisted of a huge number of letters to him which might be of interest, but with replies which reveal little or nothing."

However, the voluminous general files of the White House during his Presidency are preserved in the Library of Congress, and the author has combed through them. They contain illuminating Coolidge correspondence and memoranda in his own hand which have been incorporated into this book. Also, the transcripts of Coolidge's press conferences have been found recently. During his Presidency, Coolidge used a protective shield by speaking to the press off the record with only indirect attribution to himself. The most informative portions of the press transcripts were published in 1964 by the University of Massachusetts Press in a volume entitled *The Talkative President.*

Newspapers and magazines of the period have been used. Newsmagazines as we know them today did not exist then. The most popular was the *Literary Digest,* which collected press opinions from around the nation on prominent or interesting topics. The *Outlook* and the *Independent,* which *Outlook* swallowed up, focused their interpretations on the more serious side of the news. *Time,* which was started in 1923, was quite skimpy compared to today, though much in the same style, and has provided vignettes on people and events for this book. The *Nation, New Republic, Harper's,* and *Atlantic Monthly* strongly resembled today's magazines, but the mortality in journals appealing to the highly literate population is striking, including the *Forum, Scribner's, North American Review, Century,* and *American Mercury.*

Only Yesterday by Frederick Lewis Allen, published in 1931, fastened public attention on the bizarre nature of the preceding decade. Allen had been strongly influenced by a book of 1928, *The Great American Bandwagon,* by Charles Merz, a prolific journalist who wrote in trenchant vein about the aberrations of the era. Since Allen's book there has been a great deal of interest in the twenties. Isabel Leighton in *The Aspirin Age* edited a collection of essays about high-spot events, and George E. Mowry in *The Twenties: Ford, Flappers and Fanatics* collected articles of the period. Joe Alex Morris in his *What a Year!* described more than the year 1929, and John Montgomery has contributed his *The Twenties: An Informal Social History. American Heritage* has put out in book form its August, 1965, issue, *The Twenties,* and *Life* magazine has put out its 1964 articles entitled *War, Boom and Bust,* written by Ernest May and the editors of *Life.* Most recently we have had *Babbitts and Bohemians* by Elizabeth Stevenson. George H. Knoles has compiled *The Jazz Age Revisited: British Criticism of American Civilization During the 1920s,* and the Englishman Beverley Nichols gave his reactions to Coolidge America in *The Star Spangled Manner.*

Histories of this century covering a wider span of years than the twenties have proved valuable for this book: *Since 1900* by Oscar Theodore Barck, Jr., and Nelson Manfred Blake; *Our Recent Past* by Thomas Bonner; *America in Midpassage* by Charles and Mary Beard; *From Versailles to the New Deal* by Harold U. Faulkner; *Between the Wars, 1919 to 1941* by David S. Shannon; *Contemporary America* by Harvey S. Wish; and *American Epoch* by Arthur S. Link and William B. Catton. *The Great Crusade and After, 1914–1928,* by Preston William Slosson is deserving of special mention for its success in interweaving political and economic facets of the era.

CHAPTER I—CALVIN COOLIDGE

The most reliable book concerning Coolidge must necessarily be his *Autobiography,* despite his almost studied effort not to be self-revealing, and a certain tongue-in-cheek quality in some parts of the book. A few brief books about Coolidge were published in the early years of his Presidency; of these *President Coolidge: A Contemporary Estimate* by Edward Elwell Whiting is worthy of note. After his Presidency, in 1932, when his reputation was on the downgrade in the economic crisis, there was *The Rise of Saint Calvin* by Duff Gilfond, the subtitle—*Merry Sidelights on the Career of Mr. Coolidge*—conveying the tenor of the book. In 1938 the noted Republican editor William Allen White published *A Puritan in Babylon.* White had an ill-concealed dislike for Coolidge from the time of his nomination for Vice President in 1920, and this book did little to aid Coolidge's reputation for posterity. His general theme was that Coolidge had turned the country over to Wall Street interests, "another crew which was to devastate the country more terribly than Harding's greasy playfellows." In 1940 there was a friendly book, *Calvin Coolidge* by Claude M. Fuess. Mrs. Coolidge supplied Fuess with family letters, and Frank Waterman Stearns made available his correspondence with Coolidge. Fuess was far more accurate with his facts than White but failed to grapple with the central problem of Coolidge's responsibility for the Crash, and he concluded lamely, "His task was to keep the Ship of State on an even keel before a favoring wind." There was no further biography of Coolidge for more than a quarter of a century when, in 1967, Donald R. McCoy put out *Calvin Coolidge: A New Appraisal.* Since Coolidge's death in 1933 many people had occasion to provide their recollections of this peculiar personality, and Edwin Connery Lathem collected these in a 1960 book, *Meet Calvin Coolidge: The Man Behind the Myth.*

Lowry's article, "Calvin, the Silent" appeared in the *New Republic,* September 28, 1921. H. L. Mencken's estimate of Coolidge appeared in his *American Mercury* in April, 1933, three months after Coolidge's death. Coolidge's life in Northampton as a fledgling lawyer was described by his friend Alfred Pearce Dennis in the *Saturday Evening Post,* September 20, 1924. Frank Waterman Stearns, though a resident of the White House, received surprisingly little attention from the press during the Coolidge Presidency. However, *Independent* magazine once alluded to him: "His heart and soul are completely wrapped up with the welfare of Mr. Coolidge. He would cut off his right hand, he would put out his right eye if he thought for a moment that it would aid the President. He doesn't pretend to understand Mr. Coolidge, he simply worships him."

The detailed account by Fuess of the Boston police strike is by far the best I have encountered. Mark Sullivan in his *The Twenties,* the last volume of *Our Times,* explains the turndown of Senator Lenroot in favor of Coolidge in the 1920 convention in terms of the aversion for Lenroot's association with La Follette. Samuel Hopkins Adams' essay "The Timely Death of President Harding" appears in *The Aspirin Age.* See also his *Incredible Era.* Mark Sullivan in his *The Twenties* has an excellent discussion of the Harding regime which concludes *Our Times.* The young newspaperman at the kerosene swearing in, Joe H. Fountain, later wrote of it in *Homestead Inaugural,* and his recollections were included in the account in *American Heritage* by C. M. Wilson in December, 1963. Harry Daugherty's memoirs, *The Inside Story of the Harding Tragedy,* appeared in 1932.

The correspondence about Coolidge's attitude toward the Klan is in the White House files. From the time that Coolidge took office, the White House secretariat was busy denying rumors that Coolidge was a member of the Klan. Thus, in a December, 1923, letter, secretary Clark wrote a Reverend Plomer, "You can be very positive in your statements that neither President Harding or [*sic*] President Coolidge has been a member of this body." For articles about Vice President Dawes, see "Charles the Bean-Spiller," by F. Ray, *New Republic,* March 18, 1925; "Dawes and Delay" by C. Field, *Outlook,* March 25, 1925; "Dawes, the Melody Man," by E. C. May, *Collier's*, August 1, 1925; and "General Dawes" by J. T. McCutcheon, *Century*, May, 1928.

Everett Sanders, who worked more closely with Coolidge than any other man, discussed him in "The Coolidge Character" in the *Saturday Evening Post* of January 17, 1933. Life in the White House in the Coolidge days has been described by Ona Griffin Jeffries in *The Ins and Outs of the White House* and Irwin H. "Ike" Hoover in his *Forty-two Years in the White House*, which appeared the year after Coolidge's death. The relations between Coolidge and Hoover were not cordial, Hoover admits, and Mrs. Coolidge took angry exception to some of Hoover's statements, such as the one that White House employees were filled with "fear and trembling" about their jobs while Coolidge was President. Dr. Kolmer's report of Coolidge at the bedside of his son appeared in *Time* magazine of July 18, 1955, from an article in the Temple University medical journal. Mrs. Coolidge discussed her husband in articles in *Good Housekeeping* from February to June, 1935, entitled "The Real Calvin Coolidge." For further discussion of their relationship see the book, by Ishbel Ross, *Grace Coolidge and Her Era* and "Presidents and First Ladies" by Mrs. Coolidge's social secretary, Mary Randolph, in the *Ladies' Home Journal* of June, 1936.

Charles Merz in his article "The Silent Mr. Coolidge" in the *New Republic* of June 2, 1926, made a statistical analysis which showed that Silent Cal in speeches, press conferences, and official statements was silent only one day out of four and that he was drowning the nation in a torrent of words. Mencken wrote an estimate of Coolidge in the Baltimore *Evening Sun* of October 17, 1927, and praised his writing ability in the same paper on December 24, 1928. "Mr. Coolidge" by Frank Kent appeared in the *American Mercury*, August, 1924; "Coolidge in Spite of Himself" by John Spargo, *North American Review*, September, 1927; "The Genius of the Average" by Gamaliel Bradford, *Atlantic Monthly*, January, 1930; and "The Great Coolidge Mystery" by Bruce Bliven, *Harper's*, December, 1925. Governor William J. Bulow wrote the story of Coolidge's sojourn in the Black Hills of South Dakota in the summer of 1927, along with his impressions of the President, for the *Saturday Evening Post* of January 4, 1947, "When Cal Coolidge Came to Visit Us." The book *Starling of the White House* was published in 1946. Coolidge gems were collected by John H. McKee in his *Coolidge Wit and Wisdom*. Sinclair Lewis' "The Man Who Knew Coolidge" was first published by Mencken in his *American Mercury* of January, 1928.

Budget Director Lord sent reports directly to Coolidge, which are in the White House files, about recommendations he had made to the departments for saving money. Coolidge, in turn, sent letters of congratulation to Cabinet officers for their accomplishments in economy.

The fiction of the White House Spokesman was apparently well enough known to the reading public so that Will Rogers could poke fun at it in his *Saturday Evening Post* article of January 8, 1927, "Letter from a Self-Made Diplomat to His Constituents." He told of his visit to the White

House where he met Coolidge, who had the Spokesman by his side. "You can't hardly tell the Spokesman or double from the President. I have seen lots of doubles in the pictures when I was out there [in Hollywood]. But this one the President has is the best I ever saw. When he is just there not doing anything, you would swear it was Mr. Coolidge." The comment by Drew Pearson about Coolidge's amazing press popularity was in the Washington *Post* of March 10, 1963.

CHAPTER II—THE REACTION

For the mood of conservatism in politics, see *The Republican Ascendancy 1921–1933*, by John Donald Hicks; *America in the Twentieth Century* by Frank Freidel; and the section concerning Coolidge in *The Crisis of the Old Order*, the first volume of *The Age of Roosevelt* by Arthur M. Schlesinger, Jr. André Siegfried's view is contained in his *America Comes of Age: A French Analysis*. For the attitude of Wilson's Attorney General, A. Mitchell Palmer, on the Red danger see his "Case Against the Reds" in the *Forum* of February, 1920.

Coolidge's management of the news was discussed by Oswald Garrison Villard in "Press and the President," *Century*, December, 1925. A careful treatment of the Ku Klux Klan of the twenties is in the 1965 book *The Ku Klux Klan: A Century of Infamy* by William Peirce Randel. See also *Hooded Americanism: The First Century of the Ku Klux Klan* by David M. Chalmers. Imperial Wizard Hiram Wesley Evans explained "The Klan's Fight for Americanism" in the *North American Review* of March, 1926. There are two diatribes in book form about David C. Stephenson: *The Mad Mullah of America* by Edgar Booth and *So They Framed Stephenson* by Robert A. Butler. Robert Couglan of Time-Life as a small boy in a Catholic family was an eyewitness to "Konklave in Kokomo," which he described in *The Aspirin Age*. For other good accounts concerning Stephenson, see "Indiana's Mystery Man" by W. G. Shepherd in *Collier's*, January 8, 1927, and "Gentlemen from Indiana" by Morton Harrison in the *Atlantic Monthly*, May, 1928. The facts concerning the sex attack on Madge Oberholtzer have been taken by the author from those stated by the Supreme Court of Indiana in upholding Stephenson's conviction, 205 Indiana Reports 141 (1933). The paradox of the dwindling of lynchings in the South during the Klan era was thus explained by the *New Republic*: "The persistence of lynching as an institution was possible only as long as it remained respectable. The Klan cheapened it and diverted the awful instrument of inter-racial terrorism to all sorts of trivial and even political ends, and so brought it into universal contempt."

Prothro's analysis of the businessman outlook during the decade, published by the University of Louisiana Press in 1954, was the result of an industrious sifting of journals for business. Coolidge's probusiness bias is evidenced by memoranda in the White House files marked "Confidential"

299

from William E. Humphrey to secretary Edward T. Clark, asking him to convey to the President what he had done and what he planned to do to strangulate the Federal Trade Commission. Richard Washburn Child defended Coolidge in the articles "President" and "More of the President" in the *Saturday Evening Post* of April 17, 1926, and in the *Forum* of February, 1927.

For the Child Labor Amendment, see "Battle on the Child Labor Amendment," *Literary Digest*, December 6, 1924; "Child Labor Amendment Defeated," *New Republic*, May 20, 1925; and "Defeat of the Twentieth Amendment" by T. F. Cadwalader, *Annals of the American Academy of Political and Social Science*, January, 1927.

The perplexity of liberals is evidenced by an amusing contest carried on in the *Nation* in early 1924 by William Hard for the best definition of Progressive, the prize being a lock of Senator Henrik Shipstead's hair (the Farmer-Laborite from Minnesota had quite a mane). For the life of George W. Norris, see *Fighting Liberal: Autobiography of George W. Norris* and *Integrity: The Life of George W. Norris* by Richard L. Neuberger and Stephen B. Kahn. For the Muscle Shoals debate, see "Muscle Shoals: Bonanza or White Elephant?", in *Scientific American*, May, 1925, and "The Problem of Muscle Shoals," *Current History*, August, 1928.

For the position of labor in the Coolidge Era, there are good accounts in *The Lean Years: A History of the American Worker 1920–1933* by Irving Bernstein and in *American Labor* by Henry Pelling. The autobiography of Samuel Gompers, entitled *Seventy Years of Life and Labor*, appeared in 1925, after his death. Concerning Gompers, see Benjamin Stolberg's "What Manner of Man Was Gompers?", *Atlantic Monthly*, March, 1925, and "Karl Marx and Samuel Gompers," by J. R. Commons, *Political Science Quarterly*, June, 1926.

Concerning the strife in Gastonia, a running barrage of articles can be found in the *Nation* and *New Republic* in the latter half of 1929. Other helpful articles are "Gastonia" by Mary Heaton Vorse, *Harper's*, November, 1929; Sinclair Lewis' "North Carolina's Labor War," *Literary Digest*, November 9, 1929; "Religion as a Cloak for Injustice," *Christian Century*, October 30, 1929; and "Lesson of Gastonia," *Outlook*, September 11, 1929. The literature about Sacco and Vanzetti is abundant. For a view in retrospect more than twenty years afterward, see *The Legacy of Sacco and Vanzetti* by G. Louis Joughlin and Edmund M. Morgan.

CHAPTER III—THE EXPERIMENT THAT FAILED

Highly readable histories of Prohibition are *The Dry Decade* by Charles Merz and *The Great Illusion* by Herbert Asbury. See also *Pressure Politics: The Story of the Anti-Saloon League* by Peter H. Odegard and *Prohibition: The Era of Excess* by Andrew Sinclair.

Malcolm Cowley discussed the spread of Greenwich Village standards in his *Exile's Return,* published in 1934, after his return from expatriation to France a few years before. The loosening of morals is taken up in *Fantastic Interim: A Hindsight History of American Manners, Morals and Mistakes Between Versailles and Pearl Harbor* by Henry M. Robinson. Practical methods of evading the Prohibition restrictions are described by Charles Merz in *The Dry Decade,* and they are also detailed in "Profession of Bootlegging" by Joseph K. Willing in the *Annals of American Academy of Political and Social Science* of May, 1926. Discussions of Assistant Attorney General Mabel Walker Willebrandt include "Woman in Law" by A. Strokosch, *Saturday Evening Post,* September 24, 1927; "Where Duty Lies," *Collier's,* October 27, 1928; and "Mrs. Willebrandt's Appeal to the Methodists," *Literary Digest,* September 29, 1928.

I have found no correspondence regarding Prohibition involving Coolidge in the White House files, a conspicuous omission which may have some bearing on the question of how deeply he was committed to the cause. There is a letter from Prohibition Commissioner Haynes to Coolidge's secretary C. Bascom Slemp in February, 1924, outlining plans to make Cleveland, the site of the Republican National Convention, bone-dry. Haynes was as good as his word. H. L. Mencken wrote that Cleveland was his worst experience during Prohibition: "Even the local cops and newspaper reporters were dry, and many of the latter spent a large part of their time touring the quarters of the out-of-town correspondents, begging for succor."

For the battle by General Smedley Butler to dry up Philadelphia, see "Leatherneck Wallops the Small Gods" by J. Stuart, *Collier's,* January 17, 1925, and "General Butler's Dramatic Exit," *Literary Digest,* January 9, 1926. Al Capone is the subject of the book *The Biography of a Self-Made Man* by Fred D. Pasley, and he is the major figure in *The Bootleggers and Their Era* by Kenneth Allsop. See also the articles "I Know You, Al" by Edward D. Sullivan, *North American Review,* September, 1929, and "Rise of a Racketeer" by L. W. Hunt, *Outlook,* December 10, 1930. In the years following the St. Valentine's Day Massacre, many clues from gangland were pieced together, and as authoritative a reconstruction as any is the *St. Valentine's Day Massacre* by Boris O'Hara.

CHAPTER IV—A-U-T-O

Books on the history of the automobile include *Combustion on Wheels: An Informal History of the Automobile Age* by David L. Cohn; *The Automobile Industry: Its Economic and Commercial Development* by Ralph C. Epstein; *Treasury of the Automobile* by Ralph Stein; and *And Then Came Ford* by Charles Merz. A recent collection of instructive and entertaining material on the automobile is the British book edited by Derek Jewell entitled *Man and Motor: The 20th Century Love Affair.* Mark Sullivan in his *Our Times* devoted considerable attention to the automobile revolution in Volume I, *Turn of the Century*, and Volume IV, *The War Begins.* On fear that the auto market might be saturated, in the June, 1920, issue of *Review of Reviews*, J. G. Frederick discusses the question "Can the Automobile Business Go On Growing?" The *Literary Digest* recurrently in the decade took up the question—see the issues of September 11, 1920, November 21, 1925, and June 18, 1927. The symptoms of automania were discussed by William Ashdown in the *Atlantic Monthly* of June, 1925, "Confessions of an Automobilist." That many Americans preferred an automobile and a life on wheels to the roots and comforts of a home was taken up in "Automobile Gas Gypsies" in the *New Republic*, August 11, 1926, and "Gasoline Gypsies" in the *Survey*, December 1, 1924.

For Aaron Sapiro, see "Sapiro the Spectacular" by E. C. Lindeman in the *New Republic* of April 13, 1927. Books consulted for the section on Henry Ford have included *Ford: The Times, the Man, the Company* by Allan Nevins with Frank Ernest Hill, *The Last Billionaire* by William C. Richards, and *We Never Called Him Henry* by Harry H. Bennett. Amid Ford's great personal popularity in the twenties, there were some sharply critical articles about him, such as a series that Robert Littell wrote for the *New Republic* in October and November, 1923, and "The Canonization of Henry Ford" by Charles Merz in the *Independent*, November 27, 1926.

For the career of William Crapo Durant, see "Record in Industrial Growth: W. C. Durant and the General Motors Corporation" by F. W. Parsons in the *Saturday Evening Post*, February 7, 1920, and "Riders of the Whirlwind" in *Collier's*, January 19, 1929. Durant was undoubtedly better known to the public for his offer in 1928 of a $25,000 prize for the best plan for enforcing Prohibition than for all his achievements in the world of industry and finance. For Walter P. Chrysler, see his autobiography in 1938, *Life of an American Workman.*

CHAPTER V—PERSONALITY CRAZE

Walter Lippmann's views on Calvin Coolidge as a fascinating public personality were in an article for *Vanity Fair* in May, 1926, and he expanded his assessment for his 1927 book *Men of Destiny.* "The Meaning of Lindbergh's Flight" by John W. Ward appeared in *American Quarterly X.* The book by Kenneth S. Davis is *The Hero: Charles A. Lindbergh and the American Dream,* and a more recent book, *The Last Hero: Charles A. Lindbergh* is by Walter S. Ross. The visit of the Prince of Wales with Coolidge is described by "Ike" Hoover in his book. Among the many articles about the prince in contemporary journals, note "He's a Prince!", *New Republic,* September 10, 1924, and "On the Trail of His Royal Shyness," *Literary Digest,* September 20, 1924. The visit of Queen Marie to the White House is also described by "Ike" Hoover. The ballyhoo about the queen is reflected in a series running from May to October, 1926, in *Good Housekeeping* by M. P. Daggett, "Close-Up of a Queen." For an uncomplimentary appraisal of the queen, see "Marie of Rumania" by Charles Merz in the *New Republic,* October 20, 1926, and for a summing up of the public fuss, see "Mr. Babbitt Draws a Queen" by H. N. Denny, *Forum,* March, 1927. The account of Marion Talley's lunch with President Coolidge is in *A Puritan in Babylon* by William Allen White, who was a guest on the occasion. For the debate in the press on whether the artistic merits of Miss Talley qualified her as a new Melba, see the *Literary Digest* of March 6 and 20, 1926. The long groundwork for Miss Talley's sensational debut is indicated by this excerpt from the *Nation* of October 14, 1925: "When the date is finally announced when she will sing, we suspect that there will be a prodigious activity in Missouri, a refurbishing of opera hats, a vast purchasing of gowns and cloaks. . . ."

Mencken's article concerning his dinner with Valentino appeared in his *Prejudices: Second Series.* Had Valentino become fed up with being a film idol long before? See an interview with him by John K. Winkler in *Collier's* of January 16, 1926, "I'm Tired of Being a Sheik." The summary of Valentino's career and last illness is based on news accounts, and there is some divergence from the 1967 book *Valentino* by Irving Shulman.

"Grover, the Magnificent" by Henry F. Pringle appeared in the *American Mercury* of July, 1929. Gene Fowler wrote a comprehensive book about Mayor Walker entitled *Beau James.* Pringle discussed Walker in the *American Mercury* of November, 1926. For Walker's peregrinations, see "His Honor Jimmy Walker, Mayor of Europe," *Literary Digest,* October 8, 1927. For unflattering portraits of Walker, see "New York's Jimmie" by C. F. Thompson, *Nation,* August 28, 1929, and "Musical Comedy Mayor," *Outlook,* May 20, 1931. Coolidge's impression of Walker was reported by his secretary Herman Beaty in *International-Cosmopolitan* of April, 1933.

For new interest in recreation and sports which swept the nation, see "The Age of Play" by Robert L. Duffus in the *Independent* of December 20, 1924. Duffus pointed out that this was a major social revolution, a change in fundamental folkways, since play had been considered sinful as a form of idleness only a century before. Sports personalities of the era are depicted in *The Golden People* by Paul Gallico. For William Tatem Tilden II, see "Greatest Tennis Player of All Times" by Allison Danzig in the *New York Times Magazine,* December 22, 1963. The wave of public excitement about the Battle of the Century between Dempsey and Tunney is described by Charles Merz in *The Great American Bandwagon.* See also "Commercialized Prize Ring" in *Outlook,* September 28, 1927. For Gene Tunney as an atypical sports hero, see "Gentleman Gene" by Grantland Rice in *Collier's,* November 5, 1927; "Corbett to Tunney on How to Win the Mob," *Literary Digest,* January 14, 1928; and "Tunney's Bout with Shakespeare," *Literary Digest,* May 2, 1928.

CHAPTER VI—CULTURE—HIGHBROW

The Twenties: American Writing in the Postwar Decade by Frederick J. Hoffman is a sharp and comprehensive dissection of American life and letters in a formative period, integrating the issues of the day—the changes in the moral code, postwar cynicism, and the economic boom. A perceptive evaluation and representative selection are found in *The American Twenties: A Literary Panorama* by John K. Hutchens. For a discussion of the rebels and avant-garde of the decade, see *Garrets and Pretenders: A History of Bohemianism* by Albert Parry. Gilbert Seldes in his *Seven Lively Arts* has a good commentary on the intellectual trends. Harold Stearns, who had so pessimistic an outlook on the culture of the twenties, wrote in 1937 *America: A Re-Appraisal,* in which he found little cause for expecting a regeneration of the arts.

There are two worthy books about Mencken: *The Irreverent Mr. Mencken* by Edgar Jerome Kemler and *Disturber of the Peace* by William Manchester. Maxwell Geismar has a critical essay on the place of Lardner in literature in the *Ring Lardner Reader.* Irving Howe wrote the book *Sherwood Anderson.* Geismar in *The Last of the Provincials* has essays on Mencken, Sherwood Anderson, and F. Scott Fitzgerald. The most comprehensive study of Sinclair Lewis and his work is *Sinclair Lewis: An American Life* by Mark Shorer. For the interrelationship of Fitzgerald with Mencken, Lardner, and Hemingway, with all of whom he was on close terms, see *Fitzgerald and His Contemporaries* by William Goldhurst. *F. Scott Fitzgerald: The Man and His Work* by Alfred Kazin is a collection of views on Fitzgerald, including an essay by Kazin. A study in depth of the man is *The Far Side of Paradise: A Biography of F. Scott Fitzgerald* by Arthur Mizener. Frederick J. Hoffman has written the book *The Great Gatsby: A Study.* In *The Twenties,* edited by Richard E. Lanford and William E. Taylor, there are twenty critical essays on literary figures of the era, including one on Robinson Jeffers by Frederick I. Carpenter, on William Carlos Williams by Richard J. Calhoun, on Sinclair Lewis by Maurice Kramer, on Mencken by M. K. Singleton, on Willa Cather by John H. Randall III, and on Hemingway by Robert O. Stephens. Hoffman in *The Twenties* has an excellent discussion of expressionism.

CHAPTER VII—CULTURE—FOR THE MASSES

Lloyd Morris in his *Not So Long Ago* discussed the development of the movies, radio, and automobile in this century as means of popular entertainment in an age when entertainment became an end in itself. For the history of the cinema, see *The Rise of the American Film* by Lewis Jacobs, *The Movies* by Richard Griffith and Arthur Mayer, *The Hays Office* by Raymond Moley, and *The Fifty Years Decline and Fall of Hollywood* by

Ezra Goodman; for a history of the German cinema, *From Caligari to Hitler* by Siegfried Kracauer; for the comedy, *Harold Lloyd's World of Comedy* by William Cahn, *Keaton* by Rudi Blesh, and "Comedy's Greatest Era" by James Agee in *Life* magazine, September 5, 1949.

For the tonic to the ego in the new movie palaces, see Lloyd Lewis on "The Deluxe Picture Palace" in the *New Republic,* March 27, 1929. The actress Mary Astor gave her reminiscences about the advent of talkies in the New York *Times,* October 5, 1967, II,1:6. For the strides in technology that made talkies feasible, see "The Amazing Story of the Talkies," *Popular Mechanics,* December, 1928. For two critical views of the talkies, see "Movies Try to Talk" by Robert F. Sisk, *American Mercury,* August, 1928, and "Movies Commit Suicide" by Gilbert Seldes, *Harper's,* November, 1928.

Aldous Huxley discussed the degrading role of radio in "The Outlook for American Culture," *Harper's,* August, 1927. Paul Schubert gave a comprehensive survey in his 1928 book *The Electric World: The Rise of the Radio.* For the fortuitous circumstances which brought radio into the home, see "Signing Off on the First Ten Years" by George W. Gray, *World's Work,* December, 1930. Stuart Chase probed whither radio was heading in his "Inquiry into Radio," *Outlook,* April 18, 1928. For the heart throb of radio, Rudy Vallee, see "God's Gift to Us Girls" by Martha Gellhorn, *New Republic,* August 7, 1929, and "Riding the Crest," *Outlook,* September 11, 1929. For Graham McNamee, see "Baritone Out of Work," by W. Davenport, *Collier's,* January 14, 1928.

There are two good articles on jazz, which by coincidence bore the same titles, "Anatomy of Jazz," and appeared in the same month, April, 1926, one by Don Knowlton in *Harper's* and the other by H. O. Osgood in the *American Mercury.* There was considerable argument about the new art form—that is, if it was art. See "Jazz Is Music" by George Antheil, *Forum,* July, 1928, with a reply by Sigmund Spaeth in the August issue. "George Gershwin and Jazz" appeared in the *Outlook* of February, 1928.

Martin Mayer in his book *Madison Avenue* gives a history of the services rendered by the advertising agencies. The role of advertising in the new age was discussed by Stuart Chase in "The Tragedy of Waste," *New Republic,* August 19, 1925.

Analyzing the content of newspapers, E. S. Martin wrote "Newspapers," *Harper's,* May,1927, and Silas Bent wrote "The Art of Ballyhoo," *Harper's,* September, 1927. See also Charles Merz in the *New Republic* of December 30, 1925, "What Makes a First-Page Story." For Brisbane, see *Citizen Hearst* by W. A. Swanberg and an interview with him by S. Crowther in *Collier's,* February 20, 1926, entitled "Richest Hired Man." For Bernarr MacFadden in journalism, see Oswald Garrison Villard in *Atlantic Monthly,* March, 1926, "Sex, Art, Truth and Magazines." His wife, Mary Williamson MacFadden, wrote of her life with him in the book *Dumbbells and Carrot Strips: The Story of Bernarr MacFadden.* It was written with Émile Gavreau, who was the editor of the *Evening Graphic,* and contains much of the history of the *Graphic* which only Gavreau would know.

For the obsession with murder in newspapers see "Wanted—Bigger and Better Murders" by Charles Merz, *Harper's*, August, 1927, and "The Hall-press-Mills Case" by Bruce Bliven, *New Republic*, December 1, 1926. Damon Runyon described the defendants in the Snyder-Gray case in the New York *American* of April 19, 1927. Alexander Woollcott had an essay on the case in his book *Long, Long Ago*. H. L. Mencken had his own comment on Gray in his essay "A Good Man Gone Wrong," *American Mercury*, February, 1929. The paradox, he said, was that Gray was actually the perfect model of the YMCA virtuous and God-fearing American. Such a man cannot differentiate between one sin and another. "His initial peccadillo shocked him so vastly that he could think of himself thereafter only as a sinner unspeakable and incorrigible. In his eyes the step from adultery to murder was as natural and inevitable as the step from the cocktail-shaker to the gutter in the eyes of a Methodist bishop."

CHAPTER VIII—THE RULE OF MELLON

There is an excellent study of Mellon by Harvey O'Connor entitled *Mellon's Millions: The Biography of a Fortune*. There are some interesting additional facts about Mellon in a book by Philip H. Love entitled *Andrew W. Mellon*. A recent discussion of the Mellon fortune appeared in articles in *Fortune* magazine of October, 1967, "The Mellons of Pittsburgh." Articles of value about Mellon in the Coolidge administration are by Frank Kent in the *New Republic*, March 24, 1926; by S. Bent in *Scribner's*, January, 1928; and "Powerful and Shy," *Collier's*, November 12, 1927. Details of the fight against Mellon are contained in the book *Independent Man: The Life of Senator James Couzens* by Harry Barnard. The New York *Times* of April 12, 1924, discussed Coolidge's sharp rebuke to the Senate for its approval of Senator Couzens' investigation of Mellon. Senator Thomas J. Walsh said that no Executive had addressed a lawmaking body in such an arrogant tone "since the days of the Tudors and Stuarts."

Commenting on the Democratic support for the Mellon tax bill, Frank Kent wrote in the *New Republic*, "It is not the Democrats who have changed in the country but the country that has changed the Democrats. The crumbs from the prosperity banquet table at which for four years the big fellows have been gorging are so numerous, succulent and satisfying to the little fellow that all his truculence toward the 'interests' has disappeared." For discussions of Joseph P. Grundy, see the *Literary Digest* of November 16 and December 28, 1929, and "Of, for and Buy," *Collier's*, December 14, 1929.

"Mr. Coolidge on Business as a Spiritual Force" was discussed in the *Literary Digest* of December 5, 1925. For the primacy of business, see "Dogma of Business First" by Stuart Chase, *Harper's*, September, 1926. For business as a science, see "The Dawn of a New Science" by Arlington J. Stone, *American Mercury*, August, 1928. For business and the cult of service, see "Business and Ethics" by John T. Flynn, *Forum,* October, 1928; also John T. Flynn's "Business and the Government," *Harper's,* March, 1928. For business as a religion, see "Religion in Business" by Jesse Rainsford Sprague, *Harper's,* September, 1927. Frederick J. Hoffman in *The Twenties* deals with the reverence for business as a religion and as a dominant motif in the literature of the age.

There is a full discussion of the Pecora investigation into the securities markets in *America in Midpassage* by Charles and Mary Beard. For Samuel Insull, see the book *Insull* by Forrest McDonald; "From Insull to Injury" by N. R. Danielian, *Atlantic Monthly,* April, 1933; and a series of articles, "Up and Down with Sam Insull," by John T. Flynn, in *Collier's* in December, 1932.

CHAPTER IX—THE SUPREME ILLUSION—THE NEW ERA

Prosperity Decade by George Soule gives a rounded economic background for the Coolidge Era. Professor Thomas Nixon Carver in his 1925 book *The Present Economic Revolution in the United States* expounded the doctrine that with the widening ownership of shares of stock, industry would belong to the people in the new era.

The correspondence between Coolidge and Secretary of State Kellogg is in the White House files. The circumstances of Coolidge's review of the fleet are narrated by his naval aide Wilson Brown in the *American Heritage* of February, 1955. For the revelation of the activities of William B. Shearer at Geneva, see "Keeping the Profit in War," *New Republic,* September 18, 1929, and "Mr. Shearer's Tale," *Nation,* October 16, 1929. The diplomatic maneuvering that preceded the Kellogg Peace Pact is given in detail in the book by Robert H. Ferrell covering the administrations of two Secretaries of State entitled *Stimson-Kellogg.* There are two books about Borah, *Borah of Idaho* by Claudius O. Johnson and *Borah* by Marian C. McKenna. There are some acid articles by Charles Merz: entitled "This Man Borah," *New Republic,* May and June, 1925, and "Androcles and the Lion," *Century,* April, 1926.

For the initiation of the easy money policy and its impact on the stock market, see *The Great Crash* by John Kenneth Galbraith. Hoover in his memoirs asserts that he saw the danger ahead and implored Coolidge in 1927 to halt the low interest policy, but Coolidge replied that it was within the exclusive jurisdiction of the Federal Reserve Board. On the Florida land boom, see "Florida Frenzy" by G. M. Shelby, *Harper's,* January, 1926. On the Wall Street speculation, see "New Era in Wall Street" by J. Moody, *Atlantic Monthly,* August, 1928; "Wall Street Hysterics," *Literary Digest,* June 28, 1928, and "Capeadores in Wall Street" by Ralph W. Robey, *Atlantic Monthly,* September, 1928. Robey claimed that Mellon and Coolidge invariably made optimistic statements about business whenever Wall Street faltered. The difficulty in making a case against Coolidge on this ground is that business prospects were a favorite topic on which he sounded off in all seasons. The memoirs of Senator Watson were entitled *As I Knew Them.*

There were some doubts raised about the solidity of the nation's prosperity. See "Explaining Our Puzzling Profitless Prosperity" in the *Literary Digest,* November 19, 1927, and "Prosperity Without Profit" by Jesse Rainsford Sprague in *Harper's,* June, 1928. Stuart Chase in a series in the *Nation* beginning in October, 1929, raised the question of how widely the blessings of prosperity were diffused; his articles were entitled "Prosperity, Believe It or Not." A journalist showed more foresight than the economists—Elmer Davis in "If Hoover Fails," *Harper's,* March, 1929, expressed his fears that the props under the economy, such as the auto market, were weaker than generally believed. The distress in the farm sector of the economy was repeatedly discussed. See "Farmers' Situation, a National Danger" by Senator George W. Norris, *Current History,* April, 1926; "What the Farmer Wants," *New Republic,* February 10, 1926; and "Agricultural Depression" by A. P. Chew, *New Republic,* June 6 and 13, 1928.

CHAPTER X—DREAM'S END

The recollections of Everett Sanders in this chapter are from his article "The Coolidge Character" in the *Saturday Evening Post* of January 17, 1933, and "Last Letters of Calvin Coolidge" (to Sanders) in the *Saturday Evening Post* of March 25, 1933. Allegations that Coolidge was not sincere in his "I do not choose . . ." statement are based on the most tendentious evidence. "Ike" Hoover's book has been cited for proof that Coolidge wanted to be drafted, but Hoover's "proof" consists of the following: that the White House staff knew that Coolidge really wanted to stay on, that his December message to the Republican National Committee was vague (it could not have been more unequivocal), and that when Herbert Hoover was nominated, Coolidge was so upset that he locked himself in his room without eating dinner. For a vivid account of the 1928 Presidential campaign, see *A Catholic Runs for President* by Edmund A. Moore.

For the Crash and the onset of the Great Depression, in addition to Galbraith's book, see *Herbert Hoover and the Great Depression* by Harris G. Warren and *The Crisis of the Old Order 1919–1933* by Arthur M. Schlesinger, Jr.

Claude M. Fuess in his biography of Coolidge has a good description of his life in Northampton after his Presidency. The view of Coolidge in his post-Presidency days by F. W. Plummer is from the Boston *Globe* of May 18, 1930, and his last talk on public affairs with Henry L. Stoddard was in the New York *Sun* of January 6, 1933.

INDEX

309